Gilles Paquet and Christopher Wilson

Intelligent Governance

A Prototype for Social Coordination

Collaborative Decentred Metagovernance Series

This series of books is designed to define cumulatively the contours of collaborative decentred metagovernance. At this time, there is still no canonical version of this paradigm: it is *en émergence*. This series intends to be one of many 'construction sites' to experiment with various dimensions of an effective and practical version of this new approach.

Metagovernance is the art of combining different forms or styles of governance, experimented with in the private, public and social sectors, to ensure effective coordination when power, resources and information are widely distributed, and the governing is of necessity decentred and collaborative.

The series invites conceptual and practical contributions focused on different issue domains, policy fields, *causes célèbres*, functional processes, etc. to the extent that they contribute to sharpening the new apparatus associated with collaborative decentred metagovernance.

In the last few decades, there has been a need felt for a more sophisticated understanding of the governing of the private, public and social sectors: for less compartmentalization among sectors that have much in common; and for new conceptual tools to suggest new relevant questions and new ways to carry out the business of governing, by creatively recombining the tools of governance that have proven successful in all these sectors. These efforts have generated experiments that have been sufficiently rich and wide-ranging in the various laboratories to warrant efforts to pull together what we know at this stage.

This eleventh volume in the series proposes some guideposts for a prototype of intelligent governance. Its intent is not formulaic. We proceed in three steps: first, to clear the mind of cobwebs and mental prisons in order to proceed mindfully to the diagnosis phase of problem definition; second, to develop an inquiry with a new toolbox capable of generating both a synthetic perspective and collaborative arrangements based on *affectio societatis*; and third, to gauge the impact of culture governance on the evolution of the governance *problematique*, and to propose a protocol to design creative and imaginative responses to wicked policy problems – smartly, wisely, cognitively and heuristically.

Interested parties are invited to join the Chautauqua.

– Editorial Board

Other titles published by INVENIRE are listed at the end of this book.

Gilles Paquet and Christopher Wilson

Intelligent Governance

A Prototype for Social Coordination

INVENIRE

Ottawa, Canada
2016

University of Ottawa **Press**
Les **Presses** de l'Université d'Ottawa

The University of Ottawa Press (UOP) is proud to be the oldest of the francophone university presses in Canada and the oldest bilingual university publisher in North America. Since 1936, UOP has been enriching intellectual and cultural discourse by producing peer-reviewed and award-winning books in the humanities and social sciences, in French and in English.

www.Press.uOttawa.ca

Library and Archives Canada Cataloguing in Publication

Title: Intelligent governance : a prototype for social coordination / Gilles Paquet and Christopher Wilson.
Names: Paquet, Gilles, author. | Wilson, Christopher, 1953- author.
Series: Collaborative decentred metagovernance series.
Description: Series statement: Collaborative decentred metagovernance series | Reprint. Originally published: Ottawa, Canada : Invenire, 2016. | Includes bibliographical references.
Identifiers: Canadiana (print) 20220285241 | Canadiana (ebook) 20220285276 | ISBN 9780776638409 (softcover) | ISBN 9780776638416 (PDF) | ISBN 9780776638423 (EPUB)
Subjects: LCSH: Organizational effectiveness. | LCSH: Institutional cooperation. | LCSH: Social learning. | LCSH: Interagency coordination.
Classification: LCC HD58.9 .P36 2022 | DDC 302.3/5—dc23

Legal Deposit: Library and Archives Canada, Third Quarter 2022
© University of Ottawa Press 2022, all rights reserved.

This book was initially published by Invenire Books in 2016. The cover design, layout and design were produced by Sandy Lynch. The University of Ottawa Press reissued this book thanks to the support of Ontario Creates.

Invenire

Invenire Books, an Ottawa-based idea factory that operated from 2010 to 2019, specialized in collaborative governance and stewardship. Invenire and its authors provide creative practical and stimulating responses to the challenges and opportunities faced by today's organizations. The list is now carried by the University of Ottawa Press.

Profession: Public Servant
The Entrepreneurial Effect: Practical Ideas from Your Own Virtual Board of Advisors
La flotte blanche : histoire de la compagnie de navigation du Richelieu et d'Ontario
Tableau d'avancement II : essais exploratoires sur la gouvernance d'un certain Canada français
The Entrepreneurial Effect: Waterloo
The Unimagined Canadian Capital: Challenges for the Federal Capital Region
The State in Transition: Challenges for Canadian Federalism
Cities as Crucibles: Reflections on Canada's Urban Future
Gouvernance communautaire : innovations dans le Canada français hors Québec
Through the Detox Prism: Exploring Organizational Failures and Design Responses
Cities and Languages: Governance and Policy – An International Symposium
Villes et langues : gouvernance et politiques – symposium international
Moderato Cantabile: Toward Principled Governance for Canada's Immigration Policy
Stewardship: Collaborative Decentred Metagovernance and Inquiring Systems
Challenges in Public Health Governance: The Canadian Experience
Innovation in Canada: Why We Need More and What We Must Do to Get It
Challenges of Minority Governments in Canada
Gouvernance corporative : une entrée en matières

Tackling Wicked Policy Problems: Equality, Diversity and Sustainability
50 ans de bilinguisme officiel : défis, analyses et témoignages
Unusual Suspects: Essays on Social Learning
Probing the Bureaucratic Mind: About Canadian Federal Executives
Tableau d'avancement III : pour une diaspora canadienne-française antifragile
Autour de Chantal Mouffe : le politique en conflit
Town and Crown: An Illustrated History of Canada's Capital
The Tainted-Blood Tragedy in Canada: A Cascade of Governance Failures
Intelligent Governance: A Prototype for Social Coordination
Driving the Fake Out of Public Administration: Detoxing HR in the Canadian Federal Public Sector
Tableau d'avancement IV : un Canada français à ré-inventer
A Future for Economics: More Encompassing, More Institutional, More Practical
Pasquinade en F : essais à rebrousse-poil
Building Bridges: Case Studies in Collaborative Governance in Canada
Scheming Virtuously: The Road to Collaborative Governance
A Lantern on the Bow: A History of the Science Council of Canada and its Contributions to the Science and Innovation Policy Debate
Fifty Years of Official Bilingualism: Challenges, Analyses and Testimonies
Irregular Governance: A Plea for Bold Organizational Experimentation
Pasquinade en E: Slaughtering Some Sacred Cows

The University of Ottawa Press gratefully acknowledges the support extended to its publishing list by the Government of Canada, the Canada Council for the Arts, the Ontario Arts Council, the Social Sciences and Humanities Research Council and the Canadian Federation for the Humanities and Social Sciences through the Awards to Scholarly Publications Program, and by the University of Ottawa.

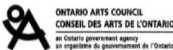

ONTARIO ARTS COUNCIL
CONSEIL DES ARTS DE L'ONTARIO
an Ontario government agency
un organisme du gouvernement de l'Ontario

Canada Council   Conseil des arts
for the Arts   du Canada

Canadä

uOttawa

| Table of Contents

"Intelligent governance is anti-bureaucratic."
Nicolas Berggruen and Nathan Gardels

| Not a Plan, But a Prototype, and Indications Along the Way

"Il ne faut pas faire de plan, il faut suivre les indications."

Charles Péguy

All organizations, whether they be centralized or decentralized, operate through the coordination of the many uses of different resources, under the control of various individuals or groups, using variegated processes, in order to reach their own desired outcomes. This may happen by self-organization or by a compounding of deliberate actions by members. Despite the seeming linearity of specific processes, overall coordination of the whole organization (intra and between processes and with the organization's external environment) is rarely linear. It requires a significant amount of tacit knowledge, guesswork, experimentation, trial and error, and social learning – often across organizations and stakeholder groups – in order to achieve the right fit and best use of resources and the most beneficial outcomes.

Striking this 'right fit' between resources, processes and outcomes in complex environments, where different groups have something to contribute towards joint outcomes even though they partake in joint operations in the pursuit of their own objectives – this is what we call "intelligent governance." As

Berggruen and Gardels (2013) suggest, "intelligent governance" is the practical application of an evolving worldview that is a less conflictive, more intelligent, more cooperative, and wiser mode of human coordination.

This short book proposes some guideposts for intelligent governance.

It does not put forward a rigid blueprint or a recipe that could mechanically and blindly be followed, but a prototype for any process of inquiry seeking to help organizations find a way forward (through innovation, and value adding), some general indications about the most toxic pitfalls likely to materialize that must be avoided along the way – mental prisons, lack of mindfulness, etc. – and about the most promising opportunities or initiatives likely to nudge the coordinating inquiries into successful directions.[1]

In this context, prototyping means:

1. identifying some top requirements as quickly as possible;
2. putting in place a quick-and-dirty provisional medium of co-development;
3. allowing as many interested parties as possible to get involved as partners in designing a promising arrangement; and,
4. through playing with prototypes, encouraging all to get a better understanding of the problems, of their own priorities, and of themselves (Schrage 2000: 199ff; Paquet 2009: Introduction).

Any proposed wayfinding prototype must be mindful of the dangers of approaching intelligent governance with a formulaic mindset or on the basis of too narrow a perspective when it

---

[1] Alain Finkielkraut has epitomized on Péguy's epigraph above. *"L'homme qui fait des plans croit pouvoir tirer la vérité de son propre fonds et plier la réalité à ses modèles. L'homme qui suit des indications subordonne sa pensée au visage que présentent les choses et les événements. Celui qui fait des plans trace sa route, celui qui suit les indications demande à la réalité qu'elle lui montre le chemin. Celui qui fait des plans décide de tout, celui qui suit des indications s'attend à tout"* (Finkielkraut 1992: 72).

comes to problem, issue and organizational definitions. Each situation must be contextually ascertained, its complexity and circumstances fully appreciated, its plurality of stakeholders and their worldviews taken into account, its various dynamics probed, and the wayfinding for the organization or the socio-economy must be understood as distilled by a mix of self-organization and the work of evolving inquiring systems constantly fuelled by testing social learning.

No system of inquiry is quite the same, and no experience of social learning unfolds exactly in quite the same way, but all of them are exposed to the same challenges:

- the crippling nature of the mental prisons inherited from the past;
- the inadequacy of the *outillage mental* in use;
- the difficulty in appropriately taking into account the polyphony of stakeholders' information, viewpoints and preferences;
- the propensity to hyperfocus on the mechanics of governing boards and associated plumbing issues, instead of the broader philosophical and architectural underpinnings that shape the conditions of wayfinding in a collective setting; and,
- the failure to be mindful about the forces of self-organization, or to imagine ways to make sense of seemingly unresolvable paradoxes and conundrums, or to elicit the required collaboration of partners in overcoming them.

These are some of the most perilous threats to the three phases of an inquiring system – the diagnostic phase, the design of response phase, and the mobilization of partners phase – in order to develop the organization's capacity to make sense of what is going on and to find its way in the complex, turbulent and disordered world of ours. These phases are occasions to invent new ways to overcome the challenges they face and to build on the occasion, through a mix of reframing, restructuring, retooling and virtuous scheming, and by establishing and sustaining the various collaborative links necessary to carry on a concerted task.

Mindfulness is a central element of the diagnostic phase; imagination is a crucial component of the design phase; and some form of *affectio societatis* is fundamental for the mobilization phase.

None of these capabilities are ever to be harnessed overly tightly without their positive force being neutered somewhat. The reference points we will draw attention to in building a prototype of intelligent governance and in using it are those most likely to matter for an open and informed diagnostic process, an unimpaired and unrestricted creative design process, and a mobilization process likely to meet with success simply because people are dissatisfied with what is going on and want to make a change.

The assemblage of sensors and levers on which we focus do not represent a comprehensive checklist of all the relevant forces at work in all situations. But they do constitute an 'enabling core checklist' for a wide range of inquiring processes – helping to guide an inquiry through its initial and evolving stages by constantly examining and re-examining the environment and the players in order to avoid major pitfalls.

It is crucial, however, not to restrict the attention too narrowly by these reference points. The art of diagnosis, design and mobilization depends for its success on relying on a relatively broader and encompassing synthetic perspective of the situation and its context – such as might be exhibited from atop a tall crane or building – a view that broadens both space and time horizons and is often more important for what it evokes loosely than for what it shows precisely (Normann 2001: Part V).

Consequently, this book, while identifying new frameworks and assumptions, tends to feature practical springboards, triggers and pressure points that help open the minds of actors to connections that need to be made by mindful and creative collaborators. While we insist on certain elements or 'dots' that governance experts should pay attention to, connecting these dots, evoking patterns, discovering ways in which they can be made use of, etc. are the essential initiatives that are meant to be activated throughout the inquiring process.

We propose to deal with this vast space of dramatic perspectives in an unusual way – from the more tractable to the more daunting, from ways to escape from mental prisons to ways to bring forth enabling capabilities as perplexing as those evoked by the interactive notions of 'goodness of fit' or 'burden of office'. Yet the path to intelligent governance does not always move forward linearly. It often meanders, from this experience to that, from one worldview to another, from one understanding to another, all the time distilling the connoisseurship that enables one to distinguish what may constitute good governance for a given situation.

This approach requires a bit of investment from the reader, and the more so as the book unfolds. For this is a book intent on nudging the reader outside the comfort zone of *les idées reçues*, and urges him/her to press on, to explore further, to prototype an inquiring system of one's own, to take a leap ... for this voyald is meant to be transformative.

References

Berggruen, Nicolas and Nathan Gardels. 2013. *Intelligent Governance for the 21st Century: A Middle Way between West and East*. Cambridge, UK: Polity Press.

Finkielkraut, Alain. 1992. *Le mécontemporain*. Paris, FR: Gallimard.

Normann, Richard. 2001. *Reframing Business: When the Map Changes the Landscape*. New York, NY: John Wiley & Sons.

Paquet, Gilles. 2009. *Crippling Epistemologies and Governance Failures: A Plea for Experimentalism*. Ottawa, ON: University of Ottawa Press.

Schrage, Michael. 2000. *Serious Play: How the World's Best Companies Simulate to Innovate*. Boston, MA: Harvard Business School Press.

| Escaping from Mental Prisons and Designing New Arrangements

"Nous risquons de faire deux erreurs liées:
penser le nouveau avec les catégories du passé
et croire qu'il se substituera à l'ancien,
alors qu'il s'y ajoutera tout en le transformant
et en étant transformé par lui."
Marc Guillaume

Over the last 75 years, much of the attention given to governance in public debates has been focused on the choice between centralization and decentralization as modes of governance. Whether the focus was national economies – as in the debates of Hayek *et al.* (1935) with the central planners in the 1930s – or on particular organizations – as in the recent books by Brafman and Beckstrom (2006) or Laloux (2014) – the key question has always been whether one can govern most effectively from the centre. The broad conclusion from all those debates has been that one cannot, and should not do so (Calame and Talmant 1997; Cleveland 2002).

Despite the rich assortment of examples and cases used to develop the main points of this denunciation of centralization, the outcomes of most academic and professional debates would appear to have had little impact on the real world experiences of organizations confronted with complex governance challenges.

The current canonical patterns of governing practices appear to flow perversely from the very opposite of the conclusions of these studies. Central planning fantasies continue to be celebrated widely, and tall tales of romanticized leadership are still regarded as gospel truths. Hierarchical arrangements remain the dominant pattern of organization, despite decentralized organizations being shown to immensely outperform centralized ones, not only in financial terms, but also when it comes to the innovation and adoption of new ideas, or the reporting of misconduct (Kleiner/Seidman 2012; Paquet and Ragan 2012: 92-93).

This has persuaded us that intelligent governance arrangements will not come to prevail over ineffective, dumb and otherwise imprudent ones, unless and until:

- more detailed and practical arguments for intelligent governance are put forward than those that have been available up to now;
- the nature of their advantages are conveyed more effectively to those who have some influence on the design of such governing arrangements; and,
- there is a shift in the overall governance culture, and a new paradigm of distributed governance is embraced.

This calls for a more sophisticated statement of the governance *problematique* than the ones that have been previously been put forward, and for a better packaging of its tenets in presentations to interested publics.

A *problematique* in four movements

Constructing such a *problematique* requires some refurbishment of the four clusters of activities that typically underpin much of what constitutes governance work: (1) prior problem description and learning; (2) analytical tools and frameworks; (3) the *problematique* itself; and (4) the implementation of correctives and repairs.

That refurbishment includes:

- a *mise en garde*, a cautionary attitude, to help innoculate against a variety of mental prisons and crippling epistemologies (inherited either from the past or from ideologies or from constraining disciplines) that are likely to limit unduly the scope of any inquiry, and consequently the depth of understanding of governance failures;

- an enrichment of the collective capacity to get a grasp on socio-economies and complex organizations as instituted processes through the use of conceptual or analytical frameworks[2] that are likely to elicit meaningful diagnoses. One can usefully build on a combination of sub-processes, that are dynamically integrated through the operations of structures and sub-systems;

- a *governance problematique* that, as the object of the inquiry, is an ensemble of the related problems and that is built on diverse conceptual frameworks and multiple vistas in order to provide a synoptic perspective on the ways in which effective coordination and collaboration can be generated, but also to enable the effective engagement of stakeholders when power, resources and information are widely distributed; and,

- an insight into the complexity and power of stewardship and its important role in designing the apparatuses of coordination, and its pivotal role in the redesign of the evolving wayfinding apparatus fuelled by social learning, and in evincing what protocols might be useful to ensure that the governance message is appropriately conveyed to partners and publics alike – who may remain skeptical, and in need of nudging forward.

In the following sections, we identify clusters of governance activities – which we have called 'movements' because of the level of orchestration involved in them and through them – with the idea to provide checklists of dimensions that practitioners

---

[2] A conceptual or analytical framework is taken to mean in this context what it means for Harvey Leibenstein (1976: 17), i.e., a set of relationships that frame the issues of interest but do not lead to specific conclusions about the world of events because the parameters are not sufficiently specified to lead to falsifiable conclusions.

should be mindful of, because they are not only crucial to the success of each movement, but also because these movements are interdependent and central to the production of balance in intelligent governance.

Practitioners cannot approach intelligent governance without first freeing themselves from the crippling epistemologies and mental prisons which surround them; or without entertaining a broad cosmology of heuristics and tools; or without generating comprehensive understanding and innovative solutions; or without ensuring effective implementation of the emerging repairs. This cannot be done without attending to sub-processes, sub-systems, synoptic views, wayfinding exercises and stewardship.

Our four 'movements' are therefore meant to bring together four checklists of issues of import. Even though not all of these dimensions are likely to be of equal importance at all times or in all circumstances, not keeping them in mind is perilous. Together, they constitute an *outillage mental*, a mental toolkit that will be useful and practical in most circumstances.

First movement: Dealing with mental prisons and crippling epistemologies

There are a number of crude ideological mental prisons that are well-known and uniformly denounced both in the governance literature and in practice. They correspond to biased, non-dialectical views or representations of the lifeworld that are sufficiently distortive as to lead to completely inappropriate diagnoses, and therefore to inadequate or even toxic remedies to existing situations. Nationalism or socialism or progressivism are illustrations.

In the same way, very simplistic methodologies like hyper positivism are readily recognized as crippling epistemologies because they unduly restrict the process of acquisition of knowledge. But similar pathologies can also come in less obvious and toxic forms. For instance, too many observers have a tendency to make simplifying assumptions, such as the choice of rationalistic positivism as the only road to sound knowledge. While such assumptions are convenient to make analysis easier, they also generate unrealistic understandings and misguided directions, not only for any governance inquiry, but also for subsequent coordination and collaboration efforts. This being said, any time a person selects one perspective on an issue or a research strategy as opposed to another, it may be said that one is courting a potential mental prison or a crippling epistemology – if and when their choice is made to the absolute exclusion of other perspectives as useful sources of knowledge. These truncated perspectives become ever more toxic, the narrower and the more restrictive the chosen approaches are. Yet most practitioners do not question either their basic assumptions, or their initial perspectives on most issues (Katouzian 1980; Paquet 2009: 32ff).

These mental prisons and crippling epistemologies are the product/source of *apophenia* – a fundamental human tendency to seek patterns in random information. Sometimes, however, those affected by those beliefs can fall prey to the "pneumopathological" – a word proposed by Eric Voegelin and most recently used by Robert Sibley to describe the state of "those who are morally insane, 'living' as it were in a fantasy-world of self-righteousness" (Sibley 2013). For instance, the belief in 'the perfection of the unfettered markets' or that 'organizations can't function without top-down leadership' are two such crippling fantasies.

Cleansing and synthesizing

Therefore, much of the work in Parts I and II of this short book will focus on:

- cleansing our approaches to complex wicked problems of governance of some key unhelpful concepts in good currency;
- while establishing the foundations of a broader framework that will enable governance practitioners to design effective governance inquiries.

Even though the word 'governance' has gained significant popularity in public usage over the last 40 years, it has also been sanitized, bowdlerized or anathematized to such an extent by a plurality of lawyers, political scientists and organizational behaviourists that it has been widely emasculated as a useful conceptual tool for fostering social coordination of all types. Therefore, much of the governance literature is unable to contribute significantly to the sort of re-conceptualization of governance practices that is currently required.

Nevertheless, there has been some serious work that has shown how governance provides a more powerful conceptual framework for understanding organizational dynamics than traditional management approaches, a more powerful lens to approach public policy and public administration, and a better guide for designing more effective wayfinding and stewardship for both organizations and socio-economies (Paquet 2013). However, this work has not yet succeeded in toppling the obsolete, analytical frameworks that have continued to enjoy good currency since early in the last century.

This failure of the governance argument to prevail is ascribable in part to the aggressive conservatorship flavour of traditional government structures and social science disciplines, and of the outdated epistemologies they are built upon (Terry 2003; Paquet 2009). These particular mental prisons have blocked our capacity to transform our socio-economies and organizations, and therefore to adjust to new and unforeseen circumstances. But this failure is also in part ascribable to the impatient, hurried, and unduly scattered ways in which the notion of governance has been presented to audiences who have remained hesitant to abandon their deficient mental toolkits until they could be assured that the alternative is shown (i.e., proven) to be compellingly more effective.

This aversion to uncertainty, often associated with experimentation and exploration, versus the supposed certainty of established belief is another type of mental prison. A template or model or prototype cannot be simultaneously general, precise and simple (Thorngate 1976), so undue simplification of either the problem or its solution for communication purposes inevitably entails less precision and less generality, and thereby becomes less persuasive. Academics have tended to prefer simplicity whereas practitioners prefer applicability for results.

Some crippling epistemological prisons can only be remedied by a *changement de la garde*, for it is difficult for most persons and groups to shake off the conceptual frameworks that have for years been cozy mental prisons, and the source of much intellectual comfort. For some, these paradigms and tools have become part of their culture and identity, much like the Stockholm syndrome – the psychological capture-bonding that brings the captured victim to identify with and defend its captor.

Much can be done to limit the damage of such prisons, by explicitly bringing to light not only the way retrospective assumptions may constrain an inquiry from proceeding in certain directions, but also the potentialities that new avenues may offer. In attempting to do so, we hope the arguments of intelligent governance are persuasive (Hirschman 1986). Herein lies the central purpose of this book.

Minimum changes required

The basic intent is not to propose a comprehensive survey of all the mental prisons plaguing traditional governance practice or to catalogue of all the insights generated by the alternative governance approaches that have developed over the last half century. Rather, the intent is to provide a very lean and explicit statement of the minimum changes required in the foundations and pragmatics of an approach of intelligent governance, a kernel if you will, that would make better social coordination reveal itself to others as both more promising and heuristically achievable.

This entails a two-step procedure:
- first, freeing governance inquiries from the unduly constraining assumptions and unhelpful conceptual quagmires that have become concatenated merely to simplify an analyst's life, or to simplify the complex problems at hand and make them more tractable; and,
- second, to open governance inquiries up to a broader range of ownership, perspectives, and contributions,

in order to find better ways of designing collective responses to the problems at hand.

For our purpose, intelligent governance represents an abbreviation for an ensemble of principles, mechanisms, practices, norms, conventions, etc. that constitute a governing or coordinating apparatus capable of coping with evolving circumstances and the exigencies of the context (complexity and uncertainty), while ensuring effective performance (through shared competencies) and ultimately adaptability and antifragility.

In this regard, we focus on meso-phenomena, and on the ebb and flow of information and communication flows as the major sources of influence in configuring the nature and texture of organizations.

Second movement: **Outillage mental** *for an enlightened inquiry*

One can stylize a complex organization or socio-economy as a 'going concern,' or as an "instituted process," in the sense of Karl Polanyi (1957) – a real-life process, evolving through time, and defined by changing structures, rules of operation, organizational arrangements, and institutions to reconcile the changing values, plans, and preferences of individuals or groups, and the geo-socio-technical constraints imposed by the real world. This accommodation work is performed by all sorts of contraptions, rules, conventions, organizations, institutions, etc. At any point in time, the instituted process may harmonize these two families of forces well, so that the rules of operations, etc. may catalyze some form of armistice between all of them. Or they may not – resulting in the hindering, deflecting, or even stalling of the evolution of the 'instituted process.'

When one wishes to gauge the capacity to transform a socio-economy or complex organization, one must focus on the forces that shape the anatomy of the informational/material sub-processes of the organization, and the physiological sub-systems of the organization:

- first, the informational dynamics of the various sub-processes: including the impact of demography or state intervention, the importance of the income distribution, the nature and efficacy of financial and credit instruments, and changes in the psycho-social-cultural conditions, business climate, etc.; and,

- second, the dynamics of the various sub-systems: each sub-system is a metabolic relationship involving interdependencies between the organization and its external environment; among the various subsystems of the internal environment (structural, technological, functioning, governance); and the interactions between the public informational texture of the organization and its physical/material back-end processes.

Anatomically speaking

The great diversity and heterogeneity of most socio-economies or complex organizations make national averages or aggregate measurements somewhat suspect, and the common references to the 'whole instituted process' are also often unhelpful since the sub-processes may be instituted quite differently from place to place, and it is the ways in which the sub-processes and sub-systems interact with one another that may hold more in the way of explanation for aggregate performance than superficial measures that average performance over the whole system.

It is therefore useful to analyze a socio-economy or an organization as complex structured games, which can be partitioned into more or less separable sub-games, which underpin more or less separable dynamics. We do this to determine which sub-games may have asymmetric impacts on the other games at specific moments or points in time.[3]

The following are six basic sub-processes or sub-games we have found to be most useful in understanding the operations of complex organizations or socio-economies.

1. The **demographic sub-process** — corresponds to the population and the labour supply it generates. Slow growth in the demand for labour, for instance, may be the

---

[3] The partitioning into sub-processes or sub-games has come to be regarded by historians and economists as heuristically powerful (Akerman 1944/1955; Paquet and Wallot 2007; Paquet 2014: chapters 2 and 6).

result of a low level of capital accumulation generating a high level of frustration among new entrants into the labour force, but also among the new generation of potential managers whose vertical mobility will be considerably reduced.

2. The **financial sub-process** — refers to the set of activities and institutions which regulate and mop up savings from individuals, re-allocating them throughout the economy. The implicit assumption in good currency is that our financial sub-processes are very efficient, and that they are not the source of any significant impediments to the investment activities.

   In fact, the contrary is indicated. The implications of the 2008 financial meltdown and recession are that the structure of our financial system may not always act in the most efficient way to stimulate investment and capital formation. It may suffer from a great deal of sclerosis, from too much opaqueness, and it might benefit immensely from increased competition. Moreover, it may not handle many financing functions, especially with regard to risk capital, well or at all exposing markets to manipulation by self-serving individuals.

3. The **production and exchange sub-process** crystallizes not only as a result of comparative advantages, but also as a result of protective tariffs, from a multitude of tax holidays and subsidies by federal, provincial and municipal governments, in addition to echoing foreign direct investment and foreign ownership. One important impact of this last factor is that Canada is frequently viewed as a miniature replica of the US economy although using similar but older technology. Therefore, it has to bear a consistent burden of real and perceived inefficiency, generated by shorter production runs and a less efficient use of capital equipment and technology in general.

4. The **distribution of income and wealth sub-process** is a force at centre stage in policy debates, nationally and

internationally, especially since the post Second World War, and becoming even more of a focus since the 1960s. New social rights have been propounded and legitimized through various legislations, with the consequence that distribution of income and wealth has ceased to be a mitigation tool of the socio-technical production and exchange process. It has become such a prominent part of the culture governance that distributive goals are presented up front, often commanding adjustments to the production and exchange process prior to realizing any gains for redistribution.

5. The **state sub-process** has been elevated by many to the role of grand definer of the 'common good' or the 'public interest' in the second half of the 20th century. And yet the state does not nor can it speak with one voice. The last 50 years have witnessed a genuine fragmentation of the state (Naím 2013). The overly ambitious distributional roles that the state accepted to shoulder have translated into a proliferation of interventions and regulations as a result of the larger number of activist governments that often pit one group against another.

6. Lastly, the **socio-cultural sub-process** resulting from the broad ecology of groups and their motives is one of the key reasons why a national consensus on any matter of significance is unlikely to materialize, and why there remains a high degree of social dissonance. What used to be regarded as a societal *mélange* of regional, ethnic, linguistic, social, and occupational groups, forming an open and pluralistic society, has become a society that is micro-fragmented, divided, balkanized, and disjointed. This fragmentation is a reflection of individual identity that has evolved from being primarily associated with one or another major social groups to being a unique compilation of these and other characteristics. As a result, no one group speaks for 'me,' resulting in an erosion of the accepted rules of social cohesion and a decline in public spiritedness or even enlightened self-interest.

This has generated a motivational crisis brought on by a delinking between the motivations demanded by our production and state process, and the motivations supplied by the socio-cultural system. This has reduced our ability to act together to deal in a concerted way with the difficulties that threaten our socio-economy and our complex organizations. Most socio-economies have broken down into a number of bargaining arenas associated with different narrowly defined groups having a very limited interest in expending resources for the collectivity, but unbounded appetites for exorbitant self-serving entitlements from the socio-politico-system or any organization in which they are located or on which they depend.

Physiologically speaking

While the six sub-processes discussed above may be said to have a semi-autonomous dynamic, their intermingling will inevitably produce more or less asymmetric impacts on each other. These interactions will also operate within a system of relationships with the external environment, and the relationships among the four sub-systems internally (Laurent and Paquet 1998: 30-32).

Therefore, we can describe an organization's metabolic sub-system (at the interface of the external environment and the internal system) as that which regulates the ways in which the system draws physical, human and informational resources from the environment, metabolizes them, and transforms them into energy for the organization.

The internal sub-systems of a socio-economy or of a complex organization are:

1. the **technological sub-system** that provides the texture of the existing physical and social technologies at any point in time;

2. the **functional sub-system** that connotes the ensemble of operational relations that combine physical, informational, and inter-personal resources into arrangements that support the capacity for smooth functioning, social

learning, collaboration, trust, etc. within given structures organizing certain activities, actors and resources;

3. the **structural sub-system** that connotes the set of arrangements instituting the capacity to learn and transform the system and constituting the limits of its inner adaptive capacity to learn, innovate and survive; and,

4. the **governance sub-system** constitutes the set of basic wayfinding relationships that both monitor and execute its collective actions in order to align with the rough directions on which a modicum of agreement has been reached, while registering the various tensions generated among partners in the course of such actions that may call for adjustments in standards, guideposts or assumptions (and therefore new forms of organizations and learning processes to be developed) (Laurent, Paquet and Ragan 1992).

The intermingling of sub-processes and sub-systems: the genius of reconstruction

In the different segments of a socio-economy, or complex organizations, sub-processes and sub-systems do not always intermingle in predictable or harmonious ways. Sometimes, one sub-process or another may dominate, but this is frequently only temporary; most of the time, the organization is a composite of forces from many sub-processes that in balance explain the way in which a sector or a region or a complex organization is likely to evolve. However, under the impact of environmental changes, as well as internal tensions and technological changes, the systemic forces underpinning the rules of operations can often run into conflicting pressures that generate structural adjustments, modifying the governance wayfinding sub-system as a result. This is a non-linear result.

It is therefore neither obvious nor predictable as to why or how complex organizations crystallize in certain patterns as a result of the forces within an evolving socio-economic system or organization. The interplay of sub-processes within an organization's process of social learning is especially interesting as it can create novel and unpredictable responses. However, it is clear that the structure and the operational rules within complex organizations tend to crystallize in ways that echo their social milieu and collective consciousness – be it in terms of available resources, socio-cultural background, ethos, or organizational behaviour – as international comparative studies have shown (Hampden-Turner and Trompenaars 1993). What constitutes a resource, an acceptable motivation, an acceptable behavior, or even a proper goal are all socially determined.

Moreover, there is no assurance that the multiple forces at work, which are anchored in the different sub-processes and sub-systems, will coalesce smoothly or coherently into an organizational pattern or form, or that they will coalesce into a stable pattern in an acceptable time frame.

Social learning may take some time. In large and complex socio-economic-political entities, it may take generations. "Conflictive equilibrium" – a situation where each group realizes that it cannot rid the system of its opponents, that it will have to live with them, and work to compromise with them to achieve the objectives that it does not have the capacity to achieve on its own – this situation may endure for quite some time. Consequently, there may be a need to nudge socio-economies or complex organizations in desired directions – softly at times or more brutally at others – if resilience, survival, and antifragility are to ensue (Paquet 1972: 10).

One reason why collaboration may be slow in developing is that citizens have lost confidence in the possibility of increasing their welfare through greater social collaboration and integration via the agency of the state (Nanos 2012). Another is the generalized lack of knowledge of collaborative frameworks, tools and skill sets in our managerial culture that has put a premium on top-down control. But it does not follow that collaboration will **never** materialize. Paquet and Ragan (2012), for instance, have identified families of similar organizational failures and have shown how a mixture of design responses and sufficient mindfulness can prove remedial.

Such reconstructive work starts with the present structure and reconstructs the process that has resulted in this structure, so as to gain *"une compréhension proprement historique de la situation donnée"* (Ferry 1996: 9ff). But the Deweyan inquiry goes a bit further: it also factors in the future, so that the inquiry takes into account the possibilities. Ours is a world of "affairs" (as Dewey (1935) calls them) that is never frozen; it is a world of actualities open to a variety of possibilities, and knowledge is awareness and sensitivity to these possibilities. Indeed, it is often only the seeming inevitability of some of these possibilities that can trigger action, and without them one cannot even imagine how an action-oriented inquiry could progress (Boisvert 1998).

Third movement: Foundations of a proposed governance problematique

There are five pillars that underpin our approach to governance – a governance perspective that is not only broader, but also more dynamic and evolutionary than the governance plumbing approaches in good currency today.

First, our approach builds on the obvious core assumption that the problem context for all stakeholders is characterized by complexity, deep uncertainty, and turbulence. As a result, most of the time it is neither easy nor possible for any stakeholder to develop a comprehensive and deterministic map of this evolving context.

This type of problem context remains opaque due to its many interacting elements, and observers are plagued by ignorance. Consequently, systemic contingencies are omnipresent in the partial understandings and representations of all the stakeholders, making it imperative for the different participants to communicate with one another in order to acquire a less incomplete set of information and to learn the things they do not know.

Second, our approach adopts an informational lens to the organizational world: socio-economic organizations are considered as systems of information and communication exchange and they are characterized by the nature of the messages exchanged. This informational device focuses the attention of the actors away from the usual emphasis on material and mechanistic aspects of organizations and socio-economies (flows of production and allocation of goods and services) toward the exchanges of information (flows of communications, messages, and conversations, orchestrated by conventions, organizations and institutions) that underpin, trigger and catalyze those flows of production and allocation of goods and services, and that are closely linked to the processes of coordination and guidance operating in the organization or social system.

In defining organizations by the messages that are exchanged (decrees in centralized systems, anonymous messages in markets, and empathetic signals in communities) this communicational approach allows one to X-ray the pattern of signals in the informational dynamic of the organization, to detect blockages to these exchanges, to better analyze the coordination failures, and to find ways to repair communication failures, and thereby ensure more effective coordination, collaboration and stewardship (Paquet 1966, 1968, 1998).

It puts the different patterns of relationships (cognitive, collaborative, operational) at the centre of these exchanges, while shining a light on the filtres and mental prisons that may prevent different persons and groups from getting access to a completely informed dialectical view of reality. It shifts the focus of governance attention away from stylized and romanticized notions of leadership in the traditional management model toward routines, heuristics, patterns of action and social learning styles essential to effective cooperation. And it focuses governance away from management decisions *per se*, toward the design of loci for conversations and social learning to affect distributed governance (Hubbard and Paquet 2015: chapter 5).

Third, our approach adopts a dynamic perspective of social learning *ab ovo*. The complexity, uncertainty, and quasi-chaotic nature of the environment (that fuels turbulent organizational responses), combined with the plurality of conceptual frameworks and perspectives of the different stakeholders, and the constantly changing design of organizations (that are evolving to keep up with both changing environments and conceptual frameworks) interact in a process that maintains effectiveness and innovativeness by adapting and transforming governance through social learning.

This social learning unfolds through continual modifications of operations, systems, structures, the trade-offs made among the various norms, cosmologies, principles and conventions used to guide the organization, but also through the relative and changing valence of the different partners (and the inclusion or exclusion of some of them) in the collaborative venture. These tensions are sketchily illustrated in Figure 1.

FIGURE 1.

MRI of the Governance Process

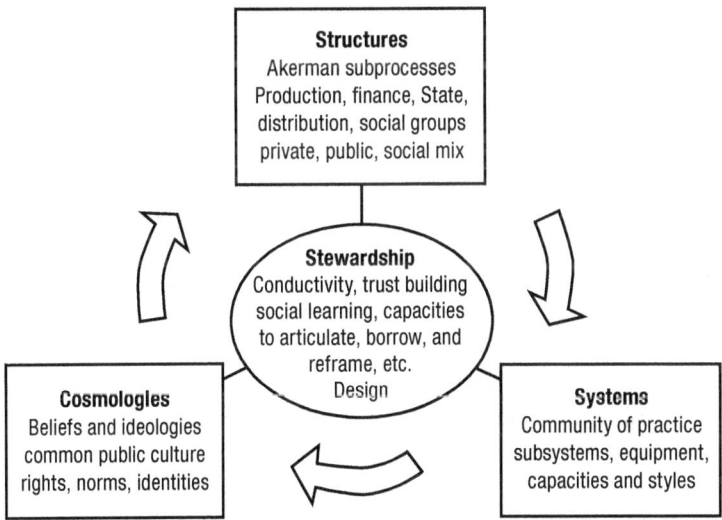

Structures
Akerman subprocesses
Production, finance, State,
distribution, social groups
private, public, social mix

Stewardship
Conductivity, trust building
social learning, capacities
to articulate, borrow, and
reframe, etc.
Design

Cosmologies
Beliefs and ideologies
common public culture
rights, norms, identities

Systems
Community of practice
subsystems, equipment,
capacities and styles

Source: Paquet, 2014, p. 8.

Fourth, our approach defines governance as effective coordination when power, resources and information are widely distributed in many hands and heads, and puts the coordination/collaboration interface squarely at the core of the governance *problematique*: the progress of stewardship from coordination (i.e., the harmonization/complementarity of frames of reference or reference points of the different partners into an aligned communicative order) toward collaboration (i.e., harmonization/complementarity of arrangements for joint action in order achieve collective results) – is a point made most forcefully by Helmut Willke (2007: 14-18). It develops a capacity to work together regardless of prior relationships, whether trust is present or not, and whether a full understanding of the situation is shared by everyone (Paquet 2011).

The distributed nature of governance implies that a governance inquiry must be designed to support the probing of a problematic context together with the existing organizational arrangements and with sufficient care and mindfulness so as to understand what does and does not work well for all partners. This necessitates facilitating both co-ownership and a capacity for effective stewardship in order to yield fruitful collaborative governance – whether or not stakeholders share common values, or common aims, or even *affectio societatis* (Cuisinier 2008), but only what Aristotle would have called concord (*homonoia*). This 'concord' is "a relationship between people ... who are not strangers, between whom goodwill is possible, but not friendship ... a relationship based on respect for ... differences" (Adrian Oldfield cited in Paquet 1999: 203).

Fifth, this governance approach zooms in on the on-going process to organize and reflexively re-organize patterns of communication among stakeholders, so that organizations and socio-economic systems can:

- respond to a contingent environment faster and better in real time;

- contribute to the design of effective multi-stakeholder communication systems to foster ongoing cooperation; and,
- orchestrate sufficient social learning among pluralist groups in such a way that collective innovation and collaborative action are both doable and capable of generating the required competencies for antifragility – i.e., the increasing capacity to cope better with ever more daunting challenges (Taleb 2012).

Long ago, James March (1971/1988: 264) hinted at the need for this type of governance renewal around some key notions of strategy, evaluation, and accountability. We will deal further with these matters in Part II.

Fourth movement: Stewardship – efficient, effective, smart, wise, cognitive, heuristic ...

Stewardship is akin to a process of wayfinding which must not only be **efficient** (doing the thing right from the perspective of using the minimal amount of resources), and **effective** (doing the right thing, and ensuring that wayfinding contributes to the achievement of the hoped for value-adding), but also be **smart** (doing the job in imaginative and innovative ways) and *wise* (do it in ways that are perceived to be socially acceptable, and politically not too destabilizing) – in order to provide a foundation for governance that is simultaneously seen as legitimate, ambitious, creative and robust (Paquet and Wilson 2011, 2015).

We handle this sort of 'intelligence in action' approach to governance in two steps.

Firstly, through the two exploratory essays in Part III that tentatively gauge the many boundaries against which the governance inquiry runs – the lack of *affectio societatis* and the drifting governance culture. We suggest that the first blockage is likely to be a fixture in most collective situations, and can be managed with the right collection of skills and affordances. However, the second blockage responds more slowly to change efforts, but it has such a carrying capacity for accelerating change that it might bring forth a revolutionary new wave of governance practice.

Secondly, through a conclusion that will not only provide guidance as to directions and mechanisms, but also focus on clarifying the notion of 'virtuous scheming'.

Envoi

This book owes much to the formal collaboration with the fellows at the Centre on Governance over the years, but also to collaboration with extramural researchers since the 1960s – both sources being mentioned explicitly in the text.

Daily conversations at the Centre on Governance over the last 20 years have created very difficult problems of attribution. Over this period of some 1,000 weeks, the Centre has produced scores of books, research reports, evaluations and articles, but it has also been the locus of thousands of conversations, piercing questions, skeptical queries, stinging satirical remarks, and most insightful suggestions, etc. that no one ever bothered to carefully minute. For all this flood of help, we would like to express our profound appreciation, together with the hope that we have succeeded in acknowledging these fruitful exchanges appropriately and fully whenever this was called for. Finally, the material, financial and moral support of the Centre on Governance of the University of Ottawa and of Invenire is gratefully acknowledged.

References

Akerman, Johan. 1944. *Ekonomics Theori II*. Lund, SE: CWK Gleerups Forlag. (French translation – 1955) *Structures et cycles économiques*. Paris, FR: Presses Universitaires de France).

Boisvert, R.D. 1998. *John Dewey – Rethinking our Time*. Albany, NY: State University of New York.

Brafman, Ori and Rod A. Beckstrom. 2006. *The Starfish and the Spider – The Unstoppable Power of Leaderless Organizations*. New York, NY: The Penguin Group.

Calame, Pierre and André Talmant. 1997. *L'État au coeur – Le Meccano de la gouvernance*. Paris, FR: Desclée de Brouwer.

Cleveland, Harlan. 2002. *Nobody in Charge*. San Francisco, CA: Jossey-Bass.

Cuisinier, Vincent. 2008. *L'affectio societatis*. Montpellier, FR: Lexis-Nexis LITEC.

Dewey, John. 1935. *Liberalism and Social Action*. New York, NY: Putnam.

Ferry, Jean-Marc. 1996. *L'éthique reconstructive*. Paris, FR: Les Éditions du Cerf.

Hampden-Turner, Charles and Alfons Trompenaars. 1993. *The Seven Cultures of Capitalism*. New York, NY: Currency/ Doubleday.

Hayek, Friedrich A. *et al.* (eds.). 1935. *Collectivist Economic Planning: critical studies on the possibility of socialism*. London, UK: Routledge.

Hirschman, Albert O. 1986. "Against Parsimony: Three easy ways of complicating some categories of economic discourse," *The American Economic Review*, 74(2): 89-96.

Hubbard, Ruth and Gilles Paquet. 2015. *Irregular Governance – A Plea for Bold Organizational Experimentation*. Ottawa, ON: Invenire Books.

Katouzian, Homa. 1980. *Ideology and Method in Economics*. New York, NY: New York University Press.

Kleiner, Art. 2012. "The Thought Leader Interview of Dov Seidman," *Strategy + Business*, (67), Summer.

Laloux, Frederic. 2014. *Reinventing Organizations*. Brussels, BE: Nelson Parker.

Laurent, Paul and Gilles Paquet. 1998. *Epistémologie et économie de la relation: coordination et gouvernance distribuée*. Lyon/Paris, FR: Vrin.

Laurent, Paul, Gilles Paquet and Tim Ragan. 1992. "Strategic Networks as Five-Dimensional Bricolage," *Proceedings of the*

IMP, 8th Conference, Business Networks in an International Context: Recent Research Development. Salle, R., R. Spencer and J.P. Valla (eds.), Lyon, p. 194-206.

Leibenstein, Harvey. 1976. *Beyond Economic Man.* Cambridge, MA: Harvard University Press.

March, James G. 1971/1988. "The Technology of Foolishness" in J.G. March. *Decisions and Organizations.* Oxford, UK: Basil Blackwell, chapter 12, p. 253-265.

Naím, Moisés. 2013. *The End of Power – From boardrooms, to battlefields, to states and churches, why being in charge isn't what it used to be.* New York, NY: Basic Books.

Nanos, Nik. 2012. "Canadians Rate Highly the Issues Close to their Day-to-Day Lives," *Policy Options,* August, http://policyoptions.irpp.org/magazines/policy-challenges-for-2020/canadians-rate-highly-the-issues-close-to-their-day-to-day-lives/ [Accessed March 14, 2016].

Paquet, Gilles. 1966. "The Structuration of a Planned Economy," *Canadian Slavonic Papers,* (8): 250-259.

Paquet, Gilles. 1968. "Anatomy of Recent Economic Development in the Communist World," *Culture,* 29(11): 18-34.

Paquet, Gilles (ed.). 1972. *The Multinational Firm and the Nation State.* Toronto, ON: Collier-Macmillan.

Paquet, Gilles. 1998. "Evolutionary Cognitive Economics," *Information Economics and Policy,* 10(3): 343-357.

Paquet, Gilles. 1999. *Governance Through Social Learning.* Ottawa, ON: University of Ottawa Press.

Paquet, Gilles. 2009. *Crippling Epistemologies and Governance Failures: A Plea for Experimentalism.* Ottawa, ON: University of Ottawa Press.

Paquet, Gilles. 2011. *Gouvernance collaborative – un antimanuel.* Montreal, QC: Liber.

Paquet, Gilles. 2013. *Tackling Wicked Policy Problems – Equality, Diversity, and Sustainability.* Ottawa, ON: Invenire Books.

Paquet, Gilles. 2014. *Tableau d'avancement III: pour une diaspora canadienne-française antifragile*. Ottawa, ON: Invenire Books.

Paquet, Gilles and Tim Ragan. 2012. *Through the Detox Prism – Exploring Organizational Failures and Design Responses*. Ottawa, ON: Invenire Books.

Paquet, Gilles and Jean-Pierre Wallot. 2007. *Un Québec moderne 1760-1840 – Essai d'histoire économique et sociale*. Montreal, QC: HMH.

Paquet, Gilles and Christopher Wilson. 2011. "Collaborative Co-governance as Inquiring Systems," *www.optimumonline.ca*, 41(2): 1-12.

Paquet, Gilles and Christopher Wilson. 2015. "Governance failure and anti-government phenomena," *www.optimumonline.ca*, 45(2): 1-24.

Polanyi, Karl. 1957. "The Economy as Instituted Process" in K. Polany *et al.* (eds.). *Trade and Markets in the Early Empires: Economics in History and Theory*. Glencoe, IL: Free Press, p. 243-270.

Sibley, Robert. 2013. "Young men can be turned to good or evil," *Ottawa Citizen*, April 29. www.pressreader.com/canada/ottawa-citizen/20130429/281822871297425/TextView [Accessed March 14, 2016].

Taleb, Nassim Nicholas. 2012. *Antifragile – Things that gain from disorder*. New York, NY: Random House.

Terry, Larry D. 2003. *Leadership of Public Bureaucracies – The Administrator as Conservator*. Armonk, NY: M.E. Sharpe.

Thorngate, W. 1976. "'In General' vs. 'It Depends': Some Comments on the Gergen-Schlenker Debate," *Personality and Social Psychology Bulletin*, 2, p. 404-410.

Willke, Helmut. 2007. *Smart Governance – Governing the Global Knowledge Society*. Frankfurt, DE/New York, NY: Campus Verlag.

PART I:

Reframing

n the design of intelligent governance, one must start with a good appreciation of the context of the organization or system of interest, and of the challenges such a context generates.

Stewarding an organization or a system requires a good appreciation of its circumstances. And yet, all too often, a certain lack of mindfulness presides over the definition of the circumstances and context of an organization, as a result of an unhealthy disrespect for the art of description by social scientists. The result is often a 'cartoonization' of the context to make the problem at hand look more tractable and amenable to "the way things have always been done here" mindset. This triggers a phenomenal sanitization of actual representations, and consequently inflicts a momentous handicap on any governance inquiry, thereby condemning it to dealing with only surrogates of reality. Such trappings have to be exorcized.

In chapter 1, we examine the debilitating refusal to accept that an issue context may be inexorably characterized by deep complexity and deep uncertainty. Intelligent governance is not built on the toxic artificial world of chosism and other so-called certainty-equivalents; it embraces deep complexity and deep uncertainty as inescapable assumptions. To better take these realities into account, a communicational lens is used to probe organizations and governance.

Since the middle of the last century, there has been a frontal attack on chosistic and deterministic representations of reality that are based on mechanical and predictable objects and a view that the whole is no more than the sum of its parts (Monnerot 1946). While the physical sciences have learned from this attack, unfortunately, in the social sciences, this perverse and unreal quest for determinism and certainty has proven all too convenient for social scientists to consider discarding them.

In chapter 2, we confront head on the difficult imperative of collaboration. This follows from the fact that power, resources and information are generally distributed in a number of hands and heads in modern organizations and systems. Yet far too many still readily assume that collaboration comes to life spontaneously whenever necessary. This is quite naïve. Collaboration needs to be engineered ... one way or another.

We argue that collaboration is essential to generate social learning and wise stewardship. This entails an appropriate use of mechanisms to ensure the emergence of the requisite trust, and the highest and best use of structures, systems and cosmologies to bolster collaboration.

In chapter 3, we show that in this world of complexity, uncertainty and necessary collaboration, governance is most often faced with wicked problems – problems where objectives are ill-defined and evolving, and means-ends relationships are unclear and unstable. This calls for a governance process that includes dynamic inquiry, evolutionary social learning and wayfinding by trial and error – in which continual learning is not an endpoint but a never ending process (Geyer and Rihani 2010).

Such foundational moves in intelligent governance represent total game changers for collective coordination.

References

Geyer, Robert and Samir Rihani. 2010. *Complexity and Public Policy*. New York, NY: Routledge.

Monnerot, Jules. 1946. *Les faits sociaux ne sont pas des choses*. Paris, FR: Gallimard.

| Beyond the Blinding Search for Simplicity and Certainty

"... high levels of uncertainty challenge existing assessment methods, established decision and management procedures ..."

Roger E. Kasperson

Introduction

We have denounced earlier the limitations of deterministic Newtonian representations of the world (Paquet 2013) that claim that reality can be "understood through rational inquiry based [solely] on objectivity, certainty and chain reasoning ... based on certainty, order, structure, status, and determinism" (Slaton 1991: 42-3).

This Newtonian worldview is comprised of a number of assumptions that are well-known and widely accepted by conventional social scientists: individualism (humans as separate and self-contained); hedonistic psychology (motivations are precise, rational, and predictable); equality (each human being is commensurable and interchangeable); mutual exclusivity (humans cannot occupy the same place at the same time without conflict and power relations ensuing), and each human pursuing his own self-interest in this individualistic dog-eat-dog world (*Ibid.*: 45-47).

This Newtonian representation is far too simplistic, too absolute, and too narrow in its applicability to be able to provide much of a useful understanding of our complex and turbulent world, where uncertainty and unpredictability are the order of the day, and where collaboration is essential.

Moreover, it is routinely and most confidently presumed that, through some not-always-well-understood processes, 'leaders' can distil the 'aggregate preferences' of their deferent or fearful followers, and can rationally guide the organization or the social system in keeping with these preferences. The pretence, for instance, that the state (or any supposedly transcendent actor) can elicit commonly agreed-upon values that can serve as guideposts for a diverse society, is pure fantasy.

As it turns out, our world is more Quantum-like than Newtonian. Humans are most often defined by their environment and relationships, rather than by their innate preferences; their desires, intentions, and talents are different and unequal; they share space and collaborate with others; their behaviour is determined not only by external stimuli, but also by discourse, deliberation, and herd movements; and most often the individual-ranked preferences cannot be aggregated into a consistent community-wide ranking because they are often at odds with one another.

While stakeholders with only a portion of the resources, power, and information necessary in a given situation may not be able to take charge, they may be able to nudge the organization or the social system in certain directions by indulging in some process of redesign of the collective arrangements between parties, either alone or collaboratively. Indeed, such pressures to alter the *status quo* will influence governance by impacting the collective capacity for stewardship and continuous learning, although not always in the ways anticipated (Hubbard *et al.* 2012).

The challenges of a more enigmatic world

For some time, Newtonian-type thinking has sanitized our views of the world in the social sciences. To a certain extent it was possible to preserve a sense of security and certainty by denying or occluding a number of emerging phenomena – such as a more diffracted and volatile distribution of power; a more complex determination of causes and responsibilities; a more unstable and diffuse definition of stakeholders, etc. in organizations and social systems.

But, in the last while, as Innerarity (2012) has shown, it has become less and less easy to rationalize the use of those comforting Newtonian assumptions in the face of socio-political-economic realities that regularly reveal increasing complexity and uncertainty due to latent forces and secondary effects like unintended consequences, unsuspected threats, system inertia, etc. (Beck 2001). The growing chasm between simplified representations that fit existing tools and the complex nature of reality has made those representations more opaque and less and less helpful.

Recognizing the more enigmatic nature of our world has triggered a reframing of our way of dealing with governance: from an unhelpful science of the precise, to a more constructive approach of the imprecise (Paquet 2013). The foundations of this approach will be developed in this section of the book.

It will proceed in two phases: first, by identifying a shift from a chosistic to a communicational perspective that is less constraining and static; and second, by a recognition that deep complexity and deep uncertainty call for governance issues to be generally recognized as wicked problems.

A communicational perspective

Friedrich Hayek (1945) contributed significantly to a reframing of perspectives on the socio-economic system. He suggested that one might be able to gain more insight into the functioning of complex organizations and socio-economies if, instead of focusing on material flows of goods and services, one were to focus on the flipside of these material flows: the information flows (messages, communications, conversations, etc.) that underpin them. That is the information exchanges that occur via the intermediation of conventions, organizations and institutions, and that underpin the dynamics that trigger the production, allocation and distribution of material goods and services, and the coordination and orientation of these material processes.

This informational perspective emphasizes the centrality of coordination among all those senders and receivers who have a portion of the information, knowledge, power and resources, as well as the systems of communication that connect them with one another.

Hayek used this approach in the 1930s to criticize the vacuity of the promises made by central planners. He argued that it was impossible for a few to acquire sufficient information in a complex system when that information is widely distributed throughout an organization or socio-economy in order to make the necessary and accurate decisions to intervene effectively and regulate top-down the whole organization or system. Since then his approach has been used to debunk not only the pretentions of central planners, but also:

1. to describe organizations and socio-economies by the nature of the messages they exchange (decrees in centralized concerns, anonymous messages in markets, etc.) (Hurwicz 1960);

2. to X-ray organizations and socio-economies in order to identify informational patterns characterizing the organization, to decode their dynamics, and to understand the information blockages and coordination failures (Paquet 1966, 1968); and,

3. to develop repair initiatives to improve organizational effectiveness by designing better devices for informational coordination (Paquet 1998).

Ultimately, as Jacob Marschak (1966) would have put it, "the economic organization problem degenerates into the problem of choosing the optimal information system." Consequently, this perspective also provides insights into the process of coordination with all its psycho-social textures (opinions, assumptions, beliefs, lies, misrepresentations, etc.), while probing beyond individual instrumental rationality to take into account all sorts of pathologies, including disloyalty and disinformation, that may have an impact on the success or failure of individual and social learning. By defining organizations as information systems (i.e., as networks of relationships that may be analyzed as networks of information flows), it focuses attention on the causal signals that ultimately trigger the movements of goods and services.

Information and knowledge cannot be regarded as a quasi-commodity any more than management or entrepreneurship can be regarded as just another factor of production. In both cases, they are 'enabling resources' that inform, shape, and catalyze the production and distribution of other resources. Furthermore, an exchange of information expands the resource, often becoming the precursor to the creation new resources. The understanding of the dynamics of communication and learning has, in fact, fostered emerging new fields of study like cognitive economics and evolutionary economics (McCain 1992; Nelson and Winter 1984).

Nevertheless, at the core of this communication dynamic is the notion of reflexivity that captures the full complexity of the informational underpinnings of the governing task in complex modern societies. Reflexive governance is governance:

- that is conscious of its limitations, of the broader forces interfering with/influencing its steering activities, and of the unintended consequences as a result of our limited information and rationality; and,
- that has ensured that it takes these factors into account in its operations.

Reflexive governance amounts to actively designing mechanisms capable of mobilizing diffracted and dispersed information, and of generating new knowledge and learning through recursive feedback relationships among the distributed steering activities. This reflexivity involves processes of self-organization, self-correction, and self-reconfiguration in the organization of interest, and in its steering mechanisms – indeed in the very purpose of the organization or social system itself (Voβ et al. 2006).

The communicational perspective also suggests something akin to a Quantum informational pattern – i.e., arrangements that do not follow simple, causal and easily predictable paths, but arrangements which one can only regard as contingent and stochastic, and coming with a fair degree of indeterminacy and uncertainty.

In such a world, the principles that effectively guide real human behaviour are quite different from those that prevail in a Newtonian world:

- people and organizations are unique, defined by their environments and their relationships with others;
- cause-effect determinism and rational decision making are not at the root of all human interactions;
- human systems are dynamic moving processes that most often cannot be partitioned into discrete units for analysis; and,
- there is no objective real world that exists apart from that which exists in one's own consciousness. Such subjectivity demands a reconciliation between competing understandings.

Obviously, this Quantum informational pattern calls for revisiting many assumptions in good currency – from modifying the vocabulary used in problem definitions, to refurbishing key concepts in the management toolbox and adding new ones, and to reconceiving the notion of social coordination in human systems on the basis of fundamental complexity, limited information, shared ownership, stewardship, experimentation, collaboration, social learning, and continuous interactions capable of modifying the very settings of the game.

Moreover, the broader mega-community, inclusive of the powerful impacts of the environment and the natural forces of self-organization, must be being taken seriously into account as forces that shape governance.

Not all conversations about stewardship, distributed governance, and inquiring systems will agree on all the implications of such a dramatic paradigm shift towards the centrality of information, or on the key stewardship concepts and mental tools required.

Nor will they share the same view about how combinations of forces shape the stewardship of organizations and social systems, or how organizations and social systems may be nudged in desirable directions.

But they must all agree that changes in the mindset and in the *outillage mental* will accompany any shift from the views associated with the traditional, Newtonian paradigm to a more Quantum one that is more aligned with collaborative governance[4] and the daily complexities being faced.

In fact, a communicational perspective forcefully drives home the idea that any perspective intent on sanitizing representations of turbulence, deep complexity and deep uncertainty in dealing with organizations and socio-economic systems would, in effect, condemn governance to trying to address the problems of Hamlet without taking into account that he was the Prince of Denmark.

Complexity, turbulence, and deep uncertainty ... responding to wicked problems

As complexity and diversity grow, so too does the potential for disorder and conflict, necessitating more and more frequent exchanges with the environment and stakeholders to sustain order within that complex environment.[5] Simplistic management planning based on logic model 'solutions' to more or less static puzzles are becoming more and more inadequate

---

[4] For instance, this entails a redefinition of rationality as ecological fit, and of the policy process as inquiring and wayfinding systems – freed from the naïveties of assuming that rationality is simple internal coherence of individual choices, and of the caricatures of the policy/strategy process as goal-control and bow-arrow target contraptions, as suggested by the traditional paradigm.

[5] This is a basic principle of thermodynamics that complex open systems do not succumb to disorder and remain viable by drawing order from their environments.

as ways to cope with a context that is not only in motion but prone to avalanches. What is essential in this context is a capacity to respond to challenges, to overcome previously unknown difficulties, all the while learning to cope ever better with the changing circumstances through systems of inquiry capable of guiding social learning in the organization or system to be able to adapt with increasing degrees of effectiveness.

Complexity and turbulence

This sort of complex and turbulent environment has triggered a number of new challenges for government that have forced some fundamental changes in perspective. For instance, a shift from:

- a world where it could be said that someone is 'in charge,' to situations where nobody would seem to have all the power, resources and information to be really in charge;
- an environment where common values might appear to prevail, to situations where a multiplicity of different values prevail and actively compete;
- situations that would appear to generate simple risk configurations (that can be handled by routine management calculations), to situations of deep uncertainty and ignorance, for which nothing less than new 'trial and error' governance instruments will do;
- situations that can be approximated by relatively simple, cause-effect relationships, to more complex situations where non-linear and less predictable relationships would appear to prevail, and where, in fact, truly unpredictable outcomes have to be anticipated;
- a simple world where direct action is always effective because the dynamic is relatively simple to understand, to more complex ones where the nature of the dynamic is opaque, outcomes are unpredictable, and obliquity in action is often the only option (Kay 2010);
- well-understood, static problems that submit easily to linear analysis, to ill-structured and evolving situations where only an inquiring system and social learning can

offer a means to develop a useful appreciation of the evolving circumstances and evince an effective system of wayfinding through experimentation and prototyping;

- logic models and well-structured, certain outcomes, to well-structured collaborative processes that produce outcomes that may be somewhat uncertain but useful products of 'learning as you go'; and,
- a shift from perspectives that would appear to be satisfied with conserving the *status quo*, to perspectives where anything less than ever greater courage and capacity to transform is tantamount to condemning the organization to regress.

These new complex and turbulent circumstances have heralded major transformations in the institutional order, like the erosion of 'Big G' Government (centralized hierarchical governing in organizations of all sectors) and its painful and still largely incomplete replacement by 'small g' governance (decentralized, heterarchical governing of organizations in all sectors) (Paquet 2011).

Maybe, more important, is the shift in the nature of governance that is being induced by:

- **dynamic complexity**, in the sense that problems cannot be addressed piece by piece, but only by tackling the system as a whole;
- **social complexity**, in the sense that since different perspectives and interests must prevail, different actors must be engaged in resolving the issues between them; and
- **generative complexity**, in the sense that the future is undetermined and the old 'best practices' are of little help (in fact, they are more likely to recreate the problems of the past in the future). Only the innovation of new practices will do (Kahane 2010: 5).

Deep uncertainty

As the complexity and the turbulence of our social systems have grown, the number of situations involving simple risks that can be handled by routine management calculations has continued to decline. Stakeholders are having to face ever more situations of deep uncertainty and incomplete knowledge, for which nothing less than a new governance regime will do. Complexity not only generates turbulence and a need to modify the *status quo*, but also deep uncertainty and unpredictability, where stakeholders may have little to no clue about what is going on or even where to begin.

These are the "unknown unknowns," described by former US Defense Secretary Donald Rumsfeld as, "the ones we don't know we don't know. And if one looks throughout the history of our country and other free countries, it is [this] category that tend[s] to be the difficult one."[6]

When one is faced with these situations, we can begin by using a slightly modified version of the definitions proposed by Roger Kasperson (2008: 348):

- Risk situations: where the magnitude of the events and consequences are relatively well-known, and probability distributions can be reasonably assigned to each;
- Uncertainty situations: where the direction of change is to some extent known, but the magnitude and the probability of events and consequences, and the receptors at risk, cannot be estimated with any precision;
- Ignorance situations: where even the broad directions of change are not known, and where the thresholds of change and non-linear relationships are possibly identified but not understood [the unknown unknowns].

One may imagine that families of situations range all over a knowledge continuum – from simple and clear known knowns with calculable risks, to situations involving deep ignorance and uncertainty, unknown unknowns – with different, more complex approaches being required as one proceeds along the continuum. As situations drift farther and farther away from the simple risk situation on the continuum, it becomes no

---

[6] "Defense.gov News Transcript: DoD News Briefing," February 12, 2002, Secretary Rumsfeld and Gen. Myers, United States Department of Defense (defense.gov), http://archive.defense.gov/Transcripts/Transcript. aspx?TranscriptID=2636 [Accessed March 26, 2016].

longer a matter of simply "working harder" with the same tools and the same perspectives, but as some would like to suggest, by referring to uncertainty management. As one travels along the continuum, one begins to experience actual changes of kind in the situations, and ultimately to the progressively more opaque issues that must be tackled with approaches that are altogether different in nature from the tools of certainty, in order to "imagine the possible, even if it seems unlikely" (Rumsfeld 2012).

One may legitimately extend the use of conventional risk management into territory of uncertainty even if the parameters cannot be easily gauged, and must be approximated, but there are limits to such forays. Beyond a certain point, those exercises become truly meaningless, and their use can only be regarded as illegitimate and possibly dangerous. In the same way, governance protocols that fit certain situations may be extended for use in ignorance territory, but again only to a point, beyond which their use in deep uncertainty becomes illegitimate and bogus.

In parallel, as one proceeds along the continuum, problem definition becomes more and more murky and ill-structured. Consequently, it becomes more and more difficult to translate a situation into a formulation that is analytically tractable and commonly acceptable. Unfortunately, when such a translation is effected forcefully, it often generates a problem definition that has lost most of the substantive, interesting and important features of the situation. In such cases, while the version of the situation may remain analytically sound, its implications are irrelevant, or even toxic, from a practical point of view since the substantial aspects of the case have been lost due to efforts to make it tractable.

One such sanitized concatenation is the traditional mapping routinely made by economists of any given good as a separate entity depending on its different time coordinate (t) and the state of the world coordinate(s). This may yield elegant modeling allowing the distillation of potential trade-offs among these notionally differentiated goods, the vagaries of market evolution have been excised in this 'spatialized' version of time and uncertainty. This sort of undue simplification is not unlike the US Ballistic Missile Threat Commission of the late 1990s taking the view (Rumsfeld 2012) that the lack of information about an activity was inferred to mean that an activity would not happen ... until that is September 11, 2001.

Wicked problems

One label that has been used to capture the sort of problems generated in such circumstances of deep complexity and deep uncertainty is to say that a problem is 'wicked.' The notion was first put forward by Rittel and Webber (1973), and it has been used widely in various ways in the public administration literature afterward (Paquet 1999). Recently, it has been adopted wholeheartedly by the Australian Public Service Commission (2007), and applied to a whole range of national policy decisions. Indeed, it has been made the central feature of the analytical framework of Valerie Brown's research group at the Australian National University (Brown *et al.* 2010).

'Wicked' problems evade clear definition. Rittel and Webber defined them using a number of characteristics that have been synthesized by Valerie Brown *et al.* (2010: 62-63) and boiled down further here as follows:

- they have multiple interpretations from multiple interest groups;
- they involve trade-offs between multiple goals, sometimes competing, that are often ill-defined and unclear;
- they have no definitive, clear solution;
- actions on this front often lead to unforeseen consequences;
- the means-ends relationships in the actions taken are not stable (i.e., logic models are of no help);
- they are socially complex, requiring contributions from many players;
- they rarely sit conveniently within a single discipline or organization;
- tackling them usually involves changes in personal and social behaviour;

- they cannot be generalized outside their particular context; and,
- their formulation rests on resolving paradoxes that call for open inquiries.

Even if the degree of 'wickedness' of a problem varies, and if all the above features do not always apply, the sort of challenges presented by such wicked problems can create quite messy environments of their own, especially if one were to insist on defining a problem in overly simplistic and static terms – in an attempt to free it from the impacts of turbulence, complexity, uncertainty, ignorance, or unpredictability.

Embracing deep complexity and deep uncertainty

Embracing deep complexity and deep uncertainty begins with a refusal to sanitize a problem in order to make it conform to pre-existing notions and make it more analytically tractable. Such sanitized strategies are not unlike that of the drunkard who has lost his watch in a dark alley but searches for it under a lamp post because that is where there is more light. Abandoning such a futile approach, however, may leave one in the discomforting situation of having to admit that one does not have quick answers or even all the knowledge, resources or power to resolve the problem. It's an admission of vulnerability that few are willing to accept easily, especially among those claiming leadership.

There have been many different avenues proposed to deal with a world of wicked problems: from the bold extensions of the choice-theoretic models *à la* James March, to the more free-reined exploratory inquiries *à la* Valerie Brown, to the bold epistemic redefinition of the *problematique* by Anna Grandori. We take a quick look at these three gambles.

James G. March's wild but overly focused approach

March's playful proposal was originally put forward in a Danish journal in 1971, and was reprinted later in a collection of essays (March 1988). It is deeply rooted in a choice-theoretic *problematique*, and it speculates about situations where goals are not clear (as is the case with wicked problems) and where goal discovery amounts to the central issue. March suggests one may temporarily suspend the usual rationality on the way to discovering promising goals if one uses what he calls 'sensible foolishness' and treats:

- goals as hypotheses;
- intuition as real;
- hypocrisy as a transition;
- memory as an enemy; and,
- experience as a theory.

This has the advantage of maintaining the dominance of a choice-theoretic framework but also allows for the use of lateral thinking in the sense of Edward de Bono (1957/1967), during those times when the search for coherence among the parts does not seem to materialize. At such times there is no prior experience to suggest how all the pieces of the data puzzle should ultimately fit together. As a consequence, one must make a series of informed guesses, coupled with adjustments along the way, to create the image as you go.

While this imaginative leap is quite a clever way to tackle wicked problems, it remains unduly focused on the decision-making process *stricto sensu* to the exclusion of many contextual or social dimensions – in particular the different values of the stakeholders. Moreover, the very playfulness with which March handles the matter is unlikely to generate the sort of deep reflexive questioning of the subterfuges that may be at play – such as the presumptions of simplicity and certainty that have acquired such legitimacy – despite the fantasy nature of the concatenations they may produce.

Even though this use of apparent 'foolishness' entails going back to basic assumptions and questioning them (as March explains at the end of his paper), it is unlikely that such a process, however playful or desirable, can lead to the necessary reframing among a group of diverse actors. Moving people out of their basic, often unspoken assumptions, is inherently a discomforting process, and is therefore generally resisted by rationalizations of the *status quo*. Likewise, simply tabling assumptions, or adopting new ones, is no guarantee that events will unfold productively from there or that the playful process will generate the shared commitment and willingness to collaborate that are necessary to bring about change.

Valerie Brown's eclectic basket of protocols

A more promising strategy has been proposed by Valerie Brown (Brown *et al.* 2010: chapter 6). It has the great merit of having served as the basic conceptual framework on which 15 short studies of wicked problems have been developed, but more importantly, of having been adopted by the Australian Public Service Commission (2007) as a framework for solving tough problems.

To serve as a basis for such a wide array of studies, Brown's framework proposes an array of eleven strategies that have been used successfully in earlier studies, and suggests that they can be usefully combined to tackle various types of wicked problems.

Each of the 15 studies starts with five questions:
• What is the wicked problem being addressed?
• What worldviews are involved?
• What ideals, facts and ideas are contributed from the different types of knowledge?
• How have the diverse sources of evidence been brought together?
• What are the partial, uncertain and open-ended findings from the study?

Over the course of the 15 studies, no less than 11 protocols (involving some 30 research tools) have been used, so in fact what Valerie Brown has proposed is more in the nature of a basket of protocols, a toolbox if you will, that has proved useful in generating collective, open, imaginative, and transdisciplinary inquiries.

This is a more broad-brushed approach than March and courageously presents a framework for collective inquiries capable of generating collaborative action. Yet its very openness gives it a certain Panglossian quality. It represents an invitation to explore with whatever tools might appear useful for the case in point, but its very optimism neglects the potential for resistance, uncooperativeness and outright sabotage that may come from those who benefit from the *status quo*. A look at her case studies reveals a certain commonality of language permeating them, while the five basic questions remain too general and high level for practitioners to generate a template for specific inquiries that can become actionable in a variety of different issue environments.

Even though it is a characteristic of wicked problems that they cannot be generalized beyond their immediate context, such looseness, as would appear to prevail in the inquiries *à la* Brown, may well generate additional malaise and discomfort, making its adoption by tribes of traditionalists (already quite reluctant to accept the challenges of a governance approach) even less likely.

Anna Grandori's epistemic scheme

Anna Grandori (2013) is equally frustrated by the gymnastics of the choice-theoretic approaches and by the looseness of the 'pragmatic' approaches to the world of deep complexity and deep uncertainty. She aims at developing an approach that can be as practical as necessary without sacrificing as much of the free-reined approaches in terms of rationality.

First, Grandori does this by broadening the notion of bounded rationality (away from the sheer strictures of instrumental coherence in terms of means-ends relationships) to the notion of epistemic rationality that jointly pursues a logic of justification and a logic of discovery: moving from a futile effort to foresee all possible contingencies to an effort to identify the pattern of thinking, the logically sound procedure likely to produce the largest number of meaningful conjectures "no matter what the contingencies". This leads her to focus her attention on the capabilities of the resources rather than on actions: taking advantage of the multifunctionality of resources – i.e., their potential for generating a variety of services or activities not just one ... the capacity to renegotiate previously agreed actions ... on the basis of their effects ... on the basis of 'investing in options' rather than by choosing actions (Grandori 2013: 31-32).

Epistemic rationality thus entails not 'maximizing' in a closed problem definition, but 'improving' in an open problem definition. And this is likely to materialize only through 'Popperian learning', i.e., through conjectures and refutations, without the benefit of probability assignments, but leading, through social learning, to exploration, and accepting solutions or agreements that expand the pie (shifting the Pareto frontier outward) as well as agreements that expand the joint surplus to be divided (a situation that is Nash-superior) (*Ibid.*, p.37).

As Grandori concludes, "framing multipurposeness as a 'negotiation between different objectives' no matter if they 'belong' to one or different actors can be considered an epistemically rational way of dealing with incomparable objectives" (*Ibid.*). Popperian social learning by guiding an exploring stewarding defined by continuous conjectures and refutation, and aiming at gauging new Pareto-improved and Nash-improved situations, is an echo effect of epistemic rationality (Paquet 2016).

Second, Grandori, in the name of the same objective, which is to jointly pursue a logic of justification and a logic of discovery, questions the sacredness of the notion of agreement or contract. Grandori proposes that the focus of contracting be displaced three steps backward in the causal chain: from contracting on actions to (1) contracting on decision rights, (2) to contracting on asset ownership and potential rights to decide and act, and finally (3) to contracting on right sharing and on legal entity establishing.

This establishes the ground on which organizational forms might be designed: as Grandori puts it, in the face of deep uncertainty, of tasks that are bound to depend on unforeseeable contingencies and circumstances, contracting on actions or decisions *ex ante* is by definition hazardous, contracting on procedures is challenging since one cannot define all possible circumstances, contracting on property rights is also chancy, while contracting on legal entity establishing (i.e., defining the property rights of the different parties and their enforceable responsibilities for the resource commitments and the resources in use) is more likely to generate firm-like organizations based on agreement about what resources to commit.

The natural extension of the Grandori inquiry leads her to reflect on ways to enrich the range of organizational forms that such firm-like arrangements might take, and on the variety of means of discovery that might be used in the search for new forms of organization. She is led to reject the corset of "discrete institutional alternatives" in favour of discrete coordination mechanisms that can be combined to fit particular challenges and circumstances in the design of fitting organizations. Efficiency and innovation may best be achieved through the design of multimodal forms of organizations like Lincoln Electric (Paquet and Ragan 2012).

The Grandori scheme is the most intellectually satisfactory. It remains however more in the nature of an analytical framework (in the sense of Leibenstein) than in the nature of a theoretical framework: a basis for negotiation of improvements in an open problem definition. Design is a central challenge here. So despite the elegance of the argumentation, nothing formulaic is likely to ensue – even though patterns of thinking are likely to be vividly sought. Grandori remains practically modest despite the robustness of the argumentation: "qualitative evidence may help in grasping what multimodal arrangements might be" (Grandori 2013: 111).

Operationally speaking

That said, the great merit of the work of Valerie Brown and her team (together with the foundational work that Anna Grandori has provided in support of this sort of exploratory and design-oriented work) has been to make the case for a promising alternative approach to solve tough wicked problems, and to demonstrate the potential of broad-brush and looser frameworks in a variety of circumstances. This is no small accomplishment in a social scientific world that is still very much crippled by chosism and quantophrenia.

However, in the face of the extraordinary resistance to governance by traditionalists in legal, political science, public administration, and even management studies – primarily because they find the challenges of collective, open, imaginative, transdisciplinary inquiries too daunting – it would appear unlikely that such eclectic and yet robust explorations as those of Brown *et al.* and Grandori – and the *force de frappe* of any effort combining them – will do much to sway those reluctant observers.

As a result, a relatively open prototype version of such an approach (less theoretical than Grandori's and less eclectic than Brown's) will be proposed in chapter 3. But before we get to it, we must set the stage with the challenge of collaboration.

References

Australian Public Service Commission. 2007. *Tackling Wicked Problems: A Public Policy Perspective*. Canberra, AU: Government of Australia.

Beck, Ulrich. 2001. *La société du risque*. Paris, FR: Flammarion/ Aubier.

Brown, Valerie A. 2010. "Conducting an Imaginative Transdisciplinary Inquiry" in Brown, Valerie A. *et al.* (eds.). *Tackling Wicked Problems – Through the Transdisciplinary Imagination*. New York, NY: Routledge, p. 103-114.

Brown, Valerie A. *et al.* (eds.). 2010. *Tackling Wicked Problems – Through the Transdisciplinary Imagination*. New York, NY: Routledge.

de Bono, Edward. 1957/1967. *The Use of Lateral Thinking*. London, UK: Jonathon Cape.

"Defense.gov News Transcript: DoD News Briefing," February 12, 2002, Secretary Rumsfeld and Gen. Myers, United States

Department of Defense *(defense.gov)*, *http://archive.defense.gov/ Transcripts/Transcript.aspx?TranscriptID=2636* [Accessed March 26, 2016].

Grandori, Anna. 2013. *Epistemic Economics and Organization – Forms of rationality and governance for a wiser economy*. London, UK: Routledge.

Hayek, Friedrich A. 1945. "The Use of Knowledge in Society," *American Economic Review*, 35(4): 519-530.

Hubbard, Ruth, Gilles Paquet, and Christopher Wilson. 2012. *Stewardship*. Ottawa, ON: Invenire Books.

Hurwicz, Leonid. 1960. "Conditions for Economic Efficiency of Centralized and Decentralized Structures" in Gregory Grossman (ed.). *Value and Plan*. Berkeley, CA: University of California Press, p.162-175.

Innerarity, Daniel. 2012. *La société invisible*. Quebec, QC: Presses de l'Université Laval.

Kahane, Adam. 2010. *Power and Love – A Theory and Practice of Social Change*. San-Francisco, CA: Berrett-Koehler.

Kasperson, Roger E. 2008. "Coping with Deep Uncertainty: Challenges for Environmental Assessment and Decision-making," in G. Bammer and M. Smithson (eds.). *Uncertainty and Risk – Multidisciplinary Perspectives*. London, UK: Earthscan, p. 337-347.

Kay, John. 2010. *Obliquity – why our goals are best achieved indirectly*. London, UK: The Penquin Press.

Leibenstein, Harvey. 1976. *Beyond Economic Man*. Cambridge, MA: Harvard University Press.

March, James G. 1971/1988. "The Technology of Foolishness" in James G. March. 1988. *Decisions and Organizations*. Oxford, UK: Basil Blackwell, p. 253-265.

Marschak, Jacob. 1966. "Economic Planning and the Costs of Thinking," *Social Research*, 33(1): 151-159.

McCain, Roger A. 1992. *A Framework for Cognitive Economics*, New York, NY: Praeger.

Nelson, Richard R. and Sidney G. Winter. 1984. *An Evolutionary Theory of Economic Change*, Cambridge, MA: Harvard University Press.

Paquet, Gilles. 1966. "The Structuration of a Planned Economy," *Canadian Slavonic Papers*, (8): 250-259.

Paquet, Gilles. 1968. "Anatomy of Recent Economic Development in the Communist World," *Culture*, 29(11): 18-34.

Paquet, Gilles. 1998. "Evolutionary Cognitive Economics," *Information Economics and Policy*, 10(3): 343-357.

Paquet, Gilles. 1999. "Innovations in Governance in Canada," *Optimum*, 29(2-3): 71-81.

Paquet, Gilles. 2011. *Gouvernance collaborative : un antimanuel*. Montreal, QC: Liber.

Paquet, Gilles. 2013. "La gouvernance, science de l'imprécis," *Organisations & Territoires*, 21(3): 5-17.

Paquet, Gilles. 2016. "Anna Grandori's epistemic scheme of thought," *optimumonline.ca*, 46(2), at press.

Paquet, Gilles and Tim Ragan. 2012. *Through the Detox Prism: Exploring Organizational Failures and Design Responses*. Ottawa, ON: Invenire.

Rittel, Horst W.J. and M. Webber. 1973. "Dilemmas in a General Theory of Planning," *Policy Sciences* (4): 155-169.

Rumsfeld, Donald. 2012. *Known and Unknown: A Memoir*. New York, NY: Sentinel. http://papers.rumsfeld.com/about/page/authors-note [Accessed March 16, 2016].

Slaton, Christa Daryl. 1991. "Quantum Theory and Political Theory" in Theodore L. Becker (ed.). *Quantum Politics: Applying Quantum Theory to Political Phenomenon*. New York, NY: Praeger.

Voβ, Jan-Peter *et al.* (eds.). 2006. *Reflexive Governance for Sustainable Development*. Cheltenham, UK: Edward Elgar.

| On Collaboration

"Collaboration is [seen as] an unnatural act
between non-consenting adults."
Former US Surgeon General, Jocelyn Elders

Introduction

I ssues are becoming more and more complex. They involve complex multi-stakeholder environments in which, because of the dispersion of knowledge, resources and power, any system of intelligent governance itself is likely to become more and more distributed. Like it or not, collaboration has become a crucial element for resolving just about any issue of significance today. When confronted with wicked problems, collaboration is not only helpful, it has become a matter of survival for organizations. In this chapter, we will probe the nature of collaboration, both in small groups and mass collaboration, and identify ways most likely to facilitate it.

Some organizations have understood collaboration well and have worked hard at it. For instance, Caterpillar Inc., the iconic Fortune 100 manufacturer of construction and mining equipment, restructured itself in 1998, moving from being a silo-based organization to an umbrella organization for 26 global business units. Collaboration and knowledge sharing became important 'must haves' for the organization. Yet in the process of reorganization, many of its employees lost track of one another, and as a consequence lost access to the knowledge they needed to share. "We found we were repeating the same mistakes and doing the same research multiple times from different business units," said Reed Stuedemann, a 27-year Caterpillar veteran and knowledge-sharing manager (Powers 2004).

By that time, Caterpillar's intangible assets, like intellectual capital, had grown significantly, to the point where they accounted for 85 percent of the company's overall value. This meant that collaboration and knowledge sharing had to be key elements of the organization's value adding process. In response, Caterpillar launched its *Knowledge Network* as a web-based system to reconnect its people and encourage them to share their knowledge and work together. This small, grassroots initiative has now evolved into a successful, enterprise-wide process that generated savings of US$75 million in five years.

The *Knowledge Network* thrives as a web-based knowledge exchange process that links over 3,000 tightly focused 'communities of practice' involving more than half of Caterpillar's 70,000 member global workforce. It has achieved a 200 percent ROI for its internally-focused communities and more than a 700 percent ROI for its external communities (*Ibid.*)

Sadly, unlike Caterpillar, most organizations treat knowledge sharing and collaboration either as unnecessary or inefficient steps in their operations. It is a view that was well captured by former US Surgeon General, Jocelyn Elders, who ironically observed that "collaboration is [seen as] an unnatural act between non-consenting adults" (quoted in Backer 2003: 10).

For all those who've tried their hand at collaboration and working with partners, Elders' comment may, in fact, seem all too familiar. It captures the frustration of needing to work together in the first place, as well as the discomfort most people experience because of their unfamiliarity with the tools and practices that might make collaboration easy and 'natural' for us.

Elders put it bluntly. Almost everyone, when they enter a room with potential partners, says

...we want to collaborate, but what we really mean is that we want to continue doing things as we have always done them, while others change to fit what we are doing.

Convinced as we are of the completeness of our own understanding and the 'rightness' of our proposed actions, our expectations are that others, once persuaded of our wisdom, will automatically adjust themselves to accommodate us. This is, of course, nothing short of delusional and self-aggrandizing. But unfortunately it is a commonly shared attitude.

Until we can face the fact that we may not have all the answers and that we must create an environment for others to want to work with us, there is little hope the rhetoric of collaboration, so popular in organizations today, will yield much in the way of collective benefits.

What aided Caterpillar in overcoming this common mental prison was its long established organizational culture of sharing (Caterpillar 2010: 21). For instance, Jim Coffey, a 31-year Caterpillar veteran and manager of its Quality and Reliability community, recalls how simply buying a colleague a cup of coffee and taking time to listen, permitted employees to learn just about anything they needed to know. Now, he says, that sharing can also take place virtually, achieving significant savings for Caterpillar along the way.

Failure to cooperate in the DNA of modern organizations

Unfortunately, for too many people and organizations, collaboration remains an undesirable option, perceived as hard to do, time consuming, unfocused and risky. It is regarded as fraught with situations of potential conflict, when most people studiously avoid such situations. The collaborative process also suffers from big egos, free-loaders and *saboteurs*. So why do it, goes the thinking, unless you absolutely have to?

The answer to this is quite simple – more and more, you absolutely have to. Like it or not, good collaboration has become crucial for resolving just about any issue of significance today.

For instance, the Conference Board of Canada recently came to this conclusion when it assessed governance and coordination as the main threat to Canada's emergency preparedness (Munn-Venn and Archibald 2007). The Naylor Report (National Advisory Committee on SARS and Public Health 2003: 212) made similar comments after the SARS crisis of 2003, pointing out that "our *first* theme is that the single largest impediment to dealing successfully with future public health crises is the lack of a collaborative framework and ethos among different levels of government." And, as the Club of Rome Secretary General Ian Johnson pointed out with respect to climate change,

> all these [complex] challenges have two things in common. First, they are all anthropogenic, caused by us humans, and second, to a broad approximation, these challenges are all shared problems ... Shared problems must be addressed through shared solutions. This requires all of us changing our values, and understanding the commonality of humanity's challenges on earth, and, they require new forms of governance: especially of the commons – whether local, national or global (Johnson 2013).

In recent years, the pressure on public institutions as a result of the growing distribution of knowledge, resources and power has led to an increasing demand for cooperative strategies – initially with other governments, but later with the private sector and civil society actors as well. Many observers (Gray 1989; Goss 2001; Straus 2002; Westley *et al.* 2006; Kahane 2007; Romero 2008; Block 2008; Senge *et al.* 2008; Tapscott and Williams 2010; Laloux 2014) have shown that increased cooperation leads to a range of positive, organizational and social benefits, including: shared community ownership, more comprehensive problem understanding, and more comprehensive and innovative solutions.

How this failure may be overcome

Once the recognition sets in that you can't do it alone, the next step is in designing the space where potential partners can come together and engage in dialogue. The ability to engage partners, including citizen partners, hinges on the quality of the group conversation. When successful, that conversation brings together different knowledge, perspectives and organizing metaphors, which then enrich collective understanding, foster shared ownership, catalyze social learning, secure mutual commitment and increase the likelihood of innovation. That space for conversation is the cornerstone of collaboration but it is also, as Block has astutely observed, the basis of society as well:

> ... *community is fundamentally an interdependent human system given form by the conversation it holds with itself. The history, buildings, economy, infrastructure and culture are [artifacts] of the conversations and the social fabric of any community* (Block 2008: 30).

To change society, address a social issue, or alter the *status quo* – one must first change the nature of the collective conversations that underpin them. Those conversations determine how things are presumed to work; what is relevant knowledge; what resources are assumed to be available; who can and should contribute; who has power and who doesn't; and who needs to decide – essentially, what is possible and what is not.

With respect to effective collaboration, therefore, success depends on the ability to foster these conversations in ways that are trust-affirming, inclusive, personal, non-paternalistic, open, authentic, learning-oriented, and that make use of heuristic problem-solving approaches that are mutually and equitably beneficial. Ensuring that that conversation follows this path is often a matter of fluke and the result of self-organization, but good stewardship may nudge this process along through a variety of artifices, practices, tools, or gimmicks capable of catalyzing and guiding the conversation in an effective way.

Collaboration is not only natural but it is 'hardwired' into us as human beings (Rilling *et al.* 2002; Hardin 2006). Children do it quite automatically. Robert Wright (2002) once wrote that our ability to cooperate is the defining trend of human history. Yet for far too long we've been fed a myth of individualism that has limited both our willingness and our capacity to work together.

Just as the ability to speak is natural, it still requires both training and a cultural context to develop effectively. Collaboration, too, requires both training and culture. What's needed is a greater familiarity with the skills, techniques, practices, and mechanisms of collaboration so that the whole thing becomes as 'natural' to us in our organizational lives as learning a language is with young children.

Of course, with the advent of the Internet and social media, we have so many more collaborative tools at our disposal to help us connect, but what tools should we be using and when should we use them? As it turns out social media like Wikis, Facebook, Twitter, and Digg are part of a range of physical and social technologies that can help to foster connectivity and cooperation within a wide spectrum of social collaboration.

This spectrum of social collaboration ranges from:

1. **small group collaboration** that is based on direct, face-to-face communication and is dominated by social technologies; to
2. **mass collaboration** that is based on mass communication and is dominated by physical technologies such as computers, telecommunications and the Internet (see Figure 2).

Small group collaboration

Small group collaboration involves social technologies for networking, building trust, developing relationships, sharing decision making, building consensus, getting shared commitments, establishing performance monitoring, ensuring accountability, and developing partnership agreements. Only then do we actually get around to doing something together. Once this pre-work is done, the social costs of collaboration do decline but the need for relational governance continues as long as collaboration exists.

We might characterize small group collaboration as:

• slow to start up,

- having relationships before action,
- requiring high trust,
- involving high partner monitoring,
- focusing on tacit knowledge,
- involving high customization,
- using team decision making,
- initially involving smaller scales and exposures to risk, and,
- being driven by member-dependent growth.

To illustrate, let us draw from prior work with the Ottawa-Carleton School Board where one of us was asked to reflect on the performance evaluation system for the Board's trustees and senior staff (Fine and Wilson 2007). The Board pointed towards the Peel School Board outside of Toronto as a 'best practice' of board-staff relations and effective collective learning and asked what could be learned from them?

FIGURE 2. Technology Spectrum of Social Collaboration

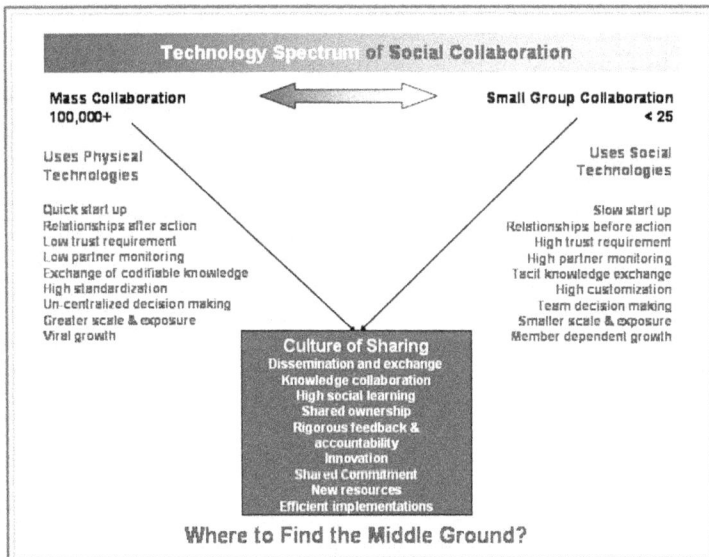

Source: Wilson, 2011, p. 18.

In an interview, the Peel Board Chair was asked about their process of staff evaluation but in response said that they didn't do anything special or different from other school boards – strategic planning, creating annual targets, negotiating metrics, conducting year end assessments, and so on. Frustrated we asked the Chair,

> How have you managed to create such a high level of trust and respect between staff and trustees? What kind of a knowledge exchange system do you have in place to head off things before they become problems? How have you managed such a high level of consensus? How do you keep focused on big picture issues?

The Chair thought for a moment, and then as if discovering it for the first time said,

> We have dinner! We all have dinner together every second week before the Board meetings. So if you have an issue, you just sit with whoever you need to talk to. There's no pressure like there is under the glare of the media. There's just a conversation. People inform each other. They learn from each other. And they make plans with each other.

In a very off hand way, the Chair identified the simple practice of 'having dinner' as the major distinguishing factor in fostering a more collaborative environment among her staff and trustees.

In small groups, collaboration is often facilitated by just such simple practices, which bring the right people together in conversation. This is because small groups are so effective at facilitating human relationships. Although often overlooked, these simple social practices can be used to great effect as tools for constructing small group partnerships.

Mass collaboration

By contrast, mass collaboration does not require relationship building at all as a prerequisite. It does require following a few basic rules. But ordinarily, action comes first with mass collaboration. Collaborators then react to some initial action by accepting it, modifying it or rejecting it, by virtue of what is referred to as stigmergic communication – communication that is based on modifications to the environment (Elliott 2006). This is the fundamental premise of the well-known 'open source' technologies such as Linux or Wikis. Complete strangers can collaborate without having to invest anything in establishing a relationship. Hence, simply from the perspective of the relationship costs associated with small groups, this form of collaboration is often considered quite efficient.

In contrast, mass collaboration may be characterized as (see Figure 2 above):

• quick to start up,
• having relationships after action,
• requiring low trust,
• involving low partner monitoring,
• focusing on codifiable knowledge,
• involving high standardization,
• using un-centralized decision making,
• involving potentially large scales and exposure, and,
• being subject to viral growth.

What's really interesting, however, is that both of these two forms of collaboration, although polar opposites in many respects, produce similar cultures of sharing, which include:

• effective dissemination and exchange of information,
• knowledge collaboration and frame reconciliation,
• collective learning,
• shared ownership and decision making,
• rigorous feedback and accountability,
• innovation,
• shared commitment,
• the development of new resources, and, most importantly,
• the effective and efficient implementation of collaborative endeavours.

One of the key differentiators between these forms of collaboration is scale. Research has shown that small group collaboration works best in groups of less than 25 people. If, for example, there are n number of partners, then in small group collaboration there are $n(n-1)$ relationships in need of attention, leading some to the conclude that the manageable upper limit for effective collaboration is 25 (requiring 600 relationships to be maintained) (Lipnack and Stamps 2000).

On the other hand, mass collaboration requires access to large audiences (Elliott 2006), ideally in the millions but at least over 100,000, which is why this form of collaboration was not particularly prevalent until the advent of the Internet era. Without that reach, mass collaboration tends to be weak, unreliable or lacking in quality. For instance, the basic premise of open source, famously captured in Linus' Law (after Linus Torvald, the originator of Linux), is "given enough eyeballs, all bugs are shallow" (Raymond 1999). Of course, its corollary is also true – fewer eyeballs, mean more bugs! But does it work?

As an example of mass collaboration, Linux software is cheaper, faster to produce, and of better quality than that of proprietary software makers like Microsoft and Apple. Says Principal Deputy Associate Director of National Intelligence, Michele Weslander, at the US Department of Defense, the Linux choice is based on "speed, efficiency and flexibility" (Weathersby 2007).

However, simply going online and signing up for Twitter or Facebook is not going to facilitate cooperation. Some tech enthusiasts have promoted social media as if it will magically generate collaboration, while ignoring the huge audience scale and the basic rules needed for social media to effectively drive collaboration. Anyone who has ever tried to create an online chat space or discussion forum knows what 'white elephants' these can be.

Conversely, some groups using relational forms of collaboration have tried to extend their reach by simply involving hundreds or thousands more people and then, when the task of relationship management proves unworkable, they are surprised by how fruitless and ineffectual their collaboration efforts have become.

Both types of collaboration have well-known rules and practices. The trouble is, most initiatives are not purely one type or the other. Their scale is somewhere in between the optimal either for small groups or for mass collaboration. So what do you do with groups larger than 25 and smaller than 100,000 that might want to work together? How do you bridge that middle ground? The answer lies in the mixing of physical and social technologies.

At Caterpillar, says Powers, the company structured its system

> so community members could communicate to others through community discussions and knowledge entries. Communities also provided space for reference materials that relate to the topic and users within a community. Community managers can select documents and links to add under Tools and Guides. (Powers 2004).

But most of the heavy lifting for Caterpillar's *Knowledge Network* was done by the managers within each of its 3,000 communities of practice who facilitate the communication work within their community. It is also interesting to observe that as big and as important as the initiative became, the staff for the *Knowledge Network* remained actually quite small – a team of six.

This strategy of local delegation has also been seen at Natural Resources Canada (Akerley *et al.* 2009) where in the development of its ground-breaking wiki site, promoters insisted that the corporate wiki have absolutely no budget, and employees were encouraged to build it themselves for their own purposes, which, as it turned out, proved to be largely social – connecting groups of people and communities of practice within the organization. By letting staff take ownership, NRCan created a network of small group communities that were linked together by wiki technologies. In effect, this was a relationship building process augmented and extended by technology.

In addition, NRCan employed a mass collaboration technique that minimized the number of rules that would apply to the wiki's development. This was achieved by negotiating a handful of absolutely 'must have' rules with Treasury Board Canada (NRCan refers to them as its wiki guardrails) in order to guide the behaviour and the content on the wiki without being overly prescriptive. Interestingly, this did not include such basic rules as the automatic translation of all content into both official languages as is the norm in the Canadian government.

As a counter example, the senior partners at a major US consulting firm tried implementing the old Lotus Notes software as a platform for firm-wide collaboration only to see it fail. Although the partners themselves were in agreement about its use and collaborative potential, only later did they discover their mistake in overlooking the different dynamics present among their more competitive junior associates. Those associates had: no culture of sharing, no incentives to cooperate, little mutual trust, and no way of knowing if their cooperation would ever be reciprocated. Furthermore, the imposed solution was not their solution. By not paying attention to these basic internal relationships, the firm virtually guaranteed the well-intended initiative would never get traction (Orlikowski 1992).

Given that collaboration usually involves unique combinations of issues, people, organizations, goals and resources, successful collaboration is resistant to templates and recipe-like formulations. Says David Straus, "there is no one right way to collaborate. At best collaborative problem solving is an educated, trial-and-error process" (Straus 2002: 31). As a consequence, partners and collaborators need to be able to draw on a range of techniques, mechanisms and practices to apply in any given situation. It is an heuristic approach that demands a lot of tools in the toolbox. Sometimes they will need to use the techniques for small group collaboration, at other times those of mass collaboration, and often they will need to discover some balance between the two.

Conclusion

Collaboration offers neither a standard template to be adhered to nor a recipe to be followed. It is essentially a process of heuristic learning that is linked to the unique combinations of partners, issues and context. What works in one situation will not always work in another. This lack of obvious transportability frustrates many, especially policy makers. What that leaves us with is the need to develop a toolbox of collaboration skills, techniques, practices and mechanisms that are likely to make a given collaboration more successful than not. The more tools available to any practitioner, the more likely will be his or her success.

The Catch-22 in all of this is that building a toolbox is itself the product of a collaboration of sorts. We need exposure to a wide range of case experience to build our respective toolboxes. Therefore, we need more opportunities to share our stories – the good, the bad and the ugly – for each story will likely reveal some new tool or practice that we might be able to apply to our next experience of collaboration.

"The real strength of [Caterpillar's] *Knowledge Network* is its bottom-up approach. People are using what they really need to use in a way they need to use it" (Powers 2004). In the end, good collaborative practitioners are like *connoisseurs* able to distinguish the subtle flavours and differences in relationships so that they can apply just the right intervention at the right time, whether it be a tool for mass collaboration or small group practice.

Until that day, we would encourage you to collect your stories and tools, and begin experimenting with the partners you've developed. If you do so, you'll be well on your way to becoming a collaboration connoisseur yourself.

References

Ahmed, Murad. 2009. "Wikipedia shows signs of stalling as number of volunteers falls sharply," *The Times*. London, UK: http://technology.timesonline.co.uk/tol/news/tech_and_web/the_web/ article6930546.ece, November 25, [Membership required for access].

Akerley, Marj, Peter Cowan and Anna Belanger. 2009. *Web 2.0 at NRCan: A Revolution in Collaboration*. Presentation to Telfer School of Management, University of Ottawa, March 30.

Argyris, Chris and Donald Schön. 1974. *Theory in practice: Increasing professional effectiveness*. San Francisco, CA: Jossey-Bass.

Backer, Thomas E. (ed.). 2003. *Evaluating Community Collaborations*. New York, NY: Springer Publishing Company, Inc., p. 10.

Block, Peter. 2008. *Community: The Structure of Belonging*. San Francisco, CA: Berrett-Koehler.

Caterpillar. 2010. *Our Values In Action: Caterpillar's Worldwide Code of Conduct*. Caterpillar Inc., www.caterpillar.com/en/company/code-of-conduct.html, (amended in 2015) [Accessed March 16, 2016].

Elliott, Mark. 2006. "Stigmergic Collaboration: The Evolution of Group Work," *M/C Journal*, 9(2).

Fine, Ed and Christopher Wilson. 2007. *Review of Evaluation Processes: Final Report*. Ottawa, ON: Ottawa Carleton District School Board, November 8.

Gormley, Ivo (Director). 2009. *Us Now: A film about Mass Collaboration*. London, UK: Banyak Films.

Goss, Sue. 2001. *Making Local Governance Work: Networks, Relationships & the Management of Change*. New York, NY: Palgrave.

Gray, Barbara. 1989. *Collaborating: Finding Common Ground for Multiparty Problems*. San Francisco, CA: Jossey-Bass.

Hardin, Russell. 2006. "The Genetics of Cooperation," *Analyse & Kritik*, 28(1): 57-65.

Johnson, Ian. 2013. The Challenge of Scarcity," *Ottawa Citizen*, September 5.

Kahane, Adam. 2007. *Solving Tough Problems*. San Francisco, CA: Berrett-Koehler.

Laloux, Frederic. 2014. *Reinventing Organizations*. Brussels, BE: Nelson Parker.

Lipnack, J. and J. Stamps. 2000. *Virtual Teams: People Working Across Boundaries with Technology*. Toronto, ON: John Wiley & Sons.

Munn-Venn, Trefor and Andrew Archibald. 2007. *A Resilient Canada: Governance for National Security and Public Safety*. Ottawa, ON: Conference Board of Canada.

National Advisory Committee on SARS and Public Health. 2003. *Learning from SARS (Naylor Report)*. Ottawa, ON: Health Canada, p. 212

Orlikowski, W.J. 1992. "Learning from NOTES: Organizational issues in groupware implementation" in J. Turner and R.E. Kraut (eds.). *CSCW'92: Proceedings of the ACM Conference on Computer-Supported Cooperative Work*, Toronto, Canada, October 31-November 4. New York, NY: ACM Press, p. 362-369.

Powers, Vicki. 2004. "Virtual Communities at Caterpillar Foster Knowledge Sharing," *T+D (American Society for Training & Development)*. June. www.vickipowers.com/writings/virtual-communities.htm [Accessed March 16, 2015].

Raymond, Eric S. 1999. *The Cathedral and the Bazaar: Musings on Linux and Open Source by an Accidental Revolutionary*. Sebastopol, CA: O'Reilly Media Inc.

Rilling, James K., David A. Gutman, Thorsten R. Zeh, Giuseppe Pagnoni, Gregory S. Berns and Clinton D. Kilts. 2002. "A Neural Basis for Social Cooperation," *Neuron*, July 18, 35: 395-405.

Romero, Jo Ann. 2008. *The Art of Collaboration*, New York, NY: iUniverse.

Senge, Peter *et al*. 2008. *The Necessary Revolution: How Individuals and Organizations are Working Together to Create a Sustainable World*. Toronto, ON: Doubleday.

Straus, David. 2002. *How to Make Collaboration Work: Powerful Ways to Build Consensus, Solve Problems and Make Decisions*. San Francisco, CA: Berrett-Koehler.

Tapscott, Don and Anthony Williams. 2010. *Macrowikinomics: Rebooting Business and the World*. Toronto, ON: Penguin.

Weathersby, John M. 2007. "Open Technology within DoD, Intel Systems," *Linux.com*, April 7, www.linux.com/archive/feed/61302 [Accessed March 16, 2015].

Westley, Frances, Brenda Zimmerman and Michael Quinn Patton. 2006. *Getting to Maybe: How the World Has Changed*. Toronto, ON: Random House Canada.

Wilson, Christopher. 1999. *"Civic Entrepreneurship at the Ottawa Centre for Research and Innovation."* Case Study. Ottawa, ON: Centre on Governance.

Wilson, Christopher. 2011. "On Collaboration," *www.optimumonline.ca*, 41(1): 15-30.

Wilson, Christopher, Erica German and Dianne Urquhart. 2008. *Best Practices in Community Knowledge Mobilization*. Ottawa, ON: Social Planning Council of Ottawa, May.

Wright, Robert. 2002. *NonZero: The Logic of Human Destiny*. New York, NY: Vintage Books.

Zander, Benjamin. 2008. *Collaborative Leadership: Awakening Possibility in Others*, address to the World Economic Forum Annual Meeting, Davos, Switzerland, January 27, www.youtube.com/watch?v=zErpOnYZZH0 [Accessed March 16, 2016].

CHAPTER 3
| Designing Social Learning

"How we might reconfigure our social discourse
in making decisions about complex problems"
John Reid

When many different but legitimate viewpoints
can exist, and there are a variety of dimensions –
economic, social, political, cultural, moral, etc. – of
import, the very notion of common understanding or shared
goals in the context of shared governance and collaboration
becomes unclear, and the means-ends relationships (so critical
to our linear worldview) unreliable. Today, on any issue of
significance to citizens, we are not only beyond the concerns
of optimization and consistency, but also beyond the powers of
science to arbitrate – we are in the world of wicked problems and
in the republic of trans-science (Weinberg 1974), where policy
problems cannot be resolved solely by the scientific method.

The governance perspective provides a way of responding
to these wicked problems in a trans-scientific way. It offers a
way of inquiring about the nature of the problem at the source of
the discomfort, of enabling collaboration among those potential
partners who have a portion of the power, the resources, and the
information (despite their different values) to contribute to its
resolution, and a way of designing and constructing modes of
stewardship *ad hoc* that are ecologically rational – i.e., matching
action and environment (in the broadest sense of the term). It

aims at creating a wholly new and unprecedented situation, a reality where all the parts can exist legitimately in a larger whole, generated by a more comprehensive knowledge built on social learning (Friedmann and Abonyi 1976; Paquet 1999).

The first section of this chapter outlines, in a general way, the sub-processes that make up this particular brand of distributed governance as social learning that has been developed over the last few decades at the Centre on Governance. The second section fleshes out the substance of the components of the social learning approach (including the development of negative capability – the capacity to keep going and collaborating when things are not going well), and it identifies some important enabling contextual resources. The third section focuses on the centrality of design thinking, and presents a skeletal roadmap for the application of design in collaborative co-governance. The fourth section explains why a change in orientation and vocabulary – from a focus on decision (on the assumption that the problem is already defined, and all the information is available) to a focus on design (with the assumption that the problem definition has yet to be constructed, and a wholly new unprecedented experimental situation has to be created) – is foundational, and how it can be operationalized. In closing, we reflect on the means to manage the transition to this new way of design thinking and vocabulary.

As a cautionary note to the reader, even though this approach may appear to some as being somewhat imprecise, its imprecision does not entail a lack of rigour (Paquet 2012).

The social learning response to the wicked problems challenge

To deal with wicked problems, practitioners must do a lot of 'on the job' learning about the configuration of relevant facts, the values defining the issues, and the possibilities desired. They must learn from both stakeholders, as well as from the mega-community, for without their combined participation (active and passive), it is unlikely that an intelligent governance apparatus can be distilled that can synthesize, reconcile and transcend the different perspectives of the different potential partners and their respective communities. Neither would it be possible to generate effective and sustained collaboration among those who hold a portion of the required power, resources and information, without their willing participation in a regime of co-ownership and a process of co-designing outcomes (Wilson 2011).

A broad gauging of the corridor of possibilities

Some decades ago, Friedmann and Abonyi stylized a simple social learning model to deal with wicked problems. They suggested that the model must respond to four questions about any possible action plan: Is it technically feasible? Is it socially acceptable? Is it too politically destabilizing? Is it implementable?

However, before responding to these questions, one must first have some appreciation of: (1) who needs to be involved; (2) appropriate theories of reality; (3) the ways social values are expressed; (4) the various future possibilities desired; (5) the political game within which the design exercise is carried out; and (6) the ways in which collective action is carried out. These six pillars of social learning are interconnected, and any change in one affects the others. A modified version of Friedmann and Abonyi's social learning model is synthesized in Figure 3.

Whereas traditional scientific approaches to problem solving focus on attempts to falsify hypotheses about some objective reality, this is too narrow a focus when the ground is in motion. For the social practitioner, what is central are efforts "to create a wholly new, unprecedented situation that, in its possibility for generating new knowledge, goes substantially beyond the initial hypothesis" (Friedmann and Abonyi 1976: 938). The social learning paradigm, built on reflection-in-action, dialogue, and mutual learning by experts and clients: i.e., on an interactive or trans-active style of planning, is one such co-creative approach.

The paradigm makes the important epistemological assumption that action hypotheses are verified as 'correct' knowledge only in the course of a social practice ... A further epistemological commitment is to the creation of a new reality,

*and hence to a new knowledge, rather than in establishing
the truth-value of propositions in abstraction from the social
context to which they are applied (Ibid.; Schön 1983).*

Similar general ideas have been explored over time by
many others, including Carl Taylor (1997) and Peter Block (2008).

This social learning framework has been used most
effectively in analyzing phenomena like multiculturalism
(Paquet 2008). Unfortunately, this formulation of social learning
has not been well adopted, operationalized or applied to the
large number of wicked problems in need of it. What appears
to be missing is a more carefully enunciated version of social
learning that occurs in stages – not in order for it to be applied
mechanically and thoughtlessly, but to make it more easily
useable as a reference protocol for practitioners interested in
applying it to various issue domains.

FIGURE 3. A Social Learning Model

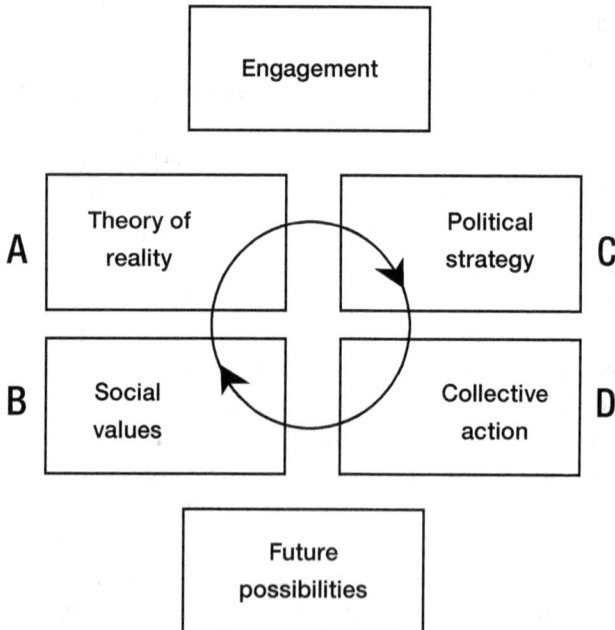

Source: Adapted from Friedmann and Abonyi, 1976, p. 933.

The contours of the Centre on Governance's version of social learning

The social learning approach, practiced at the Centre on Governance, is based on the assumptions that:

1. one does not usually have *ab ovo* a good grasp of the situation; consequently, collaborative governance requires one to start with a process of inquiry to ascertain the state of affairs, to identify those who may have something to contribute to a change in the *status quo*, and to convene them and gather the necessary information that may be spread widely among stakeholders and potential partners;

2. most potential partners have no shared values or common purposes; moreover, none has all the information, resources or power to fully take charge or to guide the group in ways assuring resilience and innovation. Recognizing this, what must therefore be constructed are arenas, spaces or platforms where these diverse perspectives can be blended into a more or less viable but evolving syncretic perspective;

3. an inquiring system and the blending of perspectives are necessary in order to elicit a mix of principles, conventions, rules, and mechanisms that can ensure effective coordination and construct the equivalent of an 'automatic pilot' to generate wayfinding, resilience and innovativeness. But these are not sufficient conditions to ensure effective problem solving or to assure commitments to implementation. An infrastructure of social learning must also include opportunities for the exploration, detection and correction by the group of incongruities as it proceeds through its social learning cycle; and,

4. it is naïve to pretend collaborative governance that is emergent like this will always be able to survive in the face of failure and tough times. It will be essential therefore to ensure the development of negative capability (in the sense of John Keats): the capability to keep going

when things are going wrong, through the operations of safe-fail and fail-safe mechanisms, and other ways of sustaining commitment.

This approach is conceived to help immunize the inquiring system against any false sense of virtue and decisiveness that leads so many to take action prematurely, and with undue haste, before a good grasp of the situation is gained. Not only is this undue haste likely to be myopic in a collaborative context, failing to embrace the full range of possibilities, but it is also likely to sabotage the nurturing and maintenance of the commitment of partners by falling prey to a premature *urgence de conclure*.

The engine of social learning and wayfinding

Whatever stewardship is present, it is unlikely to be entirely the result of a deliberate preconceived strategy, but more likely to be the product of emergent 'wayfinding', as a result of a variety of gestures and actions by partners (as their experience together unfolds) with the result that additional knowledge and validated commitments trigger yet more gestures and actions. Policy and strategy will not be simply about the efficient management of resources to some end, as gauged by some objective function (even though most managers have a tendency to reduce it to this as a matter of convenience), but about building a shared capacity to intervene by "attaining and sustaining a set of organized relationships nested within wider systems in order to experience the possibility of doing things differently and, potentially, better" (Chia and Holt 2009: ix, 112).

What may not be obvious from such a depiction is the extent to which engagement with the environment and the partners entails "local adaptations and ingenuity in everyday practical coping..." (*Ibid.*: 159). Wayfinding means

> reaching out into the unknown and developing an incomplete but practically sufficient comprehension of the situation in order to cope effectively with it. Prospective rather than retrospective sense-making is involved... [and wayfinding] is continuously clarified through each iterative action and

adjustment and not through any predetermined agenda (*Ibid.*: 159).

Social learning A: cognition and information diffusion

An inquiring system has no safe and guaranteed pathway ahead. It is an exploratory system that proactively probes for anomalies, their sources and causes, for cumulatively clarified problem definitions, for the identification of who needs to be involved in dealing with the issue, for ways in which micro-reactions might be cast in more general contexts, for groping instruments, as well as for alliances and moral contracts with other parties that might help in the process and, finally, for anything that might help accelerate the process of social learning and experimentation, and open new vistas, possibilities, and the collective capacity to get there.

The success of social learning should be gauged not so much by reference to myopic measurable temporary outcomes or metrics (that may often be quite misleading), but by the degree to which the acceptance of different but valid perspectives that lead to the modification of habits and belief systems, and by the effectiveness of the mechanisms utilized to modify the very nature of the collective process. This includes those used when the inquiring system gives signs of being derailed (either internally or from outside), or of being outside the corridor of previously accepted norms (Boisot 1995; Paquet 2009a: chapter 5).

In an effort to help identify the major obstacles to social learning, Max Boisot has suggested a simple mapping of the social learning cycle in a three-dimensional space – the information space – which maps the degree of abstraction, codification and diffusion of the information flows within organizations. The farther away from the origin on the vertical axis, the more the information is codified (i.e., the more its form is clarified, stylized and simplified); the farther away from the origin laterally eastward, the more widely the information is diffused and shared; and the farther away from the origin laterally westward, the more abstract the information is (i.e., the more general the categories in use).

The social learning cycle in Figure 4 can be decomposed into two phases, with three steps in each phase: Phase I emphasizes the cognitive dimensions of the cycle; Phase II, the diffusion of the new information.

In Phase I, learning begins with some scanning of the environment in order to detect anomalies and paradoxes. Following this first step (s), one is led in step 2 to stylize the problem (p), posed by the anomalies and paradoxes, in a language of problem solution; the third step of Phase I purports to generalize the solution found for a more specific issue to a broader family of problems through a process of abstraction (at). In Phase II, the new knowledge is diffused (d) to a larger community of persons or groups in step 4; then there is a process of absorption (ar) of this new knowledge by the population, so as to become part of the tacit stock of knowledge in step 5; and in step 6, the new knowledge is not only absorbed, but has an impact (i) on the concrete practices of the group or community.

Figure 4 enables us to identify the different potential blockages through the learning cycle. In Phase I, cognitive dissonance in (s) may prevent the anomalies from being noted; inhibitions of all sorts in (p) may stop the process of translation into a language of problem solution; and blockages (at) may keep the new knowledge from acquiring the most effective degree of generality. In Phase II, the new knowledge may not get the appropriate diffusion because of property rights (d), or because of the strong dynamic conservatism, which may generate a refusal to listen by those most likely to profit from the new knowledge (ar), or because of difficulties in finding ways to incorporate the new knowledge (i).

The mapping in Figure 4 may be interpreted as a way of identifying potential sources of blockages or failures in an inquiring system. Interventions to remove, or to attenuate the learning blockages, always entail some degree of interference with the mechanisms of collective intelligence, relational transactions, and therefore, the psycho-social fabric of the organization.

FIGURE 4. Learning Cycle and Potential Blockages

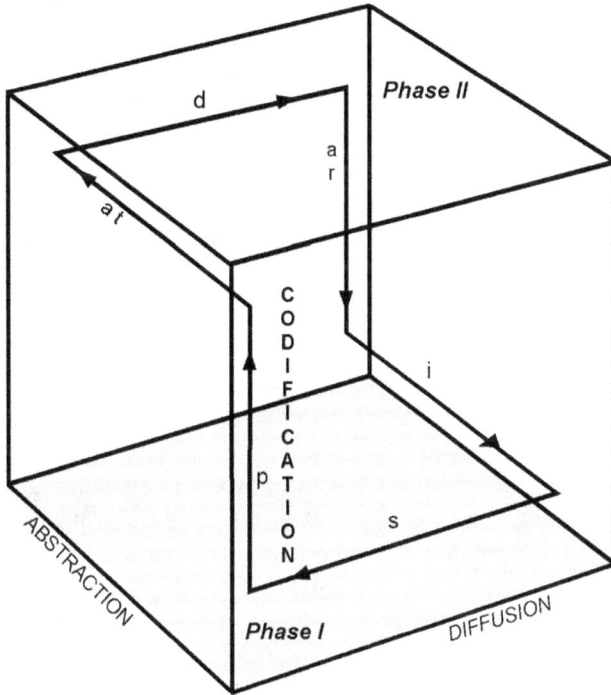

Source: Boisot, 1995, p.190.

Social learning B: collaboration

Collaboration remains a crucial component of this inquiring system – more specifically collaboration in problem definition; collaboration in solution design; collaboration in implementation; and collaboration in performance assessment and learning. For if power, resources and information are widely distributed among many hands and heads, no effective wayfinding can emerge without it. Yet often in spite of their differences, participants in collaborative forums will stay connected and willingly engage with persons with different belief systems, knowledge and motivations. This cannot be accomplished without some modicum of trust, and some evolving sense of sharing, belonging and mutual respect in this co-creative process, even though the only truly shared sentiment they may begin with is their shared discomfort with the *status quo* (Lee and Glad 2011).

Collaboration means recognizing that one cannot do it alone, that one must take a step beyond individual comfort zones "to call forth possibilities from an unknown and not-yet-possible future" (*Ibid.*) that are attainable only in concert with others. Such courage to collaborate translates into a way of being when participants can overcome their initial differences to create something unique and valued. In fact, many collaborators typically identify the process of collaborating itself as one, if not the most valuable, outcome of the experience.

This can be instituted using a variety of conventions: some explicit and rational, others tacit and quasi-emotional. Collaboration is meant to broaden the problem definition and to widen the potential responses to problems that emerge from silo-thinking, but it is never clear whether these possibilities will ever materialize. Consequently, it requires the capacity to keep going, and to endure when things may not look too promising, and also the capacity to change course when the original arrangement proves ineffective. As Chia and Holt would put it, the right balance would be the freedom "from both the obstinacy of the commonplace and the iridescent glare of the new" (2009: 212).

The ecology of activities in an inquiring system entails a cycle of social learning comprised of four phases (Table 1) that might be regarded as the standard learning process in normal times – with an observation and cognitive phase, an investigative phase, a design-cum-moral contracts phase, and an evaluative and social learning phase.

Since most responses are likely to fail, the inquiring system has to be equipped with the requisite mechanisms to ensure that the system can minimize the costs of failure: i.e., instituting routine fail-safe mechanisms (FSM) aimed at ensuring resilience, and keeping the organization within a corridor constrained by certain normative bounds. Indeed, if failure is likely, then how does one design a process to identify failure as quickly as possible in order to make the necessary adjustments on the fly and minimize the impact of failures?

TABLE 1. Provisional Checklist of Questions in the Four Phases of an Inquiring System

I Does the situation need changing?	II What is the problem?	III How will you work together?	IV How will you learn together & evaluate your progress?
1. Are there any detectable anomalies?	6. What is the task at hand?	a. DESIGN	12. What feedback and informational loops do you have to enable social learning?
2. What are the salient features of the issue domain?	7. What are the non-negotiable constraints within the mega-community?	10. What instruments of collaboration and social learning can you use to produce short-term success and long-term commitment?	13. What collective learning processes do you have in place?
3. What are the causal mechanisms at play?	8. Who are the stakeholders that must be included and how will you involve them?	b. CONVENTIONS	14. How will you gauge ongoing performance objectively?
4. Can this be resolved by a single actor?	9. What are the risks and potential rewards, and how will these be aligned among the various partners?	11. What are the conventions and moral contracts that need to be negotiated to maintain a culture of collaboration?	15. How will you gauge changes in attitudes and behaviours among partners?
5. Who are the key stakeholders?			16. How will you resolve conflicts?
			17. What fail-safe mechanisms are in place?
			18. At what point would you dissolve the collaboration?

Source: Paquet and Wilson, 2011, p. 1-12.

Social learning C: dynamic re-organizational level

It is commonly understood that organizations and systems are periodically hit by shocks that can threaten the very existence of the organization (Grove 1996). When a set of essential variables is thus affected, they can trigger step-mechanisms that command fundamental transformations if the system is to survive. When collective organizations are called on to respond to dramatic forms of creative destruction experiences, they may command self-transformation and self-reinvention as the only way to survive. For instance, safe-fail mechanisms (SFM) can trigger such effective renewal. SFMs create something tantamount to a state of exception that temporarily suspends the normal course of affairs, and plays a key role in transitioning the group from crisis to the generation of a new dissipative structure to prevent crucial loss of potential, or perhaps even implosion.

Buzz Holling[7] and other experts have suggested that both natural and human organizations go through periodic cycles of change.

According to this view, organizations move from structures capable of exploiting existing resources (phase 1 – low potential, loose connectedness, entrepreneurial), to more tightly connected forms of organization (institutionalized and more strongly connected in order to fully take advantage of a higher potential) that bump into constraints due to the very rigidities brought forth by institutionalization (phase 2 – bureaucratization, rigidity).

This inflexibility leads them to be vulnerable to change and Schumpeterian shocks and crises that are created by innovations stemming from environmental pressures or technical breakthroughs (phase 3 – crisis, fragmentation). Then, either the organization fails to adapt (with the result that it disappears or is dramatically wounded), or it reacts by a renewal that mobilizes its resources in new configurations, often much more loosely connected, as a result of creative tension (phase 4 –

[7] Stanley (Buzz) Holling, a Canadian ecologist and Emeritus Eminent Scholar and Professor at the University of Florida, is one of the conceptual founders of ecological economics.

diverse paths to renewal, high potential, weak connectedness). The cycle starts again as this new potential gets diffused in start-ups and projects of diverse sorts (Holling 1987; Hurst and Zimmerman 1994). SFMs are mechanisms to facilitate the generation of transitions from Phase 3 to Phase 4.

In order to be effective, SFMs require an early warning system, capable of detecting the existence of important but inherently unpredictable 'black swan phenomena' (Taleb 2007): either through some form of intelligent environmental scanning, or when mission reviews become mandated at particular moments of crisis. Often, as Andy Grove, one of the founders and former CEOs of Intel Corporation, has described, the change may be ongoing among front-line workers, clients or customers but go entirely unnoticed by the C-suite team caught up as they are in prior notions of the organization and its environment. Thus paying attention to the experiences of front line workers should be a requisite task for senior management.

More generally, social learning requires *fora* for deliberation and negotiation that are capable of:

- providing a refinement of the problem definition;
- suggesting ways in which improved collaboration might be generated;
- proposing mechanisms through which newly discovered impediments to such collaboration might be neutralized; and, finally,
- there must be a real possibility of experimentation on the road to renewal in full awareness of the tentative nature of the experiments (McCann *et al.* 2009).

Faced with a generative crisis, SFMs permit a break with the usual way of doing business and enable "acting when not everything is known, when all the data aren't in yet" (Grove 1996: 35).

Such actions need not necessarily result in explicit, drastic, top-down revolutions. In environments crippled by cultures of entitlement and powerful mental prisons, draconian moves are likely to lead to active and passive confrontation from which little can emerge but stalemates. Alternatively, much change can occur underground, *petit à petit*, with little fanfare, although not necessarily in a less effective way – much to the despair of those obsessed by the need for explicit deliberation theatrics. Nevertheless, when macro shifts in collective consciousness inspire changes in the culture governance of an organization or society, change may occur suddenly with little in the way of opposition – not unlike the way that icon of the Cold War, the Berlin Wall, seemed to suddenly collapse (actually dismantled by citizens on both sides) in 1989 and in days ceased to be an obstacle to the movement of people between East and West Germany.

Social learning D: three social learning orientations
The dynamics of stewardship are reflected in three families of social learning behaviours that orient practitioners in different ways: sequentially; instrumentally, through the development of competencies and affordances; and contextually, by paying attention to the mega-community, to common knowledge, and to the phenomena of emergence and synchronization. These orientations provide a basic way to focus collective attention during a process that may yield a constantly changing landscape.

1. Sequential orientation
If one had to stylize the stewardship process through social learning in a sequential way, one might make use of a template used by practitioners (Parr *et al.* 2002).

Stage I begins with some perceived gap between current reality and some desirable outcome as a trigger to direct attention toward initiating action. This originates with the recognition that the *status quo* is no longer acceptable and action is required (either individually or collectively), followed by the exploration of action possibilities. It is followed by a process of identifying who needs to be involved and the nurturing of shared ownership in a collaborative enterprise.

Stage II begins the more formal process of social learning, exploring issues and opportunities to further mobilize potential partners, and the nurturing of some prototype structure for collaboration.

TABLE 2. Three Social Learning Orientations

	Mobilization	Collaboration
Stage I	Identifying those who may be able to contribute; those who can stop change; those who have knowledge; and those who may be impacted by any decision	The establishment of co-ownership in the enterprise
Stage II	The framing of critical issues and opportunities and focusing attention on what needs to be done	The creation of platforms for a diverse group of people to work together
Stage III	The communication of key information likely to inspire, rally and motivate existing and future partners to take part in the diverse networks	The development of new relationships capable of generating tangible results, and thereby of changing mindsets, and encouraging creative thinking

Stage III has to do with efforts to sustain change through creating and renewing relationships affirming cooperation, and re-igniting the process by refocusing on new challenges and opportunities. This is another area in need of much conceptual refurbishment, and of efforts to agitate and rekindle the social learning process in order to validate performance, reframe the notion of what is now possible, validate individual contributions and benefits, and generate additional innovation.

What is obviously essential here is the development of some collective capacity to learn, i.e., to reflect on the parties different experiences and perspectives, to make sense of them, and to retool, restructure, and even to reframe some commonly held assumptions and questions that would allow the group to generate effective ways to respond to a generative challenge.

These requirements have been spelled out by practitioners of reflexive governance.

They may be summarized as follows: an iterative co-definition of broad directions by the participants; knowledge integration and learning while doing; capacity for long-run anticipation of systemic effects; scenario analysis; interactive strategy development; and ultimately the adaptation of new strategies and institutions (Drath and Palus 1994; Voβ *et al.* 2006).

But there is also a collective need to develop negative capability – the capability to continue to collaborate even when the going may be tough and disappointing. This sort of shared commitment may be rooted in *affectio societatis* at first, but this will not suffice; it must be nurtured with a regular sharing of information and attention to relationship building that permits partners to "cut each other some slack"[8] as they attempt to resolve their differences.

2. Instrumental orientation: competencies and affordances

Since dynamic co-adaptation is a core result of stewardship, such change requires behavioural competencies that need to be nudged into existence, not only by leveraging the forces of accommodation, but also by harnessing self-organization to generate entirely new possibilities.

These behavioural competencies may be divided into five categories (Michael 1993; Hughes and Weiss 2007).
1. **contextual** (embracing uncertainty and error, building bridges, reframing, improvising, adapting, overcoming);
2. **interpersonal** (consultation, negotiation, deliberation, conflict resolution, facilitation, brokering, preceptoring, educating, animating, changing roles);
3. **enactment** (enabling, empowering, responsiveness, creativity, cooperation);
4. **systems thinking** (ethics of inter-connectivity and interdependence, removing obstacles, affirming trust, freeing others to act better); and,

---

[8] This is how one Ottawa area VP of Research described why her organization encouraged relationship building in the many partnership teams in which her tech company was involved.

5. **staying the course while rocking the boat** (inclusion, imagination, experimentation, responsibility to explore, emphasis on sins of omission, learning by prototyping)

These capacities are not only individual, but collective, in the sense that rules of interaction among individuals generate emergent properties that are generated not only from the heads of individual actors but also from the dynamics of their interactions. This interaction order (in the language of Goffman) generates a sort of collective intelligence, a sort of social mind (Goffman 1959; Rheingold 2002), that can guide the behaviour of individuals working in a partnership or collaboration.

These dual (individual and collective) capacities also interact when confronted by a device or context that affords some 'action possibilities' but not others. Such 'affordances' are therefore indicators of potentialities and possibilities – like a door knob for turning, a plate for pushing, etc. Affordances are invitations to specific actions. Whether these affordances are real or just perceived is of little relevance, but their significance rests with the fact that they can open and/or limit the realm of possibilities. Therefore, while collective consciousness provides the context that generates affordances, those affordances limit the ways that individuals and collectives perceive, or learn to perceive, how to interact with that context. Learning to perceive affordances is a key kind of perceptual learning (Norman 1999). "Affordances are … relationships that hold between objects and agents… to discover and make use of affordances is one of the important ways" to deal with novel situations (Norman 2007).

Learning to perceive certain actions or behaviours as affordances (as in the Peel Board's use of dinner) is the first step in using them with intent, or developing novel ways to improve upon them in the course of social learning, and is, therefore, at the core of the innovation and design process. This is the way in which the 'automatic pilot' of governance can be improved upon.

3. Contextual orientation: megacommunity, common knowledge, synchronization

As we have suggested, the dynamic of stewardship focuses on the flow of information and communication. But it need not flow only through the heads of individual actors: it may equally emerge from a context or situation in a stigmergic way. All the dimensions explored earlier are important to pay attention to (components, guideposts, process, framework, competencies, affordances), but they may remain incomplete unless some additional enabling resources are added – like the mega-community, common knowledge, and the forces of synchronization – that act as catalysts bringing forth new information to make the other components work together, and are therefore at the core of emergence and self-organization.

This is not the place to probe these matters at great length, but they cannot be ignored altogether.

Megacommunity

A megacommunity – i.e., a public sphere in which organizations and people deliberately join together around compelling issues of mutual importance, following a pre-established set of practices and principles that make the achievement of results easier (Gerencser *et al.* 2006) – embodies both shared trust (institutional, inter-organizational, and interpersonal) and social capital (networks and norms).

Gerencser *et al.* have identified four critical elements for a thriving megacommunity: (1) shared understanding about how the problems can be resolved, the necessary players and partners, and the ways in which they affect one another; (2) the presence of partners in a listening, learning and understanding mode; (3) the designing and customizing of suitable, mutually beneficial, cross-sector arrangements; and (4) the capacity for experimentation, learning from each other, and effective collective monitoring of progress accomplished by the megacommunity.

People and groups involved in or potentially affected by, partnerships and collaborations are by definition, players in a megacommunity. For all of them, the degree of their interest in working together (and their views of it) will tend to be framed by attitudes that dominate the stewardship culture they exhibit. Although initially sparked by their common interest in changing the *status quo,* that shared mindset will evolve naturally as time passes in response to external influences, shared experiences and specific stewardship interventions.

Common knowledge

Another factor that is of key importance in the dynamics of stewardship is common knowledge. Chwe (2001: 98-99) has shown that while "coordination is often achieved through adaptation and evolution and explicit communication, but people [too] often implicitly communicate" in order to problem solve. He shows, looking at how common knowledge emerges, that it is often through communicative events like rituals, ceremonies, and other shared cultural practices. He demonstrates how the problem of indeterminacy in coordination can be resolved by the sharing of common knowledge through rituals. It indicates ways in which intervention might nudge people toward coordination through generating common knowledge, and allowing choices to be made by actors on that basis (i.e., allowing self-organization to proceed). One such ritual is the collective exercise of problem definition, which takes place together in a concerted sense rather than through independent analysis.

During one local exercise, for instance, in regional labour market coordination in Ottawa (Centre on Governance 2002) diverse business, government and community stakeholders initially interacted by advocating for their existing (failed) approaches, that were based upon independent research (and interestingly using the same data sources), until they co-designed a review of Ottawa's workforce landscape and developed in the process a tool to 'translate' their different perspectives from one to another.

This establishment of such common knowledge explicitly leverages the cultural and informational contexts of various partners likely to generate effective self-organization.

Synchronization

Yet another factor at work in the dynamics of stewardship has to do with synchronization: the fact that, for reasons that are not always clear, humans, like animals, would appear to fall into synchronized behaviour in self-organized ways (traffic flows, applause, etc.). Strogatz (2003) suggests: the spontaneous outbreak of coordinated or herd or mob behaviour, occurs above certain thresholds of shared activity (or mix of thresholds for different groups) that define tipping points where mass synchronization occurs. Strogatz has shown that, in the animal world, for instance, spontaneous coordination is an omnipresent phenomenon (fireflies flashing in unison, flocks of birds flying in formation, etc.). It has also been shown that synchronization occurs in the material world of lifeless things like clocks. It is another of those Quantum phenomenon with which social science struggles.

Synchronicity in the human world, such as experiences of group think, coordination of menstrual cycles, etc., are well documented. Given that synchronization materializes in group behaviour, we are just beginning to understand the mechanisms which underlie its generation, and the bringing of 'order out of chaos'.

For instance, the more or less spontaneous formation of 'movements' from singular events, like the protest of a single person in Tunisia and the resulting Arab Spring movement, illustrate how the forces of self-organization can operate on a social level. Consequently they need to be taken into account when dealing with collective issues. We should also mention that such forces of synchronization generate not just positive collective action. They can just as easily generate heart fibrillations or raging mobs as often as positive thrills or social cooperation. But understanding such factors is crucial if there is to be any hope of finding the equivalent of a defibrillator at the social level.

With these behavioural orientations in mind, the dynamic of stewardship that underpins the 'automatic pilot' of social learning needs to be understood as a nexus of governance mechanisms, many of which are designed with certain purposes in mind, but many others of which are simply the result of self-organization, triggered either by common knowledge, or as an unintended consequence of the interplay with context, situations, and experimental interventions, or as a result of the coherence and synchronization generated from group interactions.

While this description of stewardship does not promise the simplicity guaranteed in the literature on imperial leadership, it has the advantage of defining an approach that is immensely more promising and realistic for practitioners. It escapes from the simplistic anthropomorphic images of governing, by embracing complexity and recognizing the full extent to which mechanisms can nudge behaviours in preferred directions, as well as the extent to which experimentation and prototyping can tinker with complex non-linear systems and generate important unintended consequences as a result of the self-organization they trigger.

Most importantly, stewardship encourages shared ownership instead of the usual reliance of romanticized leadership and the general abdication of responsibility and commitment that are the dark side of leadership. If a collection of tools can help generate this type of stewardship, then any individual can step up and be given a more than fair chance to succeed, instead of deferring to the over-amped claims of specific personalities, abdicating their rights as owners.

Such an approach may not always guarantee from the outset what success will look like in governing an organization, but it does provide valuable insight into the ways in which the results of governing might become more predictable and successful through the good use of attention to context and design thinking.

Scoping design thinking

Over ten years ago, Karl Weick (2004) published a paper in which he rooted his reflections on rethinking organizational design in the testimonies of two well-known designers: Frank Gehry (the famous architect) and Dee Hock (the ex-CEO who designed VISA) (Gehry 1999; Hock 1999) – who were both blessed with an uncanny ability in design. The main lesson Weick drew from these reflections was that even though coordination is a central concern of designers, there is a danger that in fixating too much on rigid and impatient coordination imperatives one might impair the whole process of design. The job of design is fundamentally to generate contraptions that not only reconcile the pressures from the geo-technical constraints and the values and plans of the various stakeholders, but also coordinate the activities of all those who have a significant portion of the information, resources and power that need to be mobilized to ensure resilience and innovation. The risk is that coordination might be geared to static, short-term stability instead of achieving coherence among the parts in the longer term.

Weick quotes Dee Hock as observing that management is unduly focused on creating "constants, uniformity and efficiency," when what is required in our turbulent world is to understand and coordinate "variability, complexity, and effectiveness." Weick suggests that the requirements identified by Hock "are best achieved if design is recast as designing that uses transient constructs, bricolage, and improvisation" (Hock 1999: 47) in order to capture the fluid coherence possible in human systems.

This emphasis on ongoing and living processes has a Deweyian flavour: John Dewey always refused to use terms with a static connotation, like thing or object, to connote human realities and activities. He preferred using the elusive notion of 'affairs'. In the words of a Dewey scholar, "affairs are never frozen, finished or complete. They form a world characterized by genuine contingency and continual process. A world of affairs is a world of actualities open to a variety of possibilities" (Boisvert 1998).

Therefore, for Weick and others, one must design for transience and incompleteness: being satisfied to define a skeleton or bare bones framework, and to allow an emergent structure to develop around it as partners interact, argue, come together, and learn along the way. This is also what open source developers do. Stigmergic collaboration doesn't just happen.

It arises because the initial developer creates an attractive 'kernel,' or core program, that can incite the imaginations of others as to what might be possible. This is exactly what Gehry and Hock suggest. Such a kernel represents the spirit that informs a skeletal roadmap for the design of collaboration in three stages and nine steps:

a. **New attitude** and vocabulary
b. **Inquiring system:** epistemology
c. **Mental mapping;** some ethnography
d. **Thinking with our hands:** a bit of process thinking *à la* Friedmann and Abonyi
e. **Collaboration:** learning to work together
f. **Prototyping and serious play:** about reframing, restructuring, retooling
g. **Social learning:** gauging according to various metrics
h. **Engagement and storytelling:** moral contracts and learning loops
i. **Etiquette and ethics of prototyping:** corridor phenomena

These stages are not a list of mechanical steps that must be followed *seriatim* in a servile manner. The sequence is rather analogous to working through a number of transparencies (used in yesteryear with an overhead projector) that could sequentially introduce families of concerns that are overlaid one upon the other to represent cumulatively (and through an ever more sophisticated and high-definition image of complex natural or social systems) a mix of different intermingled sub-systems, that make up the whole organization or social system. It is not dissimilar from the experience in primary school where one would start with the skeleton of a human body and overlay on it the muscular system, the nervous system, etc.

While this analogy with transparent overlays is obviously imperfect, it is an attempt to capture the life of an ever more complex, ongoing process evolving over time. Each step in our roadmap would not only add static structural features (as in the primary school use of overheads) but also connote configurations of affairs, of additional ongoing nexuses of activities of different sorts. The cumulative addition of these nexuses of activities in that particular sequence aims both to enrich the perspective, and to trigger with every new transparency being added, some more and more encompassing questioning of the assumptions made in earlier steps, in addition to some consequential continuous tinkering or bricolage with how everything is assumed to fit together.

The first trio of layers (**a, b, c**) roughly connotes a phase of appreciation and description. The different steps define (a) the prerequisite attitude, discourse and vocabulary required for a meaningful inquiry to proceed; (b) the basic dynamics of the inquiry process that need to be initiated; and (c) the sort of mental map of the issue domain being explored, so as to anchor firmly the design thinking in the existing material and symbolic world of the issue domain.

The second trio of layers (**d, e, f**) corresponds roughly to experimentation *per se*. They correspond to the different stages of exploration in grappling with the new world to be constructed: (d) defines the forms that are adjusted to the circumstances, and meet some basic conditions of goodness of fit; (e) explores shared possibilities and their acceptability among crucial partners; and then (f) develops workable prototypes by trial and error, in conversations with the partners, and through experimentation.

The third trio of layers (**g, h, i**) focus more on learning *per se*. This is the moment (g) when the learning loops crystallize and when multiple reference metrics emerge; (h) when the engagement of the different partners evolve, moral contracts among partners take hold, and a new discourse takes form that allows the conversation to establish itself on a new basis; and (i) when a new appreciation of the internal and external constraints (both on the conversation and on the selection of the prototypes) emerges and gains traction.

This somewhat artificial partitioning and stylization has two main advantages: (a) it underlines clearly that, as one proceeds from stage 1 to stage 2, stage 2 forces a considerable recasting of stage 1 assumptions and activities, and proceeding to stage 3, triggers some recasting of the two earlier phases; and (b) it provides the basis for a modest checklist that might serve as a useful guidepost in the evolution of the design process.

Design attitude: why, what and how

The different steps and stages in this design process are anything but linear, since feedback loops are constantly in action. But in the process a new design attitude begins to permeate collective action. Why is the introduction of a design attitude so important? It frees us from our preconceived cognitive commitments, inspires innovations, and fosters the development of new skills and practices that can bring that innovation into reality.

Why

One is not always as fully aware as one should be of the mental prisons that haunt the sort of organizational culture in good currency, or the conventional wisdom that cripples the work of all stakeholders as potential organization designers: one of the most important of which is the focus on decision making.

The focus on making decisions, as Boland and Collopy suggest, has led to people being completely mesmerized by a concern about choice among existing alternatives, with the presumption that the problem is already well-defined, and all the possible alternatives are well-known. This is usually not the case, especially with complex problems. The design attitude recognizes that a problem definition has to be constructed (usually from competing perspectives), and that alternatives have to be created and crafted, and that they cannot be assumed to exist *ab ovo*. The design process creates a course of action that aims at creating better alternatives than those that would appear to be originally and immediately available (Boland and Collopy 2004: chapter 1; Brown 2009). This follows naturally from multiple stakeholders agreeing that the *status quo*, i.e., existing options, must change.

In order to deal with an approach based on exploring systems which are not well understood, what is required is not only a different attitude that singles out specific dimensions for careful attention, but also a different vocabulary with which to tackle them. Boland and Collopy have already tried their hand at a provisional version of a new lexicon (Boland and Collopy 2004: chapter 37) that includes: collaboration, dialogue, improvisation, prototyping, etc. These notions are essential devices in the designer's mental toolbox.

In all multi-stakeholder organizations (private, public, and social), the initial central challenge is problem definition. Each stakeholder has his own partial definition of the problem at hand, based on his imperfect knowledge and particular interests, but these partial and truncated views do not suffice to define a problem with sufficient comprehensiveness in order to produce a satisfactory response. The initial advocacy for these partial views is another mental prison that generates a dangerous blindness that can lead to actions that are likely to be misguided. Yet it is common that such partial views often succeed in hijacking the problem definition process through bullying or bribery, derailing not only meaningful inquiry but also useful learning and successful implementation.

Tabling and recognizing the extent of every stakeholder's partial ignorance helps to limit impatient, overzealous leaders who may attempt to force the process into a premature decision and nurtures the capacity to define the problem adequately, and protect the process from ready-made solutions and too quick decision-making. Using an inquiry process in a problem definition phase recognizes that most of the time the problems are wicked: (1) the goals are not known, or are very ambiguous or not agreed to by the stakeholders, and (2) the means-ends relationships are highly uncertain and poorly understood. This new awareness is a prerequisite for any meaningful future inquiry.

What

Boland and Collopy have, for instance, defined the basic elements of a design attitude that would seem to provide a more balanced approach for our complex world. For them, "a design attitude views each project as an opportunity for invention that includes a questioning of basic assumptions and a resolve to leave the world a better place than we found it" (*Ibid.*: 9).

Indeed, their 2004 book was planned to encourage a shift from a decision attitude to a design attitude. The design attitude helps to focus on stewarding the inquiring system toward inventing assemblages of arrangements likely to foster better wayfinding and resilience. To accomplish this, it is necessary to focus on the meso-level of organizations and institutions instead of individual or global levels of social coordination. Meso-phenomena are too often poorly described and apprehended, because observers insist on looking at them through micro-perspectives that focus exclusively on individuals as absolutes, denying the importance of relationships between entities. Similarly, they are equally misunderstood by approaches that focus exclusively on homogeneous macro-systems and totalities as static entities and absolutes. Good organizational design requires a vocabulary and approaches that properly focus at the meso-level to capture relationships and the nuances of a variety of contexts.

Some exploratory work has already begun on what meso elements the design process should include, and when its focus should be on efficiency, effectiveness or innovation as the prevalent guiding force (Granderi and Furnari 2008). Still other work on collaboration has focused on the process of interaction (Straus 2002) and the inter-organizational conversation (Bryant 2003, Block 2008) that emerges.

How

As discussed elsewhere (Paquet 2009b: chapter 2), the new competencies and skills that need to be developed have much to do with *savoir-faire, savoir-être*, and 'learning by doing.' Such competencies, as they are based on practical knowledge, have tended to be greatly underrated in a world where academic, technical rationality has wrongly become hegemonic: presuming as it does that knowledge flows only one way – from underlying disciplines to applied science to actual performance of services to clients and society. In contrast, knowledge in reality is a two-way street, one that emphasizes knowing-in-action, reflection-in action (Michael *et al.* 1980) and where knowledge emerges equally well from groping with situations and from implementation surprises that lead to on-the-spot experiments and knowledge creation (Wilson *et al.* 2014). Ideally, this is the way professionals are educated (Simon 1969/1981: chapter 5).

The development of skills, heuristic practices and a capacity for a 'conversation' with the situation are typically achieved through some sort of reflective practicum (residency, articling, apprenticeships, etc.) which is seen to be the only way to impart practical knowledge in a manner that aims at behaviour modification – for some of those skills are literally embodied: *savoir-faire* in the sense of *tour de main* cannot be learned and developed without a change in *savoir-être*, in identity.[9]

The task of organization design uses a variety of mechanisms to help foster a 'living organization' that has the capacity to be reliable but innovative, and to be resilient but to learn. It aims at coherence (which is different from cohesiveness), but mainly at dynamism. It cannot be accomplished only by tinkering with the hard dimensions of organizations (architecture and routines); it must also modify the behaviour and culture of the people who are the living, breathing heart of the organization. Moreover, depending on circumstances, this sort of intervention will have to be sequenced carefully if it is to be successful.

This can be an especially daunting task in the case of the exploration/exploitation split that often underpins the innovation/reliability challenge (March 1991). It is impossible to tackle this challenge without explicit efforts to transform the culture of the organization. A simple directive or partitioning of tasks or efforts is unlikely to work.

Four principles have proved useful in this sort of work (Paquet 2005: chapter 8):

- maximum participation to ensure the tapping of all relevant knowledge and greater commitment to collaboration;

---

[9] In a postsecondary context, it has proved extremely difficult to ensure the requisite training and coaching of these new competencies, for they require the development of perception skills, diagnostic skills, and the like. This explains the explosion of parallel training ventures that deal with those areas that are dramatically neglected by the formal education enterprise.

- subsidiarity, or the delegation of decision making to the most local level possible;
- some competition to squeeze out organizational slack and promote innovation; and,
- multi-stability, i.e., the partitioning of the organization into sub-systems, so as to be able to delegate to the one most able to handle a shock or perturbation the task of doing so, without the other sub-systems being forced to transform.

As for the most useful mechanisms to foster effective co-design, we observe the following:

- the setting up of ever more inclusive forums for comprehensive multilogue;
- the negotiation of moral contracts that are defined clearly and early, yet informally capture the mutual expectations of the different partners;
- the design of monitoring and learning loops, enabling the partners to revise their choice of means as the experience unfolds, but also to revise the very ends pursued through reframing the organization when it proves necessary; and,
- the invention of fail-safe mechanisms to ensure that the multilogue does not degenerate into meaningless consensus, and to prevent *saboteurs* from derailing the collective effort.

The designers must be ready to prototype and tinker together as the process unfolds. However, no organization should be permitted to act alone to ensure a sense of an experiment conducted in concert and avoid a sense of ideas being imposed.

Nadler and Tushman (1997) have suggested a blueprint of a design sequence that might serve as guide for practitioners. Their work might be stylized as follows (taking liberties with their own sequencing, and taking into account our earlier analyses):

- conduct an organizational assessment: determine what the cost is to each player;

- establish design criteria: what is the possibility that each would like to achieve and are these possibilities overlapping in some way;
- be inclusive: who needs to be involved and why is the *status quo* for them no longer acceptable;
- develop ownership: how is shared ownership affirmed initially and maintained throughout;
- establish coordination requirements: information-processing needs, tactical, strategic and cooperative data;
- encourage linking: what linking mechanisms (formal and informal) are necessary for relational governance;
- identify the properties and capabilities of the emerging assemblages of actors and mechanisms;
- conduct a provisional analysis of impacts on context and process;
- undertake simulation of both governance and solution designs in different circumstances: prototyping and serious play;
- co-design and co-plan collaborative implementation: reaffirming moral contracts of key groups, monitoring transitions, assessing impacts;
- make use of the organizational cultures: (values, beliefs and norms) as means and ends of change; and,
- establish social learning loops as mechanisms of adaptation.

Intelligent governance as protocols for learning to cope

It is not easy to capture a general shift in coordination attitudes, nevertheless it has been possible to detect such a shift in the new world battered by a sea of complexity and turbulence. Traditional attitudes that have focussed on someone being 'in charge' have shifted to a focus on developing effective coping protocols that help avoid the brunt of the malefits associated with the sort of disasters ascribable to the unexpected: avalanches, black swans and the unconceivable (Taleb 2007).

One interesting way in which this new attitude of coordination is illustrated in Weick and Sutcliffe's *Managing the Unexpected* (2008). They have identified five principles guiding high-reliability organizations in the face of turbulent environments – three of them help to improve sensitivity and the capacity to react quickly to the unexpected; while two of them have to do with the capacity to contain the toxic impacts of these avalanches:

- preoccupation with failure;
- reluctance to simplify;
- sensitivity to operations;
- commitment to resilience; and,
- deference to expertise.

These principles are built on mindfulness, the practice of being aware, moment by moment, of one's interactions with people and the environment, and their impact on the organization.

Weick and Sutcliffe suggest that these capabilities may be audited (i.e., quantified or ranked), but they may also be nudged into the organizational culture, and may be encouraged through leveraging "small wins" into the organizational culture toward greater mindfulness.

This mindfulness is but one illustration of a new skill required to be able to react helpfully in unexpected situations. It may not be optimal in all cases: some may even be repelled, for instance, by Weick and Sutcliffe's seemingly immense deference to expertise – a sentiment we would share given the degree to which expertise is becoming both narrower and more diffuse.

Other stratagems have also been put forward, that are either in the nature of 'revolutions of the mind' or expedient shortcuts, like *catastrophisme éclairé à la* Dupuy (2002). Dupuy's declaration of crisis is a ruse to deceive society into behaving in disaster mode in order to unfreeze its biases towards the *status quo*, but the appeal for ongoing disaster is unlikely to work in the long term. On the other hand, pleas for entirely refurbished conceptual frameworks and other 'revolutions of the mind' – such as *antifragility à la* Taleb (2012) – call for embracing uncertainty and disorder rather than trying in a futile way to eliminate them. These 'revolutions of the mind' occur at almost glacial speed in society in accordance with changes in culture governance and collective consciousness. Neither of these alternative approaches would appear to be as acceptable as the Weick and Sutcliffe approach. Yet the Weick-Sutcliffe approach also depends on cultural change to a certain extent, and therefore it requires much patience – even though "small wins" may indeed bring forth a change of attitude in much less than a generation. While it may not be satisfactory for those calling for instant repairs, but when it comes to cultural change, it may well be the best one can expect without the tools to alter collective consciousness directly.

One of the great merits of the Weick and Sutcliffe approach is that the authors have shown through a variety of cases that it can be very easily operationalized. Progress along the different axes defined by the five basic principles can be gauged, and "small wins" along those axes can also be gauged in terms of simple questions. Even the reliance on expertise can be made more useful if a broader range of experts are included and stakeholder expertise that is not credentialized is included. Consequently, even though the notion of mindfulness may seem elusive to many, there is a sense that the avenue opened by Weick and Sutcliffe is promising. This is all the more so because the process that they have sketched need not be rigidly adopted. Other axes of mindfulness may be invented using the same protocol they suggest to gauge progress.

One of the most interesting possibilities opened by the Weick and Sutcliffe perspective is that a whole range of economic, social and political entrepreneurs may be identified who spot disharmonies between the rules in good currency, and the sort of practices that are likely to be effective, and who may act on these anomalies due to frustration, puzzlement or sense of opportunity. This is not a job for leaders or other pseudo-masters of the game claiming to be in charge, but for anyone who may note that these anomalies exist, and are able and willing to intervene, even slightly. We will take this up again in Chapter 7.

Conclusion

Social learning is not a linear process, but it is rather an iterative process of inquiry, a process of trial and error, of experimentation and process of searching. It is the sort of reflection-in-action that Donald Schön has so aptly described (Schön 1983) – "a conversation with the situation that leads to discovery."

At the core of this process is an inquiring mind, a designer who pays attention to the evolving environment, and is willing to apply a multiple-looped learning process through which ends, means, and assumptions are continually revisited as both understanding and experimentation proceed. They are designers in the same way that the Inuit artist scrapes away at a reindeer antler with his knife, examining it first from one angle and then from another, until he cries out, "Ah, seal!" (Schön and Rein 1994: 166-67).

There have been many organizations that have made various attempts at social learning, but it has often proved easier to tinker with physical technologies than with the structures of how people interact with one another. And similarly, it has often been easier to tinker with the structures of organizations than with the organization's culture (Schön 1971). But just because tinkering with physical technologies is easier than changing an organization's culture, it would be unwise to not consider how those physical technologies impact and are impacted by culture. Within a living, learning organization they are all interconnected.

The common human reaction to puzzles is to ignore them, and to pursue the ongoing tasks as usual. Instead of being startled by anomalies, or recognizing the mysteries that they might create, the tendency is to hunker down into familiar routines and worldviews. Being compelled to find ways of understanding these emerging mysteries, to search for guidelines to help solve them, and to explore the possibilities created by them (Martin 2004) is another way of expressing this design shift in attitude towards coordination and governance.

References

Block, Peter. 2008. *Community: The Structure of Belonging*. San Francisco, CA: Berrett-Koehler

Boisot, Max H. 1995. *Information Space*. London, UK: Routledge.

Boisvert, Raymond D. 1998. *John Dewey – Rethinking Our Time*. Albany, NY: State University of New York Press, 24 (quoted by R. Garud, S. Jain, P. Tuertscher. 2008. "Incomplete Design and Designing Incompleteness," *Organization Studies*, (29): 351-371).

Boland, Richard J. and Fred Collopy (eds.). 2004. *Managing by Design*. Stanford, CA: Stanford University Press.

Brown, Tim. 2009. *Change by Design*. New York, NY: Harper Business.

Bryant, Jim. 2003. *The Six Dilemmas of Collaboration*. Toronto, ON: Wiley and Sons.

Centre on Governance. 2002. *Ottawa Works: A Mosaic of Ottawa's Economic and Workforce Landscape. Report III Ottawa's Workforce Development Strategy*, and *Ottawa Works: A Mosaic of Ottawa's Economic and Workforce Landscape; Report II Profiling Ottawa's Workforce*, and *Ottawa Works: A Mosaic of Ottawa's Economic and Workforce Landscape; Report I Ottawa's Workforce Environment*, presented to TalentWorks Steering Committee, Centre on Governance, Ottawa.

Chia, Robert C.H. and Robin Holt. 2009. *Strategy Without Design – The Silent Efficacy of Indirect Action*. Cambridge, UK: Cambridge University Press.

Chwe, Michael S.Y. 2001. *Rational Ritual*. Princeton, NJ: Princeton University Press, p. 98-99.

Dewey, John. 1935. *Liberalism and Social Action*. New York, NY: Putnam.

Drath, William H. and Charles J. Palus. 1994. *Making Common Sense*. Greensboro, NC: Center for Creative Leadership.

Dupuy, Jean-Pierre. 2002. *Pour un catastrophisme éclairé – Quand l'impossible est certain*. Paris, FR: Seuil.

Friedmann, John and George Abonyi. 1976. "Social Learning: A Model for Policy Research," *Environment and Planning, A,* 8(8): 927-940.

Gardner, Dan. 2010. *Future Babble.* Toronto, ON: McClelland & Stewart.

Gehry, Frank. 1999. "Commentaries" in M. Friedman (ed.). *Architecture + process: Gehry talks.* New York, NY: Rizzoli, p. 43-287.

Gerencser, Mark *et al.* 2006. "The Mega-community Manifesto," *www.strategy-business.com,* August 16.

Goffman, Erving. 1959. *The Presentation of Self in Everyday Life.* Garden City, NY: Doubleday.

Granderi, Anna and Santi Furnari. 2008. "A Chemistry of Organization: Combinatory Analysis and Design," *Organization Studies,* 29(3): 459-485.

Grove, Andrew (Andy) Stephen. 1996. *Only the Paranoid Survive.* New York, NY: Doubleday.

Hock, Dee. 1999. *Birth of the Chaordic Age.* San Francisco, CA: Berrett-Koehler.

Holling, C.S. (Buzz). 1987. "Simplifying the Complex: The paradigms of ecological function and structure," *European Journal of Operational Research,* (30): 139-146.

Hughes, Jonathan and Jeff Weiss. 2007. "Simple Rules for Making Alliances Work," *Harvard Business Review,* 85(11): 122-131.

Hurst, David K, and Brenda J. Zimmerman. 1994. "From Life Cycle to Ecocycle: A New Perspective on the Growth, Maturity, Destruction and Renewal of Complex Systems," *Journal of Management Inquiry,* 3(4): 339-354.

Lee, Alycia and Tatiana Glad. 2011. *Collaboration: the courage to step into a meaningful mess.* Provo, UT: Berkana Institute, berkana.org.

March, James G. 1991. "Exploration and Exploitation in Organizational Learning," *Organization Science,* 2: 71-87.

Martin, Roger. 2004. "The Design of Business," *Rotman Magazine,* Winter, p. 7.

McCann, Joseph *et al.* 2009. "Building Agility, Resilience and Performance in Turbulent Environments," *People & Strategy,* 32(3): 44-51.

Michael, Donald N. *et al.* 1980. *The New Competence – The Organization as a Learning System.* San Francisco, CA: Values and Lifestyles Program.

Michael, Donald N. 1993. "Governing by Learning: Boundaries, Myths, and Metaphors," *Futures,* 25(1): 81-89.

Nadler, David A. and Michael L. Tushman. 1997. *Competing by Design – The Power of Organizational Architecture.* New York, NY: Oxford University Press.

Norman, Donald A. 1999. "Affordances, Conventions and Design," *Interactions,* 6(3): 38-43.

Norman, Donald A. 2007. *The Design of Future Things.* New York, NY: Basic Books, p. 68-69.

Paquet, Gilles. 1999. "Tackling Wicked Problems" in G. Paquet. *Governance through Social Learning.* Ottawa, ON: University of Ottawa Press, p. 41-52.

Paquet, Gilles. 2005. *The New Geo-Governance – A Baroque Approach.* Ottawa, ON: University of Ottawa Press, chapter 8.

Paquet, Gilles. 2008. *Deep Cultural Diversity – A Governance Challenge.* Ottawa, ON: University of Ottawa Press.

Paquet, Gilles. 2009a. *Scheming Virtuously – The Road to Collaborative Governance.* Ottawa, ON: Invenire Books.

Paquet, Gilles 2009b. *Crippling Epistemologies and Governance Failures – A Plea for Experimentalism.* Ottawa, ON: University of Ottawa Press.

Paquet, Gilles. 2012. "La gouvernance, science de l'imprécis," *Organisations & Territoires,* 21(3): 5-17.

Paquet, Gilles and Christopher Wilson. 2011. "Collaborative Co-governance as Inquiring Systems," *www.optimumonline.ca*, 41(2): 1-12.

Parr, John *et al*. 2002. *The Practice of Stewardship*. Denver, CO: Alliance for Regional Stewardship.

Rheingold, Howard. 2002. *Smart Mobs*. Cambridge, UK: Perseus.

Rittel, Horst W.J. and Melvin M. Webber. 1973. "Dilemmas in a General Theory of Planning," *Policy Sciences*, (4): 155-169.

Schön, Donald A. 1971. *Beyond the Stable State*. New York, NY: Norton.

Schön, Donald A. 1983. *The Reflective Practitioner*. New York, NY: Basic Books.

Schön, Donald A. and Martin Rein. 1994. *Frame Reflection – Toward the Resolution of Intractable Policy Controversies*. New York, NY: Basic Books.

Simon, Herbert A. 1969/1981. *The Sciences of the Artificial*. Cambridge, MA: The MIT Press.

Starbuck, William H. 2006. *The Production of Knowledge*. Oxford, UK: Oxford University Press.

Straus, David. 2002. *How to Make Collaboration Work: Powerful Ways to Build Consensus, Solve problems and Make Decisions*. San Francisco, CA: Berrett-Koehler.

Strogatz, Steven. 2003. *Sync – The Emerging Science of Spontaneous Order*. New York, NY: Hyperion.

Taleb, Nassim N. 2007. *The Black Swan – The Impact of the Highly Improbable*. New York, NY: Random House.

Taleb, Nassim N. 2012. *Antifragile – Things that gain from disorder*. New York, NY: Random House.

Taylor, Carl A. 1997. "The ACIDD Test: a framework for policy planning and decision-making," *Optimum*, 27(4): 53-62.

Voβ, Jan-Peter *et al.* (eds.). 2006. *Reflexive Governance for Sustainable Development.* Cheltenham, UK: Edward Elgar.

Weick, Karl E. 2004. "Rethinking Organizational Design" in Richard J. Boland and Fred Collopy (eds.). *Managing by Design.* Stanford, CA: Stanford University Press, p. 36-53.

Weick, Karl E. and Kathleen M. Sutcliffe. 2008 (2nd ed.). *Managing the Unexpected – Resilient Performance in an Age of Uncertainty.* New York, NY: John Wiley & Sons.

Weinberg, Alvin M. 1974. "Science and Trans-Science," *Minerva,* 10(2): 209-222.

Wilson, Christopher, Wayne Foster, Carlo Sicoli and Thom Kearney. 2014. *Benchmarking Knowledge Products and Dissemination Strategies in Chronic Disease Prevention and Health Promotion.* Report. Ottawa, ON: Public Health Agency of Canada, Chronic Disease Interventions Division, March.

Wilson, Christopher. 2011. "On Collaboration," *www. optimumonline.ca,* 41(1): 15-30 [Accessed March 17, 2016].

PART II

Refurbishing

mbracing deep complexity and uncertainty entails not only a reframing of perspectives for governance, as we suggested in Part I, but also a refurbishment of a number of key concepts – not only because of the increased imprecision introduced by wickedness, complexity and deep uncertainty, but also because of the ways in which they transform how relevant knowledge is acquired. On any major issue, the relevant power, resources and information have become widely distributed (involving many hands, heads and hearts in multiple and diverse organizations), and therefore new ways are needed to steward coordination in complex arrangements.

Given that the organizational texture of social systems continues to evolve, full knowledge is not a given *ab ovo*, but is continually acquired as experience accumulates. Even the initial problem definition evolves as the process of 'learning while doing' proceeds. In such a dynamic atmosphere, governance must also change as both the understanding of the environment changes and new governing arrangements are experimented with. Such learning-based governance requires knowledge that is acquired not only through the ways typical of the humanities (α), the experimental sciences (β) or the social sciences (γ); but also by the processes of 'learning while doing' and 'reflection in action' – what we refer to as "delta knowledge" (Gilles and Paquet 1989). This delta knowledge is central to learning in the professional world, but it is also central to wayfinding in governance.

In the second part of this volume, we show how the governance challenges, presented by the opaque nature of the complex and uncertain world, demand a more holistic approach to knowledge creation and transfer – one that elevates 'learning while doing' and 'delta knowledge' to a key level of importance for the purposes of meaning-making and collective innovation. As a result, the need to acquire delta knowledge demands concomitant modifications in our traditional management notions of leadership, strategy and accountability.

In chapter 4, we explore the notion of delta knowledge *vis à vis* leadership with a view to showing how modern governance cannot count on management methods that were designed for the resolution of well-structured, static problems. Rather one must count on pooled or cumulative knowledge based on 'learning while doing' to tackle the evolving governance challenges. This leads us to question the very notion of leadership – an archaic notion that is fundamentally reductionist and ill-suited for dealing with the complexity of modern issues, or the associated need for partnerships and collaboration. Instead, we propose the concept of stewardship as being more appropriate and useful.

In the same light, we consider two subsidiary notions in chapter 5 – strategy/planning and accountability/evaluation – and show them to be lethally contaminated by mechanisms of hierarchy and control, neither of which are realistic in a distributed governance world. We show that, given the need for both upstream and downstream flows of information in the governing process, a reliance on stewardship (developed in chapter 4) commands new ways.

Reference

Gilles, Willem and Gilles Paquet. 1989. "On Delta Knowledge," in Gilles Paquet and Max von Zur-Muehlen (eds.). *Edging Toward the Year 2000*. Ottawa, ON: Canadian Federation of Deans of Management and Administrative Studies, p. 15-30.

| Delta Knowledge and the Drift from Leadership to Stewardship

"Every time we attribute everything to leadership,
we are no different from the people in the 1500s
who attributed everything they did not understand
(such as famine and plague) to God."

Jim Collins

I n the 1970s, Fritz Machlup launched a major research project on the world of knowledge[10] – its creation, distribution and economic significance. Machlup explored the different meanings, modes, types, classes and qualities of knowledge. He did not come forward with a final taxonomy, but he used a three-way classification to label the higher classes of knowledge: humanistic knowledge, scientific knowledge, social-science knowledge. There are many 'other' types and classes of knowledge he identified, but Machlup examined them in a much more cursory way.

The institutionalization of these three categories of knowledge has effectively marginalized a wide range of other, legitimate types of knowledge within institutions of

---

[10] Even though Machlup planned eight volumes, they were not all produced due to his untimely death in 1983, but the first three volumes were published, revealing the immensity of the knowledge landscape he prospected (Machlup 1980, 1982, 1984).

higher learning, ensuring that they were not recognized as valid or useable knowledge sources for dealing with human concerns (Lindblom and Cohen 1979). As a result, research – which is the process of knowledge production, and is entirely dependent on social perceptions of how legitimate knowledge is produced – has been severely biased towards the three types of knowledge above.

There is also another important class included in such "other knowledge" that we shall label "delta knowledge" (Gilles and Paquet 1989), that is fundamentally different from the other three primary classes, and also has the utmost significance for socio-economic development, and for organizational governance and social coordination.

Delta knowledge

The territory of delta knowledge spans the world of practical philosophy and reflection in action, and has its roots in the aims and activities of the Royal Society for the Encouragement of Arts, Manufactures and Commerce founded in 1754 by William Shipley. Not only does it start with the practical, as opposed to the theoretical, but it also turns on its head the basic epistemology of technical rationality.

The prevailing "technical rationality model" in science and social science presumes that everything flows from basic science or its underlying disciplines, that basic principles derived from science are then applied to problem-solutions and real-life procedures, before finding their way to the service of clients and end-users. This version of a linear cascade of knowledge production is also presumed to be a one-way street. In reality, however, knowledge may and often does evolve in other ways. It may emanate from reflection in action: from professional work in medicine, for instance, that is not an outgrowth of applied biology. It may also originate among clients and end-users who then ignite the upstream interest of professionals, policymakers and researchers.

Indeed, Schön has suggested that, for any professional, knowledge production proceeds in an obverse way: it is the 'issue' rather than theory that comes first, and 'reflection-in-action' is the technique that eliminates misfits, that ensures goodness of fit, and that finally crafts new knowledge. Research follows as a way of exploring what works in practice. The practicing professional produces new knowledge in the course of his/her job (Alexander 1964; Schön 1983).

The notion of delta knowledge is an attempt to capture this bottom-up process of knowledge production that pays particular concern to the local, the timely, and the oral, and how it flows from a reflection on experience and a conversation with the situation. This new delta knowledge is acquired by doing and observing the impacts generated by that doing. This process is best exemplified by the challenge faced by a designer who needs to search for some kind of harmony between two intangibles: a form which has not yet been designed, and a context that cannot be properly and fully described since it is still evolving (Alexander 1964). This is the sort of knowledge that emerges from case studies in management, the value of which is in providing a basis for reflection in action and meaning making, and not just as a tool for storytelling or for illustrating general principles – as is so often assumed.

Delta knowledge is different from knowledge produced via the scientific and social-scientific route, in that:

- first, it uses a very different methodology (heuristics) based on a very different epistemology (an epistemology of practice);
- secondly, it pertains to a knowledge domain excluded from the standard territory covered by theory-centric approaches in good currency and its cardinal point of reference is know-how, and not know-what;
- thirdly, the sort of knowledge acquired through 'learning while doing' has important tacit and idiosyncratic components. This explains why the process of experimentation may proceed with enthusiasm, skill and persistence in some settings, while in others, experimentation and creative problem-solving may take place only slowly and ineptly (Murnane and Nelson 1984); and,

- finally, the production of delta knowledge follows rules that are largely implicit, overlapping, diverse, variously applied, contextually dependent, and subject to exceptions and critical modifications (Schön 1988). Much of the skills training for technical and trades professions (including management, design, public administration and many other professions) is based on delta knowledge, yet this experienced-based knowledge is rarely recognized, and most certainly the implications of this link between doing and delta knowledge is not well understood. Consequently, in a world where knowledge transfer is typically a classroom-style approach of filing empty vessels, the nature of delta knowledge, the means of acquiring it, and bodies of expertise which are rooted in it, all remain underdeveloped.

Management and Design as Illustrations of Delta Knowledge

Design

Designers call their work 'projects' for they are future-oriented: each begins with a gap to be filled, but that gap can be filled only through an iterative process, an interactive conversation between local circumstances and a knowledgeable designer in search of a form that fits those circumstances and fills the gap (Topalian 1980).

Therefore, design represents a formalized process of 'reality-making'. Thus the viewpoint of design is making, and its central knowledge is 'know-how-to-make,' which constrains imagination with reality (Archer 1964). This methodology has been characterized by Lefebvre as experimental utopia:

l'exploration du possible humain avec l'aide de l'image et de l'imaginaire, accompagnée d'une incessante critique et d'une incessante référence à la problématique donnée dans le réel. L'utopie expérimentale déborde l'usage habituel de l'hypothèse dans les sciences sociales (Lefebvre 1961).

This experimental approach is forced upon the designer by the ill-structured nature of the problem being faced: how a form is created to fit a context is the result of a back and forth conversation that the designer has with the situation, and an interactive and innovative learning process (Paquet 1971). It calls for informed guesswork and experimentation in an intellectual operation that differs significantly from both deduction and induction, what Lefebvre has called *transduction*: an operation that *"construit ... un objet possible à partir d'informations portant sur la réalite ainsi que d'une problématique posée par cette réalité"* (Lefebvre 1961).

Design implies a feedback loop compressing both analysis and creation. To create something new and practical, the designer employs a process of knowledge-probing that is not unlike the manner in which one learns how to swim or how to ride a bicycle, i.e., by correction of errors, by elimination of misfits in search of "goodness of fit" (Alexander 1964). Such knowledge is acquired by the designer through experiential learning, and it becomes embodied in his/her know-how, and not in know-what. Moreover, it eventually gets embodied in both a process and a form that is no easier to synthesize or codify than the knowledge of an Olympic swimmer or that of an expert wine-taster (Archer 1964).

Management

As early as 1938, Chester Barnard – at the time one of the most distinguished management experts – introduced a distinction between 'thinking processes' and 'non-logical processes'. He emphasized the importance of the latter, and underlined the bias toward rational thinking that blinds social scientists to the non-logical processes omnipresent in effective practice (Barnard 1938/68; Schön 1983). This message was never really accepted at the time.

It is only more recently, with the emergence of the notions of complexity and distributed governance, that students of management have begun to recognize the importance of 'non-logical processes' such as vision, creativity and attitudes of mind (Sadler 1984; de Geus 2002: 16-18) in addition to those traditional elements involving rationality, logic and quantitative analysis.

This ability to think creatively is not dependent only on the academic accumulation of information, but on the development of perception and experiential learning, and sharing them with others. In contrast to the logical and purely rational sources of management knowledge, there are also important implicit, non-logical, intuitive, experimental, non-linear, and synthetic sources of knowledge. Both thinking processes contribute to the creative process (Mintzberg 1976; Paquet 1985). Newton, for instance, purportedly was first absolutely convinced by his intuition of the nature of how gravity worked, and then he applied his logical mind to invent the calculus to prove it (Dennett 2013).

Using Mintzberg's categorization of these two types of knowledge (right brain – creative and left brain – rational), one can recognize that the methodologies used in order to produce right brain/creative knowledge are quite different from those used in developing rational knowledge.

According to Mintzberg, much of a manager's work involves such processes as following hunches in the midst of a chaotic problem-solving process, and this indicates that managers have exceptionally well-developed right brains. It is this 'right-brainyness' that makes great corporate strategists capable of epoch-making leaps of conclusion (Allio 1977).

It is through lateral thinking, through cases, through techniques capable of temporarily suspending the left brain's system of reasoned intelligence, that one can develop a more creative right-brain sort of knowledge (De Bono 1967; Leenders and Erskine 1981; March 1976). Broad, sweeping strategies are not deduced, they are intuited and massaged into existence; they emerge (Mintzberg 1985; Mintzberg 1987).

The legitimacy and usefulness of this 'right-brain' knowledge and the manner of how it is generated, are matters that traditional academics typically discount, either because they are seen as unreal, or because they are unable to fit in with the usual disciplinary rubrics. But this view is unduly fundamentalist: the epistemology of practice is acceptable and it produces knowledge worth generating (Friedmann 1978).

The amazing lightness of the notion of leadership

The acceptance that deep complexity and deep uncertainty so permeate reality, implies that no one person can either perfectly comprehend and determine a context, or pretend to have all the power, information and resources to master that context. This simple admission exposes the notion of leadership as a weasel word and a fraudulent concept. "We are no more capable today of making good leaders, or reducing the effects of bad leaders, than we were forty years ago," says Kellerman (2012: xiv). "The leadership industry is a fraud."

First, leadership is anchored in the notion of hierarchy: it assumes that someone is in charge, and that this someone has all the information, power and resources to ensure the effective guidance of a host of interacting elements with an organization or social system, and therefore can be held responsible and accountable for anything good or bad that may ensue from such guidance.

Second, leadership has assumed mystical dimensions. It ascribes to the leader exceptional (if not at times super-human) qualities of clairvoyance and wisdom, the source of which is always somewhat mysterious. Such qualities permit the person 'in charge' to take the organization or social system to the 'promised land' – however that destination maybe distilled – sparing the rest of the organizational team the need to worry about where the ship is going. The followers are seen as a subservient class, wallowing in voluntary servitude to the great father leader.

No doubt the suggestion that leaders are frauds will excite much indignation, but the defence of leadership slumps quickly into circularity, seeking intellectual comfort in tautology. The leader is identified as a person who has leadership qualities, and these leadership qualities are said to be the capacity of the leader. Leadership is not unlike phlogistics for proto-chemists who centuries ago explained flammability by the existence of a flammable substance in objects.

Yet a whole literature has burgeoned around the ill-defined notions of leadership that are associated with a wide range of disparate properties that are purported to invest individuals with special and unique capacities to 'take charge.' Indeed, a certain scholarship claims to have identified those properties, and some management schools are unashamedly claiming to be able to inject them into willing souls like steroids in the bodies of athletes. Yet when the evidence is examined, "the leadership industry has not in any meaningful, measurable way improved the human condition" (Ibid.). Or, as in the case of leadership icon Jack Welch, formerly of General Electric, the leader just doesn't matter. In an interview with a *Financial Times* reporter, Jeffrey Immelt, Welch's successor at GE, shared his perception of Welch's contribution saying, "anyone could have run GE and done well in the 1990s. A dog could have run GE" (Guerrera 2009). Why? Because there were so many good people in the middle of the organization that did the actual job of running and coordinating the company for him.

Leaders, unsurprisingly, make outlandish claims to all that is great and good in their organizations. Still the mystique of leadership persists. True believers associate leaders with some sort of aura of clairvoyance-cum-influence: the leader sees things better than others, has uncommon communication capacities, and commands the unconditional following of the masses. And followers do not believe that it is at all irrational to follow a leader, because he purports to know things the rest of the group does not know. We follow the lead of Warren Buffett because we presume he is better informed than we are, more competent, and because he obviously has good reasons for doing things even though we do not fully understand them. It is a matter of faith and convenience, so that we do not have to make the effort to think things through for ourselves.

The intent here is not to deny that there are exceptional individuals who are capable of inspiring their colleagues. Most importantly, however, we want to underscore that leadership is but one tool that groups may utilize to coordinate amongst themselves. But it is not the only one. And most importantly, modern realities do not call for the attributes and skills outlined in the leadership literature. In fact, as it turns out, most often they are completely antithetical to the organizational needs of the time.

In the rest of this chapter, we suggest replacing the outdated notion of leadership with an alternative tool for coordination – stewardship – one that would appear to be better adapted to our networked world (Goldsmith and Eggers 2004) where nobody can be in charge because power, resources, and information are so widely distributed (Cleveland 2002). The notion of stewardship has the added benefit of not requiring super humans with mystical garb or magical wands. Instead it is based on the highest and best use of delta knowledge in terms of mechanisms to foster social learning, collective innovation and broad cooperation – the underpinnings of what historically has been the basis of humanity's most consistent progress (Wright 2002).

A primer on stewardship

Our central hypothesis is that stewardship underlies the governance of modern organizations and it is based on the notion that nobody is in charge, and that stewardship emerges from a network of interlacing influences that ultimately guide and coordinate some heterogeneous body of owners. Stewardship is therefore a systemic effect. Since public organizations have been drifting from large, uniform and hierarchical systems to more distributed, modular and networked systems, there has been a parallel drift in the nature of coordination – a drift from 'Big G' Government to 'small g' governance (Paquet 1999; Hubbard and Paquet 2007). The shift in the nature of an organization creates pressure for change to the organization's system of guidance in accordance to Ashby's Law of Requisite Variety, a move which we identify as a shift from leadership to stewardship models of governance.

In the world of 'Big G,' hierarchy was the order of the day, with some individuals or groups claiming (legitimately or not) to be in charge. They issued orders to subordinates who were supposed to obey to the best of their abilities. This was largely a feudalistic legacy, a world of followership, where followers followed unquestioningly, trusting in the myth of leadership and the superhuman glow of leaders to get them what they needed or wanted.

In the new world of 'small g' where nobody is in charge, where there are a variety of stakeholders, each of whom can legitimately lay claim to a portion of power, resources, and information, and where ownership must be shared, collaboration and effective coordination have become the new imperatives of social coordination.

Collaboration occurs through conversations and communications in which active owners experiment (each in their own way) with working together in the full consciousness that their actions may trigger unintended or previously unknown consequences, and that their initially intended outcomes may not be the ones realized in the end. In this light of collaboration, the attraction of leadership quickly fades, leaving erstwhile followers assuming their rightful ownership of both problems and solutions. It is here, in this space of collective interaction, that the forces of self-organization begin to emerge, often in response to deliberate interventions, which sometimes amplify the impact of self-organization; while at other times they neutralize or negate it.

As governments drift from the old top-down model of the welfare state to a new, more networked model of a strategic state (Paquet 1999), there are more inter-departmental arrangements, more inter-sectoral partnerships, and more cooperation among different levels of government, even mass collaboration – all of which have the effect of lowering the valence of the state and reducing the power of the currently powerful, including those in the upper levels of the state bureaucracies, through demands for co-governance and increased recognition of the realities of shared ownership.

This has generated forceful resistance within bureaucracies to maintain their imperium – often emboldened and supported by groups of citizens eager to retain their generous state entitlements and protections. Similar waves of transformation continue to shake organizations and institutions in the private and social sectors, often with the same resistance and lack of adaptive capacity from the managerial class.

While effective coordination is proving to be the pivotal feature of organizations seeking to survive and thrive, good stewardship, or the capacity to get people to work together well, is becoming the most sought after capacity in all sectors. It can materialize through a single person, or in small groups, like a boat with eight rowers – guided by the light touch of the coxswain. However, in more complex organizations, nothing short of a wide assortment of mechanisms for cooperation – the equivalent of an 'automatic pilot' – will ensure the requisite amount of dynamic coordination (Paquet 2007). In even larger systems, it can also emerge through stigmergic communication (communicating by modifying the environment), as we can see on the Internet.

In the 'small g' world, each stakeholder has some stake in changing the *status quo* and so contributes proportionally to the co-governance of the group and its stewardship by continually working to improve the application of cooperative mechanisms, skills and practices. As a result, any lack of critical thinking or vigilance on the part of stakeholders or partners may result in less effective experimentation, poorer prototypes, less effective social learning, poorer governance and ultimately less desirable results from cooperation (Argyris and Schön 1978; Schön and Rein 1994). In larger social groupings, free riding is easier.

An effective governance regime (i.e., the ensemble of mechanisms making up the 'automatic pilot') ensures good stewardship, as a precursor to generating the commitment and mutual responsibility needed from all parties. This co-ownership dynamic among all the parties makes those who are not fully contributing their capacities for critical thinking, collective learning, and experimentation complicit in creating collective action problems that can be individually harmful and socially toxic.

Stewardship: components and guideposts

Stewardship is an echo effect of the governance regime, and the governance regime may be regarded as the product of an attractor system – a regime that temporarily crystallizes in the presence of the complementary assets of the stakeholders, who may be motivated initially only by their shared unwillingness to continue to accept the *status quo*.

One can analyze a governance regime in its three components:

1. its emergence in parallel to an attractor system;
2. the processes through which support is rallied and sustained for the attractor system, and by which the governance regime acquires legitimacy, or not; and,
3. its capacity to generate the requisite amount of coordination, social learning, resilience, innovation, collaboration and accomplishment.

Within any such governance regime, the sustainability challenge is based on developing mechanisms of stewardship without needing them to become personalized and anchored in specific individuals who may come and go, and on generating sufficient collective resilience to accommodate both high-performance, or catastrophe.

Emergence

In certain cases, where the situation is relatively simple, an attractor system emerges organically. The contextual pressures generate some anomie among the participants who are unlikely to share the same knowledge, values or motivations beyond the desire of changing the *status quo*. This leads them to search for guideposts for cooperation, and to instigate a search for a governing regime capable of resolving the natural tensions among their different points of view.

In the case of a situation of pure and perfect competition, for instance, a price system may become the governing regime. For example, in the desolate world of POW camps in the 1940s, a barter system emerged from the fact that each prisoner received a standard Red-Cross type ration, which did not necessarily match his/her pattern of preferences. This created a situation that gave rise to a trading system within the POW camps, with cigarettes being used as the common currency (Radford 1945). Alternatively, we can witness in open source systems on the Internet, how coordination among actors is achieved by multiple, independent contributions to a shared context. In each case, coordination was not imposed but emerged via some mechanism without any need for personalized direction or planning.

Governance regimes can emerge in less obvious and more circuitous ways in more complex cases. In such situations effective coordination demands sets of principles, norms, rules, mechanisms, and other relational protocols, around which the expectations of participants can converge, in order for decision making and implementation to be defined (Paquet 2005a: 76-78). Such a regime can crystallize quite quickly when an organization is relatively small. Communities of practice, for instance, may gel on the basis of a very narrow range of shared concerns; such as described earlier with Caterpillar Inc. or as happens in a board of directors for a small high-tech startup company. Such boards typically bring together an inventive engineer, an angel financier, an important potential buyer, and a key supplier in a forum that undertakes the stewarding function.

In larger and more complex organizations that are present in all sectors, the governance regime may wear a more formal attire (more legalistic, constraining), and the board may be more layered and stylized, but the same logics are at play. Even in these more complex cases, an integrative board is not simply playing the role of financial sentinel (Type I governance) as Chait *et al.* (2005) show. It also provides space where the points of view of the different stakeholders can hopefully become harmonized and integrated (Type II governance).

However, the governance regime of a distributed organization needs even more: it must become the locus of collective discernment and meaning-making; provide a mental map of the organization and its environment; be capable of regularly distilling its purpose, its resources and its projects; and be capable of proposing the sort of transformations, innovations, and reframing that can bring the organization beyond its limits (Type III or generative governance). This generative governance unfolds through robust multilogue, framed by experimentation, prototyping and social learning, and the generation of a community of meaning as an outcome of effective collaboration (Michael 1993; Schrage 2000; Martin 2000, 2004, 2006, 2007).

Support and legitimacy

In order for a governance regime that is comprised of willing but diverse interests to be able to resolve its natural internal tensions in creative ways, it must bestow upon itself legitimacy as a facilitating mechanism. It must generate a culture of support among participants, *une manière de voir,* such that it is seen not only as the basis for realizing their individual aspirations, but also as providing the collective intelligence and capacity to facilitate their working together.

How is this collective intelligence constructed? Through multiple formal and informal channels of communication and deliberation.

A governance regime underwrites a structure, rituals, mechanisms and behaviours that facilitate interactions and stabilize expectations among group members. These constitute the visible face of the regime, triggering a rallying 'movement,' through the dual logics of synchronicity and self-organizing cascades (Sunstein 2006).

This 'movement' may materialize rationally through reasoned discussion and justification: but it may also feed off relational interactions that foster trust and shared identity in a contagious manner. It may operate through mechanisms that foster spontaneous synchronistic behaviour – like modes and fads – especially via social media. These mechanisms can also dampen the energy of a movement or amplify its impact, especially in polarizing movements (Guillaume 1987, 1989).

This latter mechanism of spontaneous, cascading propagation is generally poorly understood, but it has often been associated with governance regimes that are idiosyncratic, fragile, and often very surprising (McCann and Selsky 1984; Bikhchandani *et al.* 1998; Barabasi 2002; Strogatz 2003; Sunstein 2006).

However, it is only once a governance regime is firmly in place, that one can establish whether the fit between its internal structures, mechanisms, external context and organizational purpose are well aligned or not. In reality, many governance regimes never really finish forming, and so they have a tendency towards underperformance, necessitating ongoing attention to the collaborative process and to improving the governance 'automatic pilot.'

Obviously, the governance regime must align with and make sense of the situation, but, most importantly, it must exhibit great adaptive capacity (Bennis and Thomas 2002: 45). This capacity does not emerge from the standardized elements of corporate governance that are transportable from one situation to another, but from the characteristics and capacities of a specific regime that are often only revealed *in situ*, in a precise context (DeLanda 2006) – in the same way a specific wave determines if the surfer has the required capacities to ride it.

Effective coordination: uncertain

Do the challenges of emergence, legitimacy and contextual determinacy condemn all efforts at designing good governance to failure due to the uncertainty and unpredictability they engender? Some, like Lindblom (1990), think so. Others, like us, are more optimistic, believing that the right mix of capacities may be nudged into existence to generate good governance and good stewardship, if and only if they are suitably aligned with the local context. Still, most observers remain content to simply avoid the collective uncertainties associated with working together by emphasizing the certainties that may be described of person-leaders (e.g. Badaracco 2006; Martin 2007). As a result there have been few attempts to identify the requisite system of governance properties, or to sort out the collective capacities likely to generate good governance, or the mechanisms or practices that could foster effective system-based stewardship.

Yet one can still reasonably suggest what the principles of good governance are those that can generate dynamic, adaptive stewardship and that can foster the characteristics of inclusion, subsidiarity, multistability, and experimentalism (Paquet 2005b: chapter 8). Obviously, these principles must take into account the context in which they will be used, but one can start simply by mapping their characteristics in two dimensions.

i. Longitude: the inclusion-subsidiarity axis

The first two characteristics have to do with the best ways to assemble a team of potential partners when power, resources and information are distributed, and to structure their coordinated work. The key idea is to include as many of the most meaningful stakeholders as possible in the decision-making process – those who are willing to contribute; those who can potentially stop change; those who have knowledge and those who will be impacted (Straus 2002). The governing apparatus must be designed in such a way as to allow those closest to the situation to be allowed to take the decision (subsidiarity) because they are better informed. Thus, from the basis of their shared ownership ensues the principle of as much decentralization as possible, but only as much centralization as necessary.

Such a participative and distributed governance regime is likely to ensure continuous social learning, quick self-correcting feedback, creative conflict resolution, and the existence of shared responsibility mechanisms in order to generate the right mix of reliability and innovation.

ii. Latitude: the multistability-experimentalism axis

The other two characteristics deal with a reconciliation of the tensions between the exploitation of existing knowledge and the exploration of new knowledge (March 1991) along an axis of innovation. The principle of multistability is an important aspect in the architecture of open systems within organizational or social systems. It suggests that the best way to minimize the destabilizing influence of change in a differentiated, heterogeneous system is to recognize its component sub-systems, and then deal with them separately in order to:

a. immunize the system as a whole from the impact of change that could potentially shock and destabilize the organization completely; and,

b. delegate to a subset of the organization, the one best suited to handle any potential shock of change, the job of adjustment and experimentation.

Multistability also facilitates experimentation and proto-typing by allowing these processes to proceed *par morceaux*. It recognizes that innovation is by nature creative destruction and, therefore, it is inherently destabilizing. As a result, a good governance regime must be fundamentally experimentalist, capable of engaging the organization creatively in new avenues, but it must also do so safely and prudently – i.e., engaging in change tentatively, partially, and often *par morceaux* (Sabel 2001, 2004; Schrage 2000). This form of attentive experimentalism is an essential condition for Type III governance.

iii. Sextant

Despite the fact that these characteristics will help foster effective stewardship, and ultimately nudge a workable distributed governance regime into existence, there is no absolute assurance that effective governance will prevail. There can be many individual and systemic blockages that may prevent its emergence: an important one being that the fragmentation of ownership may well discourage cooperation and the coherent assembly of what each stakeholder believes to be a winning combination (Heller 2008). By failing to recognize the willing cooperation of others in achieving their goals, stakeholders end up pursuing 'irrational acting,' i.e., self-centred, rational acting that harms themselves by failing to produce the needed concerted action.

There may also be acts of sabotage: passive sabotage as a result of neglect, lack of vigilance or sheer incompetence; or active sabotage, by powerful vested interests or gatekeepers that may see immense benefits in the *status quo* and so work to ensure that an altered governance regime and its accompanying stewardship do not materialize (Hubbard and Paquet 2009). It may also result from a lack of collaborative skills, behaviours and practices that creates huge pressure on participants to default to the top-down leadership practices they know, but that are unsuitable for collaborative work.

Perhaps more importantly, good governance and effective stewardship may not evolve because of cognitive dissonance, and a refusal to factor in (even in a tentative way) the dynamics and the complexities of the context and the fear of unanticipated uncertainties and surprises (both good and bad) that the power of self-organization are bound to produce.

These tendencies cannot be ignored, and they cannot be entirely prepared for in advance because of their unpredictability. Instead, they must be dealt with opportunistically if and when they appear. This factor can be critical, not so much because of any inherent destructiveness in self-organization *per se*, but because of the very nature and importance of self-organization which is emergent such that its value is occluded or denied, and therefore rarely taken advantage of (even partially).

The unbearable denial of self-organization

In a world where nobody is in charge (Cleveland 2002), stewardship emerges from a good matching of the structure of governance with the dynamics of its context – together with a full awareness of the underlying forces of self-organization that are constantly being unleashed. That said, there exists a deep and profound cultural blockage among leaders and managers with respect to self-organization.

Mitchel Resnick (1994) has analyzed this blockage with much subtlety. He has shown that it is common with people who:

    i.   do not understand creative mechanisms like: probability and randomness (which open new avenues of exploration and possibility); positive feedback (that can amplify the impact of a minor shock); and emergence phenomena that are ascribable to interactions among people (as in the case of traffic jams, mobs and movements);

ii. refuse to acknowledge the very notion of self-organization – that something new can emerge spontaneously out of the interactions of system parts without any direction from anyone; and,

iii. cling to naïve explanations that assume that complex realities must somehow be orchestrated by a *deus ex machina*, and refuse to accept that there might be no leader who can legitimately claim responsibility or shoulder the blame (although leaders rarely assume blame even though they may be quick to claim credit).

Resnick tells a story about Rachel (the very young daughter of a friend of his) who has a theory about rain: clouds rain, she suggests, because the thunder orders them to (*Ibid.*). For children, there must be someone in charge. But in a surprising number of cases, many adults and scientists display the same fantasies and the same affinity to paternalism. This explains the difficulty of fully communicating the messages of Adam Smith (market and the invisible hand) and Charles Darwin (evolution) – who proposed theories that do not require anyone to be in charge. The same skepticism awaits suggestions that CEOs and orchestra leaders may be dispensable, in contrast to what is usually presumed (Cleveland 2002; Semler 1989; Seifter and Economy 2001).

It is only by disclosing the basic mechanisms at work in the governance of organizations that one can unveil the workings of an 'automatic pilot' and hope to dispel these mental blockages (Spinosa *et al.* 1997). Strangely, it has been studies of complex, non-human systems – like ant hills or synchronized flocks of birds – that have shown the way: complex coordination exists without an ant in chief or a leader bird (Resnick 1994). The lesson: coordination can be achieved by innocuous mechanisms, small changes in behaviour and by changes in the environment – via stigmergic communication – rather than by overt direction. This is also the case for coordination in human organizations, as in the case of a leaderless orchestra (Seifter and Economy 2001), or the governance of aircraft carriers' operations (Pool 1997) or open source software (Raymond 1999).

It is only through the examination of a large number of such cases in complex organizations, that the notion of stewardship – i.e., coordination without a leader – breaks the spell that many experts and lay persons fall prey to: the propensity to search always and everywhere for a *deus ex machina*. But 'looking behind the curtain' in this way cannot on its own suffice. One must also find ways to be open to the ways and possibilities of self-organization (Axelrod and Cohen 1999; Johnson 2001; Tapscott and Williams 2006; Laloux 2014). This is an equally daunting task.

For the time being, while the theories of self-organization *à la* Smith and Darwin are said to be believed, it is often more from fear of ridicule than as a result of their theories of self-organization being fully appreciated and understood, even by an educated public.

Conclusion

Since dynamic adaptation is the central process of stewardship, it requires a variety of new competencies that need to be nudged into existence, not only by leveraging the existing forces of self-organization, but also by harnessing them somewhat as heuristic tools to be pulled out, applied, set aside and picked up again as needed.

These new competencies may be partitioned into five categories (Michael 1993; Hughes and Weiss 2007):

- contextual skills: (embracing uncertainty and error, building bridges between people, reframing, improvising, adapting, and overcoming (in the manner of Clint Eastwood's *Heartbreak Ridge*));
- interpersonal skills: (consultation, negotiation, deliberation, conflict resolution, facilitation, brokering, preceptoring, educating, animating, changing roles);
- enactment skills: (enabling, empowering, responsiveness, creativity);

- systemic skills: (ethics of inter-connectedness and interdependence, removing obstacles, freeing others to act better);
- skills for staying the course while rocking the boat: (imagination, experimentation, responsibility to explore, emphasis on sins of omission, learning by prototyping).

These capacities are not only those of individuals, but they are also rooted collectively – in the sense that they may define the rules of interaction among individuals, or in how the dynamics of a situation may generate emerging properties and possibilities. They do not have to come from the heads of individual actors as inspired genius. They describe the interaction order (in the language of Goffman) that generates a sort of collective intelligence, a sort of social mind (Goffman 1959; Johnson 2001; Rheingold 2002: 179) that is capable of inspiring innovation.

These dual capacities (both individual and collective) of necessity interact, and they do so where they are confronted with a context that affords some 'action possibilities' but not others. Whether such 'affordances' are real or perceived is of less relevance than the fact that they act to constrain the realm of all possibilities. In particular, each context generates 'affordances' that individuals and collectivities perceive, or learn to perceive, as boundaries for collective action. Learning to perceive these 'affordances' thus becomes a key part of perceptual learning (Gibson 1982; Norman 1999).

In doing so, 'affordances' contribute an important element of social learning that is at the core of innovation and innovative design. It is a way that the 'automatic pilot' of governance is improved.

Still, how can one refocus social coordination away from its traditional obsession with leadership toward stewardship?

Firstly, by casting doubts on the chivalrous stories of leadership in good currency – and seeding suspicion on their alchemists, but also by showing that one can usefully replace their magic potions with a toolbox of mechanisms and practices. This quest began a long time ago with the intriguing work of scholars like the Nobel-Prize laureate Thomas Schelling (1978), who made a career of showing how some complex social phenomena can be shown to be the outcome of relatively un-mysterious mechanisms; or like Leonid Hurwicz (another Nobel prize winner, in quite a different genre) who laid the foundations for mechanism design (Hurwicz and Reiter 2006).

Secondly, one must also be bolder and agree to deconstruct complex social phenomena, to dare to put forward hypotheses that are at least as fascinating, intriguing, and perplexing in the human sphere as those that have been proposed for dealing with the animal world.

Thirdly, one must also succeed in generating for human organizations something like what Resnick has done to explain the creation of a single central cemetery in ant hills. He has shown that if an ant follows two simple rules – (1) if you stumble on a dead brother, and you are unburdened by a dead brother, take him on, and (2) if you stumble on a dead brother, and you are already carrying another dead brother, dump him – it is possible to show by the simulation of thousands of notional ants that they will construct a central cemetery without the need to assume that there is any foreman-ant.

We believe that this sort of approach represents the future challenge for governance research in organizations and in the coordination sciences: a deconstruction and compilation of what were heretofore black-box notions and concepts into their component mechanisms and simple rules.

Yet good stewardship should be seen as more than just a tool collection: it is also about developing the tacit connoisseurship, the 'know-how' to determine what tool might fit what context. The hypothesis at the core of this chapter is that to achieve a better understanding of what constitutes an effective governance regime and the dynamics of cooperation, one needs to bring together these two sets of capacities in the dynamics of collaboration – self-organization and the mechanisms to guide it.

However, the work cannot be completed without a great number of case narratives and, probably at a minimum, a new lexicon, together with new analytical tools that can provide a basis for a conceptual refurbishment.

References

Alexander, Christopher. 1964. *Notes Toward a Synthesis of Form*. Cambridge, MA: Harvard University Press.

Allio, Robert J. 1977. "Interviewing Professor Mintzberg's 'Right Brain'," *Planning Review*, 5(2): 8-22.

Archer, L. Bruce. 1964. "Systematic Method for Designers (a compendium of papers)," *Design*. London, UK: Council of Industrial Design.

Argyris, Chris and Donald A. Schön. 1978. *Organizational Learning: A Theory of Action Perspective*. Boston, MA: Addison-Wesley.

Axelrod, Robert. 1997. *The Complexity of Cooperation*. Princeton, NJ: Princeton University Press.

Axelrod, Robert and Michael D. Cohen. 1999. *Harnessing Complexity – Organizational Implications of a Scientific Frontier*. New York, NY: The Free Press, 1999.

Badaracco Jr, Joseph L. 2006. *Questions of Character*. Boston, MA: Harvard Business School Press.

Barabasi, A.L. 2002. *Linked – The New Science of Networks*. New York, NY: Perseus.

Barnard, Chester. 1938/1968. *The Functions of the Executive*. Cambridge, MA: Harvard University Press (first published in 1938).

Bennis, W.G. and R.J. Thomas. 2002. "Crucibles of Leadership," *Harvard Business Review*, 80(9): 39-45.

Bikhchandani, S. *et al.* 1998. "Learning from the Behavior of Others: Conformity, Fads, and Informational Cascades," *Journal of Economic Perspectives*, 12(3): 151-170.

Chait, R.P., W.P. Ryan and B.E. Taylor. 2005. *Governance as Leadership*. Hoboken, NJ: Wiley.

Cleveland, Harlan. 2002. *Nobody in Charge*. San Francisco, CA: Jossey-Bass.

De Bono, Edward. 1967. *The Use of Lateral Thinking*. London, UK: Penguin.

de Geus, Arie. 2002. *The Living Company*. Boston, MA: Harvard Business Press.

DeLanda, Manuel. 2006. *A New Philosophy of Society*. London, UK: Continuum.

Dennett, Daniel C. 2013. *Intuition Pumps and Other Tools for Thinking*. New York, NY: Norton.

Drath, William H. and Charles J. Palus. 1994. *Making Common Sense*. Greensboro, NC: Center for Creative Leadership.

Dupuy, J.P. 1992. *Introduction aux sciences sociales – Logique des phénomènes collectifs*. Paris, FR: Ellipses/Ecole Polytechnique.

Friedmann, John. 1978. "The Epistemology of Social Practice," *Theory and Society*, 6(1): 75-92.

Gibson, J.J. 1982. "A Preliminary Description and Classification of Affordances" in E.S. Reed and R. Jones (eds.). *Reasons for Realism*. Hillsdale, NJ: Lawrence Erlbaum & Associates, p. 403-406.

Gilles, Willem and Gilles Paquet. 1989. "On Delta Knowledge," in Gilles Paquet and Max von Zur-Muehlen (eds.). *Edging Toward the Year 2000*. Ottawa, ON: Canadian Federation of Deans of Management and Administrative Studies, p. 15-30.

Goffman, E. 1959. *The Presentation of Self in Everyday Life*. Garden City, NY: Doubleday.

Goldsmith, Stephen and William D. Eggers. 2004. *Governing by Network*. Washington, DC: Brookings Institution Press.

Granovetter, Mark. 1978. "Threshold Models of Collective Behavior," *American Journal of Sociology*, 83(6): 1420-1443.

Guerrera, Francesco. 2009. "A need to reconnect," *Financial Times*, March 12, www.ft.com/cms/s/0/822ed110-0f3d-11de-ba10-0000779fd2ac.html#axzz43CSt5h2f [Accessed March 17, 2016].

Guillaume, M. 1987. "The Metamorphoses of Epidemia" in Feher, M. and S. Kwinter (eds.). *Zone 1/2: The Contemporary City*, Boston, MA: The MIT Press.

Guillaume, M. 1989. *La contagion des passions – essai sur l'exotisme intérieur*. Paris, FR: Plon.

Handy, Charles. 1999. *The New Alchemists*. London, UK: Hutchinson.

Heller, Michael. 2008. *The Gridlock Economy*. New York, NY: Basic Books.

Himberger, D. *et al.* 2007. "When there is no cavalry," *Strategy + Business*, (48): 10.

Hubbard, Ruth and Gilles Paquet. 2007. *Gomery's Blinders and Canadian Federalism*. Ottawa, ON: University of Ottawa Press.

Hubbard, Ruth and Gilles Paquet. 2009. "Design Challenges for the Strategic State: Bricolage and Sabotage" in A.M. Maslove (ed.). *How Ottawa Spends 2009-2010*. Montreal, QC and Kingston, ON: McGill-Queen's University Press, p. 89-114.

Hughes, Jonathan and Jeff Weiss. 2007. "Simple Rules for Making Alliances Work," *Harvard Business Review*, 85(11): 122-131.

Hurwicz, L. and S. Reiter. 2006. *Designing Economic Mechanisms*. Cambridge, UK: Cambridge University Press.

Johnson, Steven. 2001. *Emergence*. New York, NY: Scribner.

Kellerman, Barbara. 2012. *The End of Leadership*. New York, NY: HarperCollins.

Laloux, Frederic. 2014. *Reinventing Organizations*. Brussels, BE: Nelson Parker.

Leenders, M.R. and J.A. Erskine. 1981. *Teaching with Cases*. London, ON: University of Western Ontario.

Lefebvre, Henri. 1961. "Utopie expérimentale: pour un nouvel urbanisme," *Revue Francaise de Sociologie*, 2-3 (July-September): 191-198.

Lindblom, Charles E. 1990. *Inquiry and Change*. New Haven, CT: Yale University Press.

Lindblom, C.E. and D.K. Cohen. 1979. *Usable Knowledge*. New Haven, CT: Yale University Press.

Machlup, Fritz. 1980/1982/1984. *Knowledge: Its Creation, Distribution, and Economic Significance*, Vols. I, II, III. Princeton, NJ: Princeton University Press.

March, James G. 1976. "The Technology of Foolishness" in J.G. March and J.P. Olsen (eds.). *Ambiguity and Choice in Organizations*. Oslo, NO: Universitesforlaget.

March, James G. 1991. "Exploration and Exploitation in Organizational Learning," *Organization Science*, 2: 71-87.

Martin, R. 2000. "The Death of Heroic Leadership," *Rotman Management*, Fall, p. 5-7.

Martin, R., 2004. "The Design of Business," *Rotman Management*, Winter, p. 7-11.

Martin, R., 2006. "Designing in Hostile Territory," *Rotman Management*, Spring-Sumer, p. 4-9.

Martin, R. 2007. *The Opposable Mind: Winning Through Integrative Thinking*. Boston, MA: Harvard Business Review Press.

McCann, J.E. and J. Selsky. 1984. "Hyperturbulence and the Emergence of Type 5 Environment," *Academy of Management Review*, 9: 460-470.

Michael, D.N., 1993. "Governing by Learning: Boundaries, Myths and Metaphors," *Futures*, 25(1): 81-89.

Mintzberg, Henry. 1976. "Planning on the Left Side and Managing on the Right," *Harvard Business Review*, July-August.

Mintzberg, Henry. 1985. *Emergent Strategy for Public Policy*. Ottawa, ON: The 1985 J.J. Carson Lecture.

Mintzberg, Henry. 1987. "Crafting Strategy," *Harvard Business Review*, 65(4), July-August.

Murnane, R.J. and R.R. Nelson. 1984. "Production and Innovation When Techniques are Tacit," *Journal of Economic Behavior and Organization*, 5.

Norman, Donald A. 1999. "Affordances, Conventions and Design," *Interactions*, 6(3): 38-43.

Norman, Donald A. 2007. *The Design of Future Things*. New York, NY: Basic Books.

Paquet, Gilles. 1971. "Social Science Research as an Evaluative Instrument for Social Policy," in G.E. Nettler and K. Krotki (eds.). *Social Science and Social Policy*. Edmonton, AB: Human Resources Research Council, p. 49-66.

Paquet, Gilles. 1985. " Entrepreneurship et Universite: le Combat de Carnaval et Careme," *Revue de gestion des petites et moyennes organisations*, 1(5).

Paquet, Gilles. 1999. *Governance through Social Learning*. Ottawa, ON: University of Ottawa Press.

Paquet, Gilles. 2005a. *The New Geo-Governance – A Baroque Approach*, Ottawa, ON: University of Ottawa Press,

Paquet, Gilles. 2005b. *Gouvernance : une invitation à la subversion*. Montreal, QC: Liber.

Paquet, Gilles. 2007. "Organization Design as Governance's Achilles' Heel," *www.governancia.com*, 1(3): 1-11.

Paquet, Gilles and John H. Taylor. 1986. "The Marksmanship of Research Grants Programs: An Evaluative Framework," *The University of Ottawa Quarterly*, 56(4).

Parker, S. and N. Gallagher (eds.). 2007. *The Collaborative State.* London, UK: Demos.

Parr, John *et al.* 2002. *The Practice of Stewardship.* Denver, CO: Alliance for Regional Stewardship.

Picard, L. *et al.* 1980. *University Management Education and Research: A Developing Crisis.* Report by the Consultative Group on Research and Graduate Education in Business, Management, and Administrative Studies. Ottawa, ON: SSHRC.

Pool, R. 1997. "When Failure in not an Option," *Technology Review*, 100(5): 38-45.

Radford, R.A. 1945. "The Economic Organization of a POW Camp," *Economica*, 12(48): 189-201.

Raymond, Eric S. 1999. *The Cathedral and the Bazaar.* Originally published at: http://www.tuxedo.org/~esr/writings/cathedral-bazaar/ [Accessed 5 April 2016 at: http://www.unterstein.net/su/docs/CathBaz.pdf].

Resnick, Mitchel. 1994. *Termites and Traffic Jams.* Boston, MA: The MIT Press.

Resnick, Mitchel. 1996. "Beyond the Centralized Mindset," *Journal of Learning Sciences*, 5(1): 1-22.

Rheingold, Howard. 2002. *Smart Mobs.* Cambridge, UK: Perseus.

Sabel, Charles F. 2001. "A Quiet Revolution of Democratic Governance: Towards Democratic Experimentalism" in W. Michalski *et al.* (eds.). *Governance in the 21st Century.* Paris, FR: OECD, p. 121-148.

Sabel, Charles F. 2004. "Beyond Principal-Agent Governance: Experimentalist Organizations, Learning and Accountability" in E. Engelen and M. Sie Dhian Ho (eds.). *De Staat van de Democratie. Democratie Voorbij de Staat. WRR Verkenning 3.* Amsterdam, NL: Amsterdam University Press, p. 173-195.

Sadler, P. 1984. "Educating Managers for the Twenty-First Century," *The Royal Society for the Encouragement of Arts Manufactures and Commerce Journal*, Vol. CXXXII, No. 5334, May.

Schelling, T.C. 1978. *Micromotives and Macrobehavior.* New York, NY: Norton.

Schön, Donald A. 1971. *Beyond the Stable State.* New York, NY: Norton.

Schön, Donald A. 1983. *The Reflective Practitioner.* New York, NY: Basic Books.

Schön, Donald A. 1988. "Designing: Rules, Types and Worlds," *Design Studies*, 9(3): 188-190.

Schön, Donald A. and Martin Rein. 1994. *Frame Reflection – Toward the Resolution of Intractable Policy Controversies.* New York, NY: Basic Books.

Schrage, Michael. 2000. *Serious Play: How the World's Best Companies Simulate to Innovate.* Boston, MA: Harvard Business School Press.

Seifter, Harry and Peter Economy. 2001. *Leadership Ensemble: Lessons in Collaborative Management from the World's Only Conductorless Orchestra.* New York, NY: Times Books.

Semler, R. 1989. "Managing without managers," *Harvard Business Review*, p. 76-84.

Simons, Robert. 2005. *Levers of Organization Design.* Boston, MA: Harvard Business School Press.

Spinosa, Charles *et al.* 1997. *Disclosing New Worlds.* Cambridge, MA: MIT Press.

Straus, David. 2002. *How to Make Collaboration Work: Powerful Ways to Build Consensus, Solve problems and Make Decisions.* San Francisco, CA: Berrett-Koehler.

Strogatz, Steven. 2003. *Sync – The Emerging Science of Spontaneous Order.* New York, NY: Hyperion.

Sunstein, C.R. 2006. *Infotopia.* Oxford, UK: Oxford University Press.

Tapscott, D. and A.D. Williams. 2006. *Wikinomics.* New York, NY: Portfolio (Penguin Group).

Topalian, A. 1980. *The Management of Design Projects*. London, UK: Associated Business Press.

Voβ, Jan-Peter *et al.* (eds.). 2006. *Reflexive Governance for Sustainable Development*. Cheltenham, UK: Edward Elgar.

Watts, D.J. 2002. "A Simple Model of Global Cascades on Random Networks," *Proceedings of the National Academy of Sciences USA*, 99: 5766-5771.

Wright, Robert. 2002. *NonZero: The Logic of Human Destiny*. New York, NY: Vintage Books.

CHAPTER 5

| Social Practice, Strategy and Accountability

"Emergence is … more wondered at than analyzed."

John H. Holland

A s explained in chapters 3 and 4, acting and knowing in the context of social practice are united in a single process of collective learning (Friedmann 1978). The stewardship process helps to bring together and coordinate the learning and actions of a variety of stakeholders each of whom has a portion of the necessary power, resources and information. It does so via an ensemble of principles, conventions and mechanisms that are capable of generating wayfinding, ongoing learning, innovation and an ever improving capacity to transform (i.e., a capacity to adapt faster and more effectively).

This 'learning-while-doing' is an evolutionary dynamic that does not operate top down, or require leaders purporting to be in charge, or an assumption of common or shared values in our pluralist society. Quite the opposite, there are multiple understandings, preferences and objectives that may be pursued by the different stakeholders. However, this heterogeneity does not prevent the emergence of principles, conventions or mechanisms that may lead the varied groups to innovatively contribute to shared outcomes that improve the situation.

This notion of an 'automatic pilot' form of stewardship as a disembodied and depersonalized nexus of arrangements, demands a dramatic rethinking of other central, traditional notions of management upstream and downstream.

From strategic planning *ex ante* to strategic thinking and social learning as you go

Planning has the same Greek root as the notion of flattening and simplification. It presumes that the problems one faces are sufficiently well-understood and well-structured, so that one can reasonably plan for their solutions. Such planning may be as complicated as putting a man on the moon, yet it can be formulated in terms of precise milestones and tasks that get the work done in a predetermined way. This is the 'bow, arrow and target' world that has dominated public policy making for decades with its static environments, content determinism and operational marksmanship, and has recently emerged in the Canadian federal government in terms of a focus on 'deliverology' – the 'science of delivery' – to compel expected performance.

The 'Big Lie' of strategic planning

Organizations can face a variety of problem types – simple, complicated, and complex (Westley *et al.* 2006). While 'bow-and-arrow' approaches may be of some use in dealing with simple and even complicated problems, they can be perilous to use when organizations are faced with the uncertainties of complex wicked problems, where goals are uncertain and evolving, and where means-ends relationships are unstable and evolving. In such situations, plan implementation is often derailed by misunderstood problems, unlooked for reactions to the implementation process and evolving contexts. Nevertheless, planners and managers frequently 'cartoonize' the messy, uncertain and complex lifeworld to fit into the comfort zone of those who have a great fear of the complexity and the unknown. This is why Roger Martin speaks of "the big lie of strategic planning" (Martin 2014).

Traditional strategy exercises are not suited to deal with issues permeated by unknowns, deep uncertainty, and unpredictability. As a result, even Mintzberg's (1985) old cautionary statements about the perils to sticking to a fixed strategy in the face of an evolving environment are too often casually ignored. So called 'best practices' are adopted holus bolus without regard to any contextual basis or without considering what might be best suited for the current circumstances and players.

The stylized presentations of conventional corporate governance have a simple recipe-like beauty: rules for board composition; neatly described board-management interactions; and uniform, stylized steps for strategic planning.[11] But when confronted by uncertainty, unpredictability and unknowable environments that change even as one thinks about them, the traditional elements of corporate governance become mental prisons that isolate the actors from the realities of the lifeworld, amounting to crippling epistemologies (Paquet 2009a). As such, they can block self-reflective inquiries that foster value adding, innovation, productivity gains, and social learning that together can provide some hope that the organization will thrive going forward. Much of the traditional literature on both corporate governance and strategic planning is unduly obsessed with a non-real world that is static and unchanging: its metaphor for problems is well-defined puzzles, for which there are already well-defined solutions that can be ferreted out with a little time and expertise.

Puzzles have a solution, but wicked organizational issues can only elicit responses – responses that are often provisional at best, and that evolve as the situation and a response evolves. In this environment, it is social learning that evinces tentative responses that may later become transformative. Yet, in the traditional corporate governance literature, strategic planning

---

[11] As long as these stylized steps are considered only as loose guidelines, or checklists, or *aide-mémoire*, this is entirely unobjectionable and should be encouraged, but if regarded as rigid recipes they are toxic (Gawande 2009).

offers little space for social learning and instead relies heavily on mechanisms of decision making, on the basis of preconceived cognitive commitments.

Indeed, the traditional management literature is prone to accept the 'cartoonesque' view that problems and solutions are always well defined, standardized and predictable, with the only management challenge being choosing which alternative, off-the-shelf response is preferred. With reference to complex wicked problems, this focus on decision making is unduly simplistic. On the other hand, wicked problems require the facilitation of cooperation where one begins by finding a way to reconcile many stakeholder points of view and elicit responses that will turn out simultaneously to be technically feasible, socially acceptable, and implementable.

This, in turn, may require (and frequently does) the design of an idiosyncratic response, often together with the design of a new structure for the participants to interact within, or sometimes a redesign of the organization, so that it can continue to do the job as it evolves. This is a crucial dynamic that is all too often missing entirely in the static and formulaic views of strategic planning: which refuses to acknowledge the dynamics of the environment and of the various players, or the need, as a result, to set in place a flexible social learning apparatus, and not the quick preparation of a catapult to launch some pre-ordained solution.

PARC organizations and stewardship

Broadly speaking, an organization – may be represented by a useful acronym – PARC – a mix of people or **P** (stakeholders of all sorts, with their skills, talents, and responsibilities), architecture or **A** (relationships of all sorts, defined by the organization charts and the like), routines or **R** (process, policies, and procedures), and culture or **C** (shared beliefs, language, norms, and mindsets) (Roberts 2004). At any given time, these PARC components are assembled in various ways – bound together by ligatures of purposes, skills, behaviours, mechanisms and practices – making them into a more or less coherent whole. Any change or disturbance to any of these components, whether originating within or without the organization, can trigger some re-alignment with all the other dimensions, whether or not the modifications are physical, or just symbolic in nature.

As complex assemblages of these PARC elements, organizations are constantly being transformed (in both their external and internal faces) as a result of the actions of new stakeholders, new and emerging relationships, new procedures, new technologies, new contexts, or changes in the material or symbolic order.

Against this backdrop, the stewardship function intervenes in real time, to improve the four-dimensional PARC configuration of the organization in a manner that hopefully generates better alignment with these changes and thereby induces better dynamic performance and resilience. This can only be done if there is a realistic and comprehensive appreciation of the nature of the environment in which the organization operates, and of the social technologies in terms of purposes, skills, behaviours, mechanisms and practices it can deploy to improve its capacity for change.

These four PARC dimensions may also be tweaked somewhat to provide even more insight into effective dynamic coordination, by:

1. a new shared vocabulary, because while description is crucial at the diagnostic phase, each participant comes to the table with their own vocabulary to describe the situation;

2. a new mindset and process of experimentalism that embraces both a tolerance of error and a 'learning while doing' attitude;

3. new types of competencies to do this work, including relational governance, and a facility for ongoing monitoring and evaluation; and,

4. windows of opportunity to 'tinker' with the organization to provide a better chance for success – by neutralizing the dynamic conservatism that prevents collaborative

efforts from being fully realized by those currently benefiting from the existing order.

However, this process will lead to nothing substantial unless one is able to have access to, or to develop, a system of inquiry and the mental toolbox of skills, practices, and mechanisms that are capable of guiding its work. Further, because this design work inevitably produces a new organizational reality out of all the contributing parts, none of the above will suffice unless the design process has succeeded in shaping a coherent organizational body, and imparting to it a style (a culture or soul) that imbues it with intelligence and legitimacy, that can underpin purposeful collective action in pursuit of change (Romme 2003).

Such a reality cannot be accomplished without its governing system acquiring learning capabilities and being able to scheme virtuously (Paquet 2009b): using the inquiring system to sort out how the different tasks can be tackled, by different parties, in different phases of collective work, and suggesting how this can be monitored, thereby revealing possible pressure points where nudging interventions might be potentially fruitful. Unless the meccano of governance ensures this sort of mindfulness and collective learning capacity, one cannot hope that governance will lead to effective collective action.

Toward forward-looking experimentalist accountability

The mechanical and simplistic ways of assessing leadership performance in implementing a strategic plan can prove counter-productive when they are used to deal with the 'upstream' risks and unintended consequences associated with wicked problems. This is because the simplistic instrument of strategic planning does not fit at all the degree of complexity of wicked problems, which require more sophisticated stewardship approaches based on mixtures of shared cognition, relational governance, collaboration, co-design and reflexivity, as sketched in chapter 3. Neither is there any way for it to account for what is known but not shared, or for what is yet to be learned.

The same may be said about performance assessment, which in its standard and simplistic version, focuses 'downstream' at the other end of the policy process. The traditional versions of evaluation (both summative and formative) are simplistic because they are a direct response to this linear, 'arrow and target' process of planning but also because they reflect simplistic assessments (achieved/ not achieved) for complex processes of experimentation and learning. To the extent that the stewardship requires more than the marksmanship philosophy of planning, evaluation of collaborations must also reflect greater sophistication and learning.

Here again all sorts of mental prisons and ideological trappings have prevented practitioners from utilizing comprehensive and intelligent accountability. The false premises inherent in compliance based accountability and derived from overly simplified planning, have led to certain pathologies in evaluation that inhibit collective learning.

One such pathology is the unwarranted belief that for each unwanted or toxic outcome there is a person responsible that must be punished. This blame-based accountability is founded on the false notion that someone is in-charge, and can therefore be faulted if things go wrong. If there is one important lesson to be learned from the analysis of complex environments, it is that this proposition is completely groundless.

Yet this is a pathology that has generated personal tragedies in cases like the tainted-blood tragedy in Canada (Paquet and Perrault 2016). The fact that failed performance can be the result of the system dynamic, and not be ascribable to any one party, is almost never discussed. Public lynchings, on the other hand, have always proved to be a popular pastime.

Another pathology is the fixation on 'gotcha accountabilities.'

To be accountable means simply to account for one's actions or inactions. Yet in a world riddled with complexity and unpredictability, cause-and-effect links may be impossible to ascertain, and, as a result officials are regularly confronted with:

1. interactions with so many different kinds of stakeholders in need of accounting, requiring different claims to many authorities (hierarchical superior, professional colleagues, clients, etc.);
2. many forms of accountings that may be demanded (political, ethical, managerial, legal, professional, etc.);
3. no clear or predictable way to determine who will make what kind of claim or when; and,
4. significant indeterminacy in the circumstances surrounding the activities for which one may be accountable, due to the complexity, heterogeneity and uncertainty that exists.

This results in a great deal of fuzziness in the definition of accountability, which often gets confused with responsibility or a willingness to accept blame.

Nevertheless, there is a great temptation to focus only on some aspects of this nexus of accountabilities (especially those that easily lend themselves to quantitative marshalling) and not to others; to some stakeholders and not to others; and to some forms of accounting and not to others. This has led to a public discourse that 'talks tough' on accountability with little in the way of actual accountability.

Typically, it is believed that people can be held accountable, that is they can be forced or coerced into being accountable. This is the language of retribution that if things don't turn out as expected, someone (not us) is at fault and should be punished. The tendency to generate black-and-white conclusions and indictments of others on the basis of very partial and reductive appraisals (*Ibid.*) is an expression of our entitlement and lack of ownership. If we have no ownership, no stake, how can we be accountable to others for the well-being of the whole? (Block 2008: 70-71). The Office of the Auditor General, for instance, has shown a particular propensity to indulge in such a blame game, 'gotcha activities' without paying too much attention to other key dimensions, such as performance results (Paquet 1999) or shared commitment or system dynamics.

A third pathology has been the false belief in openness and transparency as corrective panacea in unsatisfying performance or confused accountability.

Openness and transparency may replace deference and secrecy, but they do not necessarily generate trust or provide an antidote to deception and deliberate misinformation (O'Neill 2002: 70). Openness in the form of too much information can also smother truth and hide intentions just as easily as reticence.

However, this has not stopped phalanxes of auditors from pursuing strategies based almost entirely on calls for

... *well-intended goldfish-bowl rules ... (that) have unintended results worse than the evils they seek to forestall. They are likely to produce more secrecy, not less (only more carefully concealed), and on top of it, hamstring already overburdened administrators so as to throw their tasks into deeper confusion. Moreover secrecy is one thing; confidentiality is another. No organization can function effectively without certain amounts of confidentiality in the proposals, steps, and discussions leading up to its decisions – which should then, of course, be open, and generally will be* (Bennis 1976: 116).

Finally, there is the pathology that surrounds a great deal of reluctance to experiment and innovate.

Experimentation always entails some degree of risk. Error is an integral part of learning. Yet the tolerance for risk remains extremely low in the public sector – approximately zero. The implications of this risk avoidance attitude can be found in default behaviours for doing nothing and refraining from any type of innovation. Further, since any change is bound to expropriate from those currently benefitting from the *status quo,* change is too often interpreted as a zero-sum game where the only possible gains are those that can be taken from others. As long as change is viewed in this way, it will continue to be evaluated narrowly without proper consideration of the possible collective benefits, and so it will be avoided. It is only when one can free oneself from this mental prison and consider the possibility of a positive-sum game (Wright 2000) that appropriate accounting and learning from experimentation will become possible.

Confronting these pathologies opens the door to a collaborative exploration and "experimentalist learning accountability" through mechanisms that focus on the need to respond to chronic and urgent problems by mobilizing some process of discovery (Sabel 2001) and learning while on the go.

Intelligent accountability

However, simply avoiding the above pathologies will not suffice to generate the kind of feedback that will nourish social learning.

What is called for is a reframing of the notion of accountability to ensure that all the relevant stakeholders are fully engaged, that all the important standards are evoked in the creation of multi-stakeholder dialogue, and that the right practices are employed to encourage viable compromises to emerge. This means developing a 360-degree intelligent accountability: accountability, that avoids the above mental prisons, is forward-looking, exploratory and experimentalist in focus, and effectively feeds creative social learning.

Onora O'Neill proposed the beginnings of such a framework in her Reith Lecture:

> ... intelligent accountability, I suspect, requires more attention to good governance and fewer fantasies about total control. Good governance is possible only if institutions are allowed some margin for self-governance of a form appropriate to their particular tasks, within a framework of financial and other reporting. Such reporting, I believe, is not improved by being wholly standardized or relentlessly detailed, and since much that has to be accounted for is not easily measured, it cannot be boiled down to a set of stock performance indicators. Those who are called to account should give an account of what they have done, and of their successes and failures, to others who have sufficient time and experience to assess the evidence and report on it (O'Neill 2002: 58).

Therefore, in laying a foundation for intelligent accountability, one must recognize that:

1. the modern context is complex, and not easily reducible to simplistic, cause-and-effect, dyadic relationships;
2. standardized measures of control are not effective in generating shared commitment to the whole, and may even generate unintended consequences, like reducing the level of trust or misinterpreting the sense of the whole situation;
3. openness, transparency and quantophrenia are not always the unconditional goods that they are supposed to be; and,
4. it is absurd to pretend to manage our complex systems as if they were populated either by angelic Cartesian wantons or by a bunch of knaves and crooks.

What ensues from this understanding of intelligent accountability is a new focus on coordination and collaboration that is based on trust, that is earned over the long run, and, in the short run, requires much more attention being paid to mitigate the effects of deception and misinformation (Thomas 2007).

Dealing with deception

Disloyalty is knowingly and deliberately breaking the moral contracts that define the burden of office.

Office holders are persons with social obligations and duties. Such duties are often rather ill-defined in our complex world precisely because the notion of burden of office is an essentially contested concept (Paquet 1997, 2008). What constitutes successful performance of the burden of office is not written in stone, but is based on "a shared set of expectations and a common currency of justifications" (Day and Klein 1987: 5) that are quite difficult to define consensually.

Despite the vagaries that may surround an explicit definition of burden of office, there seems to be general agreement that disloyalty in the public sector is increasing over the last two decades (Paquet 2010). Many have ascribed this to honest disagreement ensuing from the greater complexity of policy issues, or to an increasing number of possible interpretations around these complex issues. However, this does not entirely explain the observed phenomena.

We assert that a culture of disloyalty has been developing: one that it is more than just passive disloyalty (a dwarfing interpretation of what is expected as part of the burden of office) and, in fact, verges on active disloyalty (e.g. deliberate undermining of superiors and/or betraying the trust of partners and citizens) (Hubbard and Paquet 2007). It involves both those who are elected and the public servants meant to serve them. Nevertheless, whether the deception is passive or active, it "is not a marginal moral failure. Deceivers do not treat others as moral equals; they exempt themselves from the obligations that they rely on others to live up to" (O'Neill 2002: 71).

Unless this sort of behaviour (amounting to betrayal and treachery) is seriously punished, trust in public institutions will continue to be undermined. Once that trust is lost, it can be restored only over the very long term. Yet the capacity and willingness for the public service system to shield deceivers from any sort of punishment (even rewarding such behaviour by lateral promotions, especially out of the country) stands as a constant re-enforcement of this sort of objectionable behaviour (Paquet 2014: chapter 4).

This is not an easy matter to deal with. Those who try are likely to be accused of McCarthyism by self-righteous public servants and their union representatives who may perceive an attack on one as an attack on all public servants. Yet unless deception is robustly deterred, the legitimacy of the whole institution of the public service as an independent and non-partisan organization is in peril.

However, the suggestion that calls for loyalty to the elected government should not be construed as condoning moral numbness. The notion of loyalty is not an unconditional good. Public servants have a duty (as part of their burden of office) to provide their best advice as fully as possible to their political masters. And when they have fully exercised their "voice" option to no avail, and still feel that certain policies should not be implemented and that they cannot allow themselves to be identified or associated with them, and they have also given up on the option of working patiently within the system for change, they are obligated to "exit" the system and risk being an 'outsider' (Bennis 1976: 54) in order to fulfill their primary duty to citizens.

Dealing with misinformation

The only way to counter the flow of misinformation originating from official organizations and institutions (and also from the media and special interest groups) is through a process of active checking by citizens. But this is at times very difficult, quite time-consuming, and not always possible for the ordinary citizen. Some have argued that the media are supposed to provide a critical assessment of the information they distribute, but this has become quite a quaint and naïve notion. Despite the charters and codes calling for impartiality, accuracy, fairness, giving a full view, editorial independence, respect for privacy, standards of taste, decency, etc., the media remain "erratically reliable and unassessable" (O'Neill 2002: 77, 89-90). These days, understaffed news organizations simply print whatever they may be given by public authorities or found on the Internet without assessment. Corrections can be made later on the back page.

Other checks against misinformation include the super-bureaucrats, who purportedly are the super-defenders of the highest standards on this front, but in general do not necessarily fare any better than the media. From time to time, gross disinformation has been detected and exposed – even from the desks of super-super-bureaucrats.

Some may remember the deliberate misinformation concocted by the Governor of the Bank of Canada in earlier years – a misdeed exposed in a pamphlet published by Carleton University economist Scott Gordon (1961) for which the super-bureaucrats made him pay handsomely.[12] Nothing would indicate that the propensity towards misinformation (Gordon 2016) or the tolerance of the public sector gentility have been in any way weakened over the last 50 years.

Against this, the lack of critical thinking and the deliberate *confusion des genres* in the information industry (factual reports, babbling by opinionated and less than fully-informed columnists, irresponsible rants by ideologically-tainted journalists, Twitter feeds, etc. are all presented as equally valid 'information') leave the public at the mercy of a lot of people who literally have both a licence and motive to deceive.

Social architecture required

A number of new institutions would therefore seem to be necessary to signal a determination to deal with these two major sources of organizational dysfunction – deception and misinformation:[13]

- first, a monitoring agency that would assess the quality and reliability of information;
- second, forums where governments, the private and non-profit sectors can debate important national issues in particular domains; and,

[12] The personal costs borne by Scott Gordon as a result of his drive to expose Coyne`s misinformation is a cautionary tale. His original letter was signed by 29 economists and the short book he wrote soon after demonstrated very effectively that there had been deception on the part of the Governor of the Bank of Canada. But after this event, Gordon was marginalized and shunned by the federal bureaucracy. His part-time career as a mediator in public service affairs was brought to a halt, and he was explicitly ignored by a royal commission later struck on monetary affairs (even though he was one of the best known Canadian experts in this area). He was later to depart from Canada to pursue a most successful career in the United States. This cautionary tale illustrates the perils of exposing deception and misinformation generated by the officialdom in the public sector in Canada.

[13] Distrust is not simply a loss of trust, like a loss of grace, because things went wrong. Distrust is often built into our institutions, and is a cultural norm followed consciously or not by most. As such it represents a strategy of risk management. The only way to escape the cycle of distrust is peer-to-peer discussions that lead to co-decision making and collaboration (Earle and Cvetkovich 1995)

- third, a council that would make possible promising experimentations even when they would appear to transgress 'the existing rules' (Hubbard and Paquet 2006).

Such cooperative institutions would permit the natural competitiveness between organizations to act as a watchdog, both on the reliability of information and the collective understanding it might generate.

Many other mechanisms may also be required to institute some form of soft accountability built on earned trust. But, in the very short term, matters of deception would require some form of direct action: at first, possibly a lay oversight committee might be charged with the task of defining the contours of the nexus of 'accountability for moral contracts' based on more robust definitions of different officials' burden of office (MPs and officers of Parliament, the Executive, and the public service).

The mandate and focus of such a committee[14] could attempt to clarify the reasonable expectations citizens might have of the different actors, and identify the nature of the moral contracts likely to echo the contours of their burdens of office. It could also act in the early phase of any dispute as a mediator, to ascertain the boundaries of what might be considered to be deception. Its opinions would be made public and, over time, would help to determine the nature of legitimate expectations in different cases and different contexts.

Unlike oversight committees in other areas, its purpose would not be to find blame, but to improve performance and collective learning. It would not adjudicate but merely issue opinions. In this way, it might help to break the existing mould where the senior bureaucracy acts as a solipsistic entity that intentionally crafts ineffective measures for self-regulation to ensure both accountability and responsibility can be largely avoided (Boyer 2003).

[14] The composition of such a lay oversight committee may evolve over time, but it should initially be a credible blue-ribbon group whose members are seen as above board (Monique Bégin, Claude Castonguay, Preston Manning, etc.) that would help clarify the major interfaces and define the future mission and role of such a committee.

In the matter of misinformation, active fact checking and critical thinking pose a much more difficult challenge. Hubbard and Paquet have suggested the creation of a 'Social and Economic Observatory' to ensure the dissemination of reliable information. But such an observatory cannot be expected to perform the whole, complex, Herculean task of sifting truth from fiction, and fiction from outright deception and lies in any order of government, let alone all of them. However, it may serve as a basis for the development of at least some critical appraisal of the available information.

Such an observatory could also play an important role, not only in the control of information quality but in creating a culture of critical thinking to mitigate the existing culture that acquiesces to the misinterpretation and misuse of data, and to contribute to collective meaning making. Still, one must realize that, important though such an institution may be in the short run, it is likely to take a decade or more to alter the Canadian culture of gullibility that exists within both the media and the citizenry.

A social learning framework redux

Change is always forward-looking. Therefore, looking to correct the mistakes of the past will not suffice. Experimentalist accountability is geared to social learning, based on an appreciation of the difference between what is expected and what happens, and embraces this "error" as a way to evaluate, learn and adjust collective action (Michael 1993).

But such learning only occurs under two basic conditions:

1. if the conversation with the situation is conducted within a context where the ethos is sufficiently rich and supportive to allow for a meaningful conversation to be carried out; and,

2. if the conversation, deliberation and accumulation of judgments is conducted with tact and civility, with a capacity to span boundaries, to recognize and accept different perspectives as valid, and to synthesize multiple logics.

Unfortunately, this sort of conversation does not necessarily fit into the sort of standardized and formalized rules so common in public bureaucracies. Its cumulative result remains very much tacit rather than codifiable knowledge – the capacity to deal effectively with matters of practice, and to deal with matters in a more real-time manner, and with a full appreciation of the local and the particular context. The accumulation of such tacit knowledge is predicated on the fact that through experience we learn a great deal and that at any time we know more than we have in the past and often more than we can tell (Polanyi 1966). This is the way knowledge evolves in common law: case by case, over time – a way opposed by traditional political science (Hermet *et al.* 2005).

Our conclusion is that learning or intelligent accountability cannot be defined in one single direction, or with reference to just one stakeholder. It must be defined as a framework that is:

1. focused on risk and exposure rather than program delivery; be carried out with social learning and performance in mind and not simply for compliance and conformance; and regarded as a tool for change and therefore as necessitating experiments and innovation;
2. a 360-degree process pertaining to all the stakeholders surrounding the official or the office;
3. used with considerable prudence in balancing the push or supply forces (living up to one's own perception of one's burden of office) and the pull or demand forces (the need to meet the expectations and demands of the other various other stakeholders and publics);
4. operating at many levels (legal, organizational, professional, political, etc.); and
5. instituted in interwoven layers of compatible moral contracts.

The first two components we have dealt with earlier in this chapter.

The third component of our framework has been proposed by Robert Nozick, and it is rooted in the tension between push and the pull forces of the supply and demand sides, as an economist would put it. In Nozick parlance, accountability will be satisfactory when the push forces are greater than or equal to the pull forces (Nozick 1981), when accountability isn't imposed, it is chosen. When we choose to 'own' our situation and are willing to care for the whole, accountability becomes restorative rather than retributive and collective learning is engendered. This can easily be applied to a vast network of relationships, among many different stakeholders in very many dimensions.

For the fourth component, we turn to M.J. Dubnik – who has used Nozick's push-and-pull framework and applied it to four types of institutional forms, in order to illustrate eight species of accountability (Dubnik 1996). On the pull or demand side, one finds an array of institutional factors that frame the challenges faced by any official confronted with multiple, diverse and often conflicting expectations. On the push or supply side are the more personal ways of interpreting the burden of office that materialize in some traits – the internalized sense of obligation, obedience, fidelity or loyalty, and amenability (i.e., a desire to actively pursue the interest of the public). Table 3 below summarizes these species of accountability.

TABLE 3.
Species of Accountability

	Conduct of accountability External pull	Accountability of conduct Internal push
Legal	Liabilities	Obligations
Organizational	Answerability	Obedience
Professional	Responsibility	Fidelity
Political	Responsiveness	Amenability

Source: Dubnik, 1996.

The fifth component of our framework for intelligent accountability is borrowed from Donaldson and Dunfee's integrative theory of social contracts that define different layers/lattices of moral contracts as a tool to ensure "good" performance for the organization. The moral contracts are at three levels:

- **hyper-norms** (e.g. the obligation to respect the dignity of each person, etc.) that would apply to all concerns;
- **operating conditions** for the different communities; and,
- the **microsocial contracts** regarding expectations at the operating level (Donaldson and Dunfee 1994).

This social learning framework (risk-exposure-based, performance-focused and forward-looking experimentalist accountability, pull and push *à la* Nozick; various settings *à la* Dubnik; layers of moral contracts *à la* Donaldson and Dunfee) reveals the great complexity of accountability, even within organizations with traditional hierarchical structures.

But, as we have suggested earlier, these hierarchical structures are no longer effective, and the new distributed or networked structures set to replace them are even more complex on this front.

Two major questions will thus confront those trying to employ the intelligent accountability framework in this new context:

1. what are the basic principles that should guide the creation of the necessary conditions for good performance-oriented, forward-looking and experimentalist accountability; and,
2. what priority rules should prevail when moral contracts would appear to be different and incompatible?

On the first front (basic principles), one may use the prudent principles developed over the last decade in a variety of settings as complex alternative service delivery arrangements became instituted to replace the traditional, paternalistic, state-centric systems (Tassé 1996; OAG 1999; Posner 2006).

What most people would appear to agree on is that the minimum conditions for accountability include:

- clear rules/understanding as to who is responsible for what;
- balanced expectations and capacities;
- adequate authorities and resources granted;
- adequate reporting mechanisms;
- reasonable review and adjustment mechanisms;
- appropriate transparency; and,
- full recognition that different accountability regimes are necessary depending on the nature of the government's role (master, partner, third-party).

On the second front (priority rules), much work has already been done to develop the foundations from the principle of precedence to determine ways in which the differing priorities may be ordered. It has been used effectively both by Harry Frankfurt (1988: chapter 9) and David Braybrooke (1987) to differentiate between needs and preferences. It has also some moral force in the definition of "capabilities" or "freedoms" that have to be given some priority to ensure sustainable development in a world of limited resources (Sen 1999).

Conclusion

Unintelligent accountability, in the form of standardized, narrowly defined, quantophrenic, top-down, formal rules, has quietly but firmly descended upon us over the last decades like a plague in a futile attempt to impose certainty in an uncertain and unpredictable world. It's a credo that has its own Swiss guards – a phalanx of rear-view mirror watching drivers, blame-seeking auditors, and privileged gate-keepers – who have great difficulty and little interest in disentangling the difference between challenges (which invite innovation) and calumny (which invites a call to arms).

We have offered intelligent accountability as an alternative. It is based on a better understanding of the notion of burden of office and a greater commitment towards gauging the real context and our own ownership of it. It is of necessity soft and flexible; and to be effective it must be forward-looking and geared to experimentalism, social learning and better performance.

However, intelligent accountability cannot count on panaceas like openness or transparency to do all the work. It must build on two simultaneous tracks: attacking the viruses first – deception and misinformation – and then on building trust among the relevant actors and improving co-governance. At the core of this second track is trust building and the crucial notion of moral contracts – contracts that will have to be negotiated by officials within the 360-degree range of their stakeholders, and often in different ways and in different issue domains and locales, if forward-looking, experimentalist accountability is to generate effective social learning and innovation.

This line of approach must build on elusive, human notions like conscience, loyalty, learning, burden of office, etc. – notions that are well-known to provoke hot flashes among the quantophrenic professions. We are not deterred by this because these very attributes help bind us together in common cause to create a future that all or most can buy into. Therefore, it would seem that much 're-education' is in order ... with irony used as principal therapy for those prone to the vapours.

In reflection then, to gain a good grasp of intelligent governance, it is necessary (but not sufficient) to proceed through the steps we have previously moved through in this book up to now:

- developing a communicational approach to organization and social systems;
- being better able to gain a sense of the dynamic problem;
- reframing antiquated perspectives that seek to eliminate complexity and uncertainty;
- casting the governing issue in terms of wicked problems and the institution of systems of social learning;
- refurbishing the practitioner's mental toolbox for use accordingly; and,

- redesigning the signaling systems of organizations for greater effectiveness in building for the future or accounting for performance.

However, one must also be able to scheme virtuously – i.e., to invent smart and wise ways in which the governing apparatus can be shaped. This is the next step.

References

Axworthy, Thomas S. 2005. "The Responsibility Crisis in Canada," *Canadian Parliamentary Review*, Summer: 7-12.

Bennis, Warren. 1976. *The Unconscious Conspiracy*. New York, NY: AMACOM.

Block, Peter. 2008. *Community: The Structure of Belonging*. San Francisco, CA: Berrett-Koehler.

Boyer, Patrick. 2003. *Just Trust Us: The Erosion of Accountability in Canada*. Toronto, ON: DundDurn Press.

Braybrooke, David. 1987. *Meeting Needs*. Princeton, NJ: Princeton University Press.

Day, Patricia and Rudolf Klein. 1987. *Accountabilities: Five Public Services*. London, UK: Tavistock.

Donaldson, T. and T.W. Dunfee. 1994. "Towards a Unified Conception of Business Ethics: Integrative Social Contracts Theory," *The Academy of Management Review*, 19(2): 252-284.

Dubnik, M.J. 1996. "Clarifying Accountability: An Ethical Theory Framework." Paper presented at the Fifth International Conference on Ethics in the Public Service, Brisbane, Australia, August, p. 5-9.

Earle, T.C. and G.T. Cvetkovich. 1995. *Social Trust*. Westport, CT: Praeger.

Frankfurt, Harry. 1988. *The importance of what we care about*. Cambridge, UK: Cambridge University Press, chapter 9.

Friedmann, John. 1978. "The Epistemology of Social Practice," *Theory and Society*, 6(1): 75-92.

Gawande, Atul. 2009. *The Checklist Manifesto – How to Get Things Right*. New York, NY: Metropolitan Books.

Gordon, H. Scott. 1961. *The Economists versus the Bank of Canada*. Toronto, ON: Ryerson Press.

Gordon, Stephen. 2016. "Why has federal tax revenue exceeded projections?" *Macleans*, January 2, www.macleans.ca/economy/economicanalysis/why-has-federal-tax-revenue-exceeded-projections/ [Accessed March 23, 2016].

Hermet, G. *et al.* (eds.). 2005. *La gouvernance: un concept et ses applications*. Paris, FR: Editions Karthala.

Hubbard, Ruth and Gilles Paquet. 2006. "Réinventer notre architecture institutionnelle," *Policy Options*, 27(7): 55-63.

Hubbard, Ruth and Gilles Paquet. 2007. "Cat's Cradling: APEX Forum on Wicked Problems," *www.optimumonline.ca*, 37(2): 12-18.

Malcolm, N. 1984. *Ludwig Wittgenstein. A Memoir*. Oxford, UK: Oxford University Press.

Martin, Roger L. 2014. "The Big Lie of Strategic Planning," *Harvard Business Review*, 92(1-2): 78-84.

Michael, Donald N. 1993. "Governing by Learning: Boundaries, Myths and Metaphors," *Futures*, 25(1): 81-89.

Mintzberg, Henry. 1985. *Emergent Strategy for Public Policy*. Ottawa, ON: The 1985 J.J. Carson Lecture.

Nozick, R. 1981. *Philosophical Explanations*. Cambridge, MA: Harvard University Press.

Office of the Auditor General. 1999. "Involving Others in Governing: Accountability at Risk" in the *Report of the Auditor General of Canada*. Ottawa, ON: OAG, chapter 23.

O'Neill, Onora. 2002. *A Question of Trust*. Cambridge, UK: Cambridge University Press.

Paquet, Gilles. 1997. "The Burden of Office, Ethics and Connoisseurship," *Canadian Public Administration*, 40(1): 55-71.

Paquet, Gilles. 1999. "Auditing in a Learning Environment," *Optimum*, 29(1): 37-44.

Paquet, Gilles. 2006. "Le palimposeste de l'imputabilité," *Revue générale de droit*, 36(4): 561-578.

Paquet, Gilles. 2008. "A Plea for Intelligent Accountability," *Financial Management Institute Journal*, 19(2): 9-14.

Paquet, Gilles. 2009a. *Crippling Epistemologies and Governance Failures: A Plea for Experimentalism*. Ottawa, ON: University of Ottawa Press.

Paquet, Gilles. 2009b. *Scheming Virtuously: The Road to Collaborative Governance*, Ottawa, ON: Invenire Books.

Paquet, Gilles. 2010. "Disloyalty," *www.optimumonline.ca*, 40(1): 23-47.

Paquet, Gilles. 2014. *Unusual Suspects: Essays on Social Learning Disabilities*. Ottawa, ON: Invenire Books.

Paquet, Gilles and Roger A. Perrault. 2016. *The Tainted-Blood Tragedy in Canada – A Cascade of Governance Failures*. Ottawa, ON: Invenire Books.

Polanyi, Michael. 1966. *The Tacit Dimension*. New York, NY: Doubleday.

Posner, P.L. 2006. "Third-Party Governance: Accountability Challenges," in C. Campbell *et al.* (eds.). *Comparative Trends in Public Management*. Ottawa, ON: Canada School of Public Service, p. 48-70.

Roberts, John. 2004. *The Modern Firm: Organizational Design for Performance and Growth*. Oxford, UK: Oxford University Press.

Romme, A. Georges L. 2003. "Making a Difference: Organization as Design," *Organization Science*, 14(5): 558-573.

Sabel, Charles F. 2001. "A Quiet Revolution of Democratic Governance: Towards Democratic Experimentalism" in W. Michalski *et al.* (eds.). *Governance in the 21st Century*. Paris, FR: OECD, p. 121-148.

Sen, Amartya. 1999. *Development as Freedom*. New York, NY: Knopf.

Tassé, Roger. 1996. *Background Paper for the Deputy Ministers' Task Force on Service Delivery Models*. Ministerial Accountability and the Citizen-Centered Renewal Initiative. Ottawa, ON: Treasury Board, July 9.

Thomas, Paul G. 2007. "Public Service of the 21st Century: Trust, Leadership, and Accountability," *www.optimumonline.ca*, 37(2): 19-24.

Westley, Frances, Brenda Zimmerman and Michael Quinn Patton. 2006. *Getting to Maybe: How the World Has Changed*. Toronto, ON: Random House.

Wright, Robert. 2000. *NonZero: The Logic of Human Destiny*. New York, NY: Vintage Books.

PART III

Scheming and Wayfinding Virtuously

M uch of our discussion up to now has been concerned in general with either efficiency (doing the thing right) or effectiveness (doing the right thing). Part III brings into the discussion two other dimensions of intelligent governance that need to be attended to:

- ascertaining the stewardship regime's goodness of fit in terms of its short-term capacity to transform the organization or system, while taking into account its evolving context; and,
- ascertaining the stewardship regime's goodness of fit in terms of its longer term capacity to maintain the compatibility of the organization or system with the socio-cultural and ethical milieu.

In this discussion we introduce two new terms – smartness and wisdom. Smartness pertains to the highest and best use of opportunism in governing in the short run: it focuses on designing an imaginative protocol or mixture of principles and mechanisms to achieve effectiveness – more in the nature of *techne* or craftsmanship. Wisdom, on the other hand, pertains mostly to legitimacy, propriety and ethics in governing over a longer time horizon – more in the nature of *phronesis* (i.e., a sort of judgment that expresses itself in correct action). Wisdom might be said to correspond to ensuring that governance echoes the cardinal virtues of the organization or the system, including: *temperentia* (the sense of limits, of not going too far); *fortitudo* (a capacity to take into account context and the longer time horizon); *justitia* (a sense of what is good); and *prudentia* (the sense of pursuing reasonable and practical objectives).

Smartness and wisdom both help to underpin efforts to intervene in the informational and communicational sub-systems of an organization with a view to improving its governance and stewardship. In fact, they amount to complementary pressures contributing to both effectiveness and propriety, even though their actions are often difficult to fully disentangle with effectiveness relying more fully on tactical scheming, while propriety relies more fully on virtuousness.

Chapter 6 discusses the 'smartness factor' in the context of an organization operating with an absence of *affectio societatis*. Smartness focuses on the capacity to construct a system of inquiry capable of ensuring the goodness of fit of the governance apparatus with its circumstances, and within the limitations imposed by local parameters that may constrain the transformation of a system of interest in the short or medium runs.

Chapter 7 relaxes these very limitations, i.e., the *mélanges* of principles and conventions that reflect the given state of culture governance, and that constrain its organizational governance to ensure that all partners attend to and live up to the requirements of their evolving burden of office. We underline the evolution of the meta-principles and meta-conventions as the cultural underground changes – in order to ensure the long-term antifragility of organizations and social systems – i.e., their capacity to spring back from setbacks ever faster and more innovatively, thus generating stronger performance in the face of ever more daunting challenges.

These parallel and yet intermeshed processes weave together the coordination and collaboration activities that underpin social learning, wayfinding, effective stewardship, and constructively encourage self-organization, shaping more or less explicitly the emergent processes of governing in more comprehensive and innovative ways.

| Collaboration in the Absence
of *Affectio societatis*

Traditional collaboration studies tend to presume that potential collaborators share common values and purposes. This is taking an easy, unrealistic route. Under this presumption, collaboration boils down to the simple design of adequate logistical arrangements. Our view is that such presumptions materialize only in exceptional circumstances, and should not be regarded as the norm under most conditions. This is one of several reasons why such designs tend to be academically pleasing but not very practical. Furthermore, given a variety of rationales for collaboration in the first place, such common values and purposes may not even be desirable as they can severely limit innovation.

In most circumstances, those who might benefit from collaboration live in a world where power, resources and information are widely distributed among many hands and minds, where each potential collaborator harbours different values, and pursues different purposes. In such cases, it is naïve and futile to fantasize about purposive associations *à la* Oakeshott (1975: 205) where members are all engaged in the joint pursuit of common purposes. Quite the contrary, when reality imposes itself, one has to accept the daunting challenge of designing effective 'civil associations' where members may not have common objectives, but instead pursue their own objectives within the context of their joint action.

Collaboration is a collective action challenge (Rothstein 2005). This entails (1) constructing inquiring systems capable of blending perspectives and reconciling the agonistic tensions among the different groups; (2) making use of agreed-upon principles, rules and conventions to hammer out practical trade-offs among the conflicting values and purposes of the different parties; and (3) distilling information so that a broader and more encompassing appreciative system and macro-rationality can emerge that goes beyond the exiguous instrumental rationalities of participating agents or groups (Paquet 2013; Paquet 2014: 176ff; Paquet and Wilson 2011).

As a result, the challenge of collaboration can be daunting because of three major hurdles:

Firstly, most persons involved in such predicaments suffer from a basic, willful blindness that leads them to denying the extent of the challenge of working with others, such as those who we have observed involved with shared complex problems in public health or public safety for example. In solving complex wicked problems where collaboration is essential, the participants (be they private firms, local authorities, national agencies, etc.) rarely share the same values or purposes, and often do not trust each other. Yet, they pretend that this collective action predicament does not exist, that cooperation is somehow automatic, and so they tend to carry on in a delusional way, assuming that collaboration is alive and well, when it, in fact, may be nonexistent. Multiple tragedies on these fronts have shown this delusion can be quite toxic.

Second, even when the different parties are tempted to concede that a collaborative problem does exist, they do not quite know how to tackle the problem of designing civil associations in the absence of common values, common purposes and *affectio societatis* (Cuisinier 2008).[15] As a result, they tend to default to

---

[15] This is a French legal concept that means that two or more people personally and jointly commit themselves to achieving the purpose(s) of their association. French courts have added to objective partnership criteria

the more familiar practices of logistics and management or to appeals to better leadership (whatever that might mean), because they are missing the frameworks, skills and practices of collaboration which are not in common currency.

Third, even if they decide to proceed boldly by trial and error, the different parties very quickly run into conflicts, which make most people uneasy at any time – even though the sharing of conflicting perspectives, paradoxes, etc. is a powerful source of social innovation. This leads them to recoil from such conflictive situations into antiseptic politeness or what Adam Kahane defines as "ways of not talking" (Kahane 2004: 35-70) before abandoning all efforts at finding synthetic and reasonable compromises, and pleading for someone, anyone to take charge (Block 1998).

We can do little in tackling the willful blindness problem directly (except by reiterating that it is toxic), but we can suggest ways in which the collaborative problem might be tackled more indirectly by applying the frameworks, skills and practices of collaboration as a means of reducing this fear of conflict so that whenever the attitude of denial is recognized, it can be staunched and overcome.

In the first section, we wish to state as forcefully as possible the seriousness of the willful blindness problem that is so flagrantly present in a large number of the organizations that require effective collaboration but fail miserably in recognizing its challenges, and therefore fail to apply the appropriate tools to generate it. Secondly, we sketch the contours of a non-threatening process of inquiry capable of fostering useful responses to the collaboration challenge, as well as identifying some of the frameworks, skills and practices which may be employed to implement it. Finally, we argue for bold exploration in this direction by agencies whose willful blindness to-date may be endangering public health and public safety.

---

an indispensable subjective one: the presence of a "spirit of cooperation" among the partners or *affectio societatis*, which defines their willingness to pursue their goals together. Lack of *affectio societatis* is a sufficient condition for the partnership to be dissolved (Cuisinier 2008).

Why this willful blindness?

A nasty statement ascribed to President Harry Truman suggests that experts cannot learn, because if they were to admit to their need to learn, it would reveal that they were not experts to begin with. Nevertheless, this type of mental prison is responsible for much of the resistance exhibited by experts to suggestions that they might have incompletely or incorrectly defined the problems they face, or that they might have to experiment beyond the conventional routines in good currency, in order to cope effectively with the challenges of an issue.

Our experience with groups of officials in the Canadian federal government, for instance, has revealed that while the most senior officials may be conscious of the collaboration problems their departments face, the cadre of mid-level officials (that would normally be directly engaged in such inter-organizational cooperation) tends to react quite negatively when these problems are brought to light, and actively fight against any initiative that may be proposed to repair these cooperative shortcomings in favour of measures that would attempt to impose greater control.

It would appear that, for many, admitting that there is a problem is tantamount to saying that they are not effective leaders and have not done their job well. They therefore deny that any such collaboration problem exists, even though, in many cases, there may be substantial evidence of tense relations among parties that may need to work together, or even open hostility, and clear evidence of mishaps arising from poor coordination or cooperation.

For instance, in the recent case of Canadian Naval officer, Jeffrey Delisle, who passed top secret NATO information to Russia, Canada's spy agency CSIS (Canadian Security Intelligence Service) was aware of Delisle's activities for some time but never briefed the RCMP, ostensibly for fear of exposing intelligence tradecraft in open court proceedings.[16]

---

[16] The Canadian Press. 2013. "CSIS knew of navy spy's activity, left RCMP in the dark," *CBC News*, May 26,
www.cbc.ca/news/canada/nova-scotia/csis-knew-of-navy-s-activity-left-rcmp-in-the-dark-1.1312803 [Accessed March 23, 2016].

Ultimately, it fell to the US FBI – not CSIS – to send a letter to the RCMP spelling out how a Canadian was pilfering extremely sensitive information, including highly classified US material, and sending it on to the Russians. In the end, CSIS never did transfer its thick Delisle dossier to the RCMP, preferring to keep its investigation sealed, and causing the RCMP to undertake its own investigation from scratch.

According to University of Ottawa security expert Wesley Wark, the RCMP and CSIS are supposed to be able to "seamlessly hand off cases back and forth between them." It was deeply troubling, he said, if the system indeed broke down in the Delisle case over CSIS's refusal to share its files or to bring the RCMP in at an earlier stage.

Since the most senior officials have a mighty diet of daily crises to handle, it is easy for mid-level officials to persuade their superiors that everything is under control, and that any observable symptoms of non-cooperation can be addressed through the simple imposition of additional controls. In fact, the many meetings that may be called and attended can give the casual observer confidence that something is actually going on. Hence, there will be no possibility for someone to say that the issue has not been seriously examined and dealt with, while creating plausible deniability of responsibility should things derail later. Consequently, the inevitable conclusion must be that responsible external observers who may have diagnosed problems of collaboration are either misguided or that the problem is insufficiently urgent ("we've been dealing with this for years") to call for any immediate or substantive action. Calls for a "serious parliamentary investigation" in the Delisle case, for instance, were unheeded.

In such situations, only a major catastrophe that is blatantly ascribable to a lack of cooperation among the different parties is likely to succeed in highlighting the importance of the problem. Such a cooperative failure happened in 2003 with the SARS outbreak, as the Naylor Report (National Advisory Committee on SARS and Public Health 2003: 212) identified, yet the institutional response was the creation of the Public Health Agency of Canada to simply impose or buy cooperation from all the relevant players. No new collaborative practice was instilled. But if, and when, such a catastrophe strikes again, damage control strategies typically geared to institutional preservation will kick in, involving a downplaying of the systemic failure of collaboration, and an admission to only minor mishaps that, we will be assured, can be instantly repaired. Or some fall guy is identified on whom the full burden of responsibility will be placed, regardless of systemic dysfunctions.

Such wallpapering of major institutional failures that result from a lack of cooperation, by the referencing to routine audits that have already highlighted the nature of 'minor' flaws, and the bland assurances that the needed repairs are already being made, are usually sufficient for the collaboration issue to be robustly placed on the back burner. Then with senior officials being caught up by signs of new crises, and the public exhibiting its natural tendency towards amnesia, concerns about coordination failures become systematically buried after a few brief moments of heart pounding concern when the lack of effective cooperation first raises its ugly head in the wake of an incident.

So despite the fact that the matter of a lack of effective coordination – among police and public safety organizations, among infrastructure providers, and among the many other crucial actors in Canada's public safety ecosystem – has been repeatedly raised in alarming terms with each new catastrophe over the last few decades, there has repeatedly been little significant social learning, little follow-up, and few new collaborative protocols that have been developed, let alone implemented. One can only live in fear and trembling at the potential consequences of this poor state of collaboration in the world of public safety when, for instance, it is clear to all that we may suffer mightily on this front in the near future – either from external attack or the relinquishment of civil freedoms. In fact, the Conference Board of Canada, has made it known that the biggest threat to public safety and emergency preparedness is the lack of cooperative governance (Munn-Venn and Archibald 2007: ii).

The same may be said about all the other major public health crises the country has experienced since the 1980s – from the tainted-blood crisis, to the Ebola crisis and to the current obesity crisis. With a multitude of stakeholders in each policy domain, there are just too many ways to say no, and only a few ways to say yes to achieve cooperation. Typically, efforts at collaboration become mired in self-serving competitions to see just who's in charge.

One can only hope that current early warnings will trigger a change of hearts and minds on this front, but the learning disabilities of our institutions are so profoundly rooted, we are immensely pessimistic about the plausibility of more cooperative scenarios emerging organically. Both public health and public safety institutions suffer from the expert driven cultures described by Truman. Therefore, in all likelihood, enormous catastrophes will be required before the agencies charged with these responsibilities are sufficiently shaken and destabilized for change to occur. It may well be that only through claims of criminal negligence for not addressing the collaboration issue earlier, will the importance of developing collaborative capacity in a complex and diverse society such as Canada be recognized and acted upon.

How can the collaboration issue be tackled in the absence of *affectio societatis*?

If collaboration becomes necessary, and yet one cannot rely on a sufficient amount of *affectio societatis* to be present, or hyper-competition or actual animosity are in fact present, how can one move the collaborative agenda forward? Our approach is based upon a governance process that brings together four key pillars of collaboration:

1. **Can't do it alone:** Collaboration begins with an organization's recognition that a problematic issue can't be dealt with unilaterally, meaning that both the

problem definition and any effective solution will require the contribution of several organizations or even several sectors. This recognition is a powerful tool to initially engage people and to periodically remind partners why they are working together.

Accepting the necessity of a distributed solution implies the need to find ways of identifying and engaging potential partners and stakeholders, and bringing them to the table. Who to include is the principal concern at this stage. Typically, successful collaborations include a diversity of stakeholders: those who might obviously be supportive; those who may oppose and have the power to stop a collaborative solution; those who have expert knowledge to contribute and those who may be impacted by any decisions or actions the collaborators may take. Successful collaboration takes great pains to avoid homogeneous perspectives around the table and to maximize the participation of potential collaborators with different cosmologies and purposes, and in order to increase the probability that they will bring the information, resources and power they have to the table.

2. **Collective learning**: Given the assembled diversity of viewpoints – all of which are likely to have some degree of validity – the second collaborative pillar is the promotion of collective learning when partners are likely to focus entirely and exclusively on trying to persuade all the others of the 'rightness' of their view.

Advocacy at this stage is counterproductive because of the incompleteness of knowledge held by the participants. Rather than advocacy, potential partners should try to establish some common knowledge base and engage in meaning-making around their shared knowledge in order to generate a frame that would be helpful in reconciling their different perspectives.

Like in the ancient parable of the blind men and the elephant, the fundamental question is what bigger reality allows all their individual perspectives to be true in part.

This will enable the partners to establish the relevance of varying types and sources of information, to define a more comprehensive problem accordingly, and to set priorities in the inquiry about what should be done.

3. **Designing the problem definition, collective decision taking and action**: The third pillar invloves the co-design of both the problem and its solution. While the notion of taking action to mitigate a problem is central to participation in collaboration, especially with regard to issues of public safety and public health, potential partners need to be wary of rushing to action before a comprehensive understanding of the issue has evolved. However, when the decision-taking time finally does arrive, the potential partners should be fully conscious of any power imbalances among them, and put in place mechanisms to mitigate any gross inequalities in order to ensure that the commitments partners have made collectively are lived up to.

There is no such thing as "almost equal" or "more equal than others" in collaboration. Each of the partners is there because he/she has a necessary contribution to make towards addressing a complex problem. In this context, they are peers. Therefore, the partners need to establish mechanisms of decision taking; identify specific partner commitments, and address the potential for free-rider behaviour. It also needs to be recognized that the participants have multiple accountabilities – to each other, to their home organizations, to specific stakeholder groups, and/or to the public. The partners need to determine how best to resolve these accountabilities if they conflict.

4. **Monitoring and evaluation:** The fourth pillar involves the partners' need to identify assessment and evaluation mechanisms to be used on an ongoing basis, such as developmental evaluation, to support a process of 'learning while doing.' Collaboration is most likely to be a process of experimentation, of trial and error, and of exploration. Therefore, ongoing feedback is essential both to gauge collective performance, and to evaluate the continued need for collective action –

is the project still needed, can it be done by others, should it be done by others, can we afford it, can it be spun off?

Stewardship as ongoing design of an automatic pilot

In the complex turbulent world in which collaboration becomes necessary, no one actor or group has all the relevant information, power and resources to effectively produce their desired results top-down, except in very unusual circumstances. In fact, even those whose fates may be correlated as a result of their association in a particular issue domain are unlikely to share the same values and purposes.

Therefore, the task of guiding a collection of partners in this environment becomes one of stewardship, not leadership. As we discussed in chapter 4, the model of visionary or romanticized leadership is inappropriate for coordination in environments of shared ownership and co-governance. Thus in collaboration, partner coordination involves the design of an assemblage of principles, protocols, norms, behaviours, rules and mechanisms, that make up something similar to an 'automatic pilot' (to use an imperfect metaphor) capable of steering the group in ways likely to generate wayfinding, meaningful self-organization, social learning, resilience, and innovativeness.

This 'automatic pilot' has to perform four intermingled but separate tasks:

1. gathering all the relevant information necessary to generate effective wayfinding;
2. ensuring that collaboration 'jells' by creating effective schemes or spaces that permit frame reconciliation among the different stakeholder perspectives;
3. assembling and applying a mix of incentives, mechanisms, practices and moral contracts likely to fuel a dynamic and continuous probing by the collaborators, one that translates into the requisite social learning, and results in effective coordination and collective resilience sufficient to generate creative innovation; and,

4. creating the conditions that ensure negative capability – the sort of feedback and engagement practices that support the contingent cooperation of partners and their robust commitment to the collaboration even through rough times.

However the frameworks, skills and practices of stewardship are generally lacking, due to the reasons cited above, and due to decades of indoctrination around the concepts of leadership and management 'science.' That is not to say that there is no history of effective collaboration or stewardship within government, or even within the particular domains of public safety and public health. Indeed, we have observed many examples of effective collaboration over the years, although their lessons have been largely so compartmentalized as to have had limited, if any, impact on the practice of governance in general.

In fact, one of us recently reported on two cases involving public health, the Canadian Partnership Against Cancer and BC's Public Health Services Authority, where stewardship and the capacity to catalyze effective collaboration were seen as essential core competencies for the organizations (Foster and Wilson 2014). Unfortunately, such experience continues to be viewed as being on the margin, and its lessons rarely disseminated broadly or incorporated into organizations, while decision makers resort to public displays of bravado to demonstrate their being in charge.

Blueprint for a transitional ethnographic inquiry

Despite the ongoing reluctance to engage in the design of systems for collaborative governance, there is a critical need to develop this collaborative capacity to withstand future catastrophes. It has triggered a growing appetite for transitional devices – such as potential ethnographic research that could be easily undertaken to underscore an organization's existing experience with successful collaboration and highlight its use of specific practices, tools, mechanisms, heuristics and affordances in facilitating cooperation. Such non-threatening research could kick-start an organization's process of learning based on its own successes and failures.

Having identified the elements of successful collaboration in a single organization, one may imagine the possibility of creating a training program and a field manual or checklist which aspiring collaborators could begin to use to support their work as agents of cooperation. Lastly, such an inquiry could identify lessons or suggest mechanisms and frameworks which may be generalized for broader organizational consumption.

We believe this sort of inquiry could proceed in three consecutive stages: explore the target organization's context for collaboration; identify how best to encourage effective social learning; and then codify tools that may subsequently be used to encourage successful collaboration even in conditions where there is a lack of sufficient *affectio societatis* among the participating parties.

Part I: Background and setting

First, such research would have to clarify a few key notions about the nature of collaboration when the challenge is 'wicked' – i.e., when the issue domain is opaque, its dynamics only approximately understood, when the actions needed to respond to such diffuse discomfort are neither well-defined nor agreed upon, and when the means-ends relationships are neither well-known nor stable.

Second, it would need to examine the key assumptions in good currency about the contours of the four basic collaborative sub-processes (inquiring systems, blending of perspectives, effective coordination, negative capability) and elicit the necessary minimal basis for collaboration to succeed and to yield resilience and innovation for the organization.

Third, it would need to quickly review, on the basis of both the existing literature and the heuristics developed by practitioners, a checklist of relevant dimensions that would have to be taken into account, and the skills needed for the construction of effective collaborative governance in the face of situations where there are no shared values or purposes, and no one is in charge.

Part II: Developing a social learning approach

First, it would be necessary to prepare an outline of the social learning approach. This is critical to synthesizing the observations about the four sub-processes, with an emphasis on the particular features of the particular domain of interest (public health, public safety, etc.):

a. in many issue domains like public health or public safety, a 'no failure is allowed' mentality prevails, because the potential economic, social and economic costs of system failure are perceived as too high. Yet this omnipresent possibility of failure should not be allowed to paralyze collective action or rule out space and time for experimentation and social learning;

b. when stakeholders are not like minded, and do not share perspectives or values, they need to explore the centrality of fail-safes (when failure is a limited possibility) and safe-failing (when failure is highly probable) – mechanisms that are designed to ensure that the collective inquiry is kept on track;

c. the need to address the critical trade-offs between pursuing decisions with undue haste, and having the courage not to act prematurely. The former presumes that one has a good grasp of a situation while the latter presumes that such is not the case. The frequent undue rush to decision making leads not only to premature and ineffective action, but it also does not allow sufficient attention to be given to the nurturing and maintenance of partner commitments, thus encouraging their unreliability and cold feet if the organization falls prey to reductive and myopic outlooks; and,

d. the requirement of constructing the foundations of negative capability – the capability to keep going when things are going wrong – instead of naïvely presuming that commitment is deeply grounded when it is not. This shifts the organizational assumption from 'failure cannot occur' to a fail fast: learn quickly mind set.

Second, a synthetic representation of the results of both the event analysis and key informant interviews would help flesh out the extent to which the present experience (as revealed by the studies and interviews) reveal (1) strengths and weaknesses on the fronts defined by the four sub-processes; (2) the blockages and pathologies that have materialized on these different fronts that would call for a diversity of repairs; and, (3) an action plan that would appear to be called for in the particular issue domain and context at the moment.

Part III: Modest general propositions

First, an effort must be made to distill some modest general propositions that transcend the particular issue domain (public health, public safety, etc.) and the particular context (e.g. federal Canada) in order to provide a preliminary sketch of what might be called a field manual, of the sort that some world leading engineering firms use to define the reference points in the conduct of the major projects. Such an instrument would be of use for a much broader set of issues and in a much wider array of contexts.

Second, a need to outline in a preliminary way the contours of a training package that is both generic and specific to public health, public safety, etc. that is capable of helping those involved in collaborative governance to improve their performance. This might constitute the main components of an effective training program in support of collaborative governance.

Approach summary

Methodology

- conducting exploratory work drawing from the knowledge base of each partner;
- ethnographic study of key events by examining issue files, and conducting key informant interviews;
- analysis of the relevant dimensions suggested by the four sub-processes of collaboration for each of the major events examined;

- preparation of summary papers on the four components of the 'automatic pilot' or inquiring system: wayfinding, frame reconciliation, incentives and moral contracting, negative capability;
- identifying the most critical blockages, pathologies, sources of concern, and purported sources and causes of success and failure; and,
- developing the skeleton of both a field manual and of a training program.

Anticipated results

1. A synthesis report distilling the learning from the analysis of the complex cases where common purposes and shared values are not present, and yet collaborative governance is required;
2. A first prototype of a collaboration field manual; and,
3. A first prototype of a related training program.

Conclusion – the case for bold exploration

This sort of probing is no panacea. It is only one approach to a problem that is both crucial and yet persistently denied and occluded for all the wrong reasons – mainly a stolid reluctance among pseudo-experts to concede that they have not resolved the collaboration conundrum.

While in search of irregular forms of governance capable of generating the requisite trust among those who lack it and yet are still required to work together, there are two stumbling blocks that stand out that must be overcome: conservatorship and design incapacities (Hubbard and Paquet 2015).

On the first front, one has to attack the mental prison of administrative conservatorship that suggests that the primary function of the bureaucracy is to protect, maintain and preserve the *status quo* of administrative institutions as if they were an absolute good in themselves, instead of a specific response to unique times and circumstances. This has led many senior executives to privilege the need to preserve their institution, over their need to serve the citizenry through adaptation and innovation, whilst elevating, behind the cloak of conservatorship ideals, the welfare of the bureaucratic tribe to the level of first priority over the welfare of citizens.

On the second front, one has to increase dramatically the attention devoted to the development of new prototypes of irregular governance through the cultivation of design thinking and learning as you go to replace the former blanket focus on decision making (Boland and Collopy 2004; Martin and Christensen 2013). This would prove helpful in developing requisite inquiring systems and designing the requisite stewardship for progressivity and antifragility,[17] and as well to resolve the natural conflicts and collisions by means of agreed-upon principles, rules or conventions (Spicer 2001: 22).

Whatever the dangers of exploration with these new prototypes – for they may well prove inadequate – it would appear preferable to mindlessly embracing old conceptual frameworks and antiquated organizational forms that have been shown to be grossly ineffective and well past their 'best before' dates.

---

[17] On the notions of inquiring systems and stewardship, see Paquet and Wilson, 2011. 'Progressivity' connotes not the popular notion of progressiveness (which has an income and wealth redistributive and social-democratic flavour, and is in good currency in social-democratic circles), but the notion of a capacity to transform to allow innovation to spread at optimal speed (Paquet 2013). Similarly, the notion of 'antifragility' does not connote the same thing as the notion of resilience (springing back to the *status quo ante* after a shock), but rather the more ambitious aim to ensure that organizations and social systems get stronger, more robust and innovative as a result of increased disorder and shocks in a turbulent environment (Taleb 2012).

References

Block, Peter. 1998. "As Goes the Follower; So Goes the Leader," *News for a Change*, Association for Quality Participation, 2 (7):11-13.

Boland, Richard J. and Fred Collopy (eds.). 2004. *Managing by Design*. Stanford, CA: Stanford University Press.

Cuisinier, Vincent. 2008. *L'affectio societatis*. Paris, FR: Lexis-Nexis Litec.

Foster, Wayne and Christopher Wilson. 2014. "Illustrations in Public Health of a More Collaborative Public Service," *www.optimumonline.ca*, 44(4): 21-44.

Hubbard, Ruth and Gilles Paquet. 2015. *Irregular Governance: A Plea for Bold Organizational Experimentation*. Ottawa, ON: Invenire Books.

Kahane, Adam. 2004. *Solving Tough Problems – An Open Way of Talking, Listening, and Creating New Realities*. San Francisco, CA: Berrett-Koehler Publishers.

Martin, Roger and Karen Christensen (eds.). 2013. *Rotman on Design*. Toronto, ON: University of Toronto Press.

Munn-Venn, Trefor and Andrew Archibald. 2007. *A Resilient Canada: Governance for National Security and Public Safety*. Ottawa, ON: Conference Board of Canada, November.

National Advisory Committee on SARS and Public Health. 2003. *Learning from SARS (Naylor Report)*. Ottawa, ON: Health Canada, p. 212

Oakeshott, Michael. 1975. *On Human Conduct*. Oxford, UK: Oxford University Press.

Paquet, Gilles. 2013. *Tackling Wicked Policy Problems: Equality, Diversity and Sustainability*. Ottawa, ON: Invenire Books.

Paquet, Gilles. 2014. *Unusual Suspects: Essays on Social Learning Disabilities*. Ottawa, ON: Invenire Books, p. 176ff.

Paquet, Gilles and Christopher Wilson. 2011. "Collaborative Co-governance as Inquiring Systems," *www.optimimonline.ca*, 41(2): 1-12.

Rothstein, Bo. 2005. *Social Traps and the Problem of Trust*. Cambridge, UK: Cambridge University Press.

Spicer, Michael W. 2001. *Public Administration and the State – A Postmodern Perspective*. Tuscaloosa, AL: University of Alabama Press.

Taleb, Nassim Nicholas. 2012. *Antifragile – Things that gain from disorder*. New York, NY: Random House.

Terry, Larry D. 2003. *Leadership of Public Bureaucracies – The Administrator as Conservator*. Armonk, NY: M.E. Sharpe.

The Canadian Press. 2013. "CSIS knew of navy spy's activity, left RCMP in the dark," *CBC News*, May 26, www.cbc.ca/news/canada/nova-scotia/csis-knew-of-navy-spy-s-activity-left-rcmp-in-the-dark-1.1312803 [Accessed March 23, 2016].

CHAPTER 7

| Culture Governance and the Strategic State

"An ideology, a dogma demands
certainty, not probability ...
Ours is really a quest for uncertainty,
for that continuing change which is life."

Saul D. Alinsky

The last chapter has shown us how we might be able to overcome a most important governance dysfunction: a lack of *affectio societatis* among potential partners (inside or outside organizations) that often leads to collaboration failure. We have witnessed it in a variety of public sector organizations where a long tradition of commandeering seems to have generated a habitus that prevents intermediate level executives, completely self-absorbed in the minutiae of their tasks, from even becoming aware of the need for collaboration in the dispatch of their work. Thus it becomes for them a standard toxic subterfuge to assume that the required collaboration by partners is already in place (even when there is plenty of evidence that this is a delusion) or that it will materialize in due time – in order not to have to face the challenge of constructing it, a task for which they are ill-prepared.

This sort of cognitive dissonance leaves organizations and socio-technical systems immensely ill-equipped to face catastrophes and crises where collaboration is essential but does not materialize. We have shown how this sort of dysfunction is rampant in both the worlds of public safety and public health.

While these dysfunctions in the small may be costly to an organization, serious crises often tend to make their existence quite visible and to trigger some correctives. Other dysfunctions in the large are often more toxic because the impact of broad *idées reçues* or culturally-rooted conventional wisdom is more diffuse. Conventional wisdom may smother the effect of effective and agile social learning to combat these toxic forces and it may even generate a certain fatalism about these forces because of the support they have in the culture.

Such cultural mental prisons and lethargies have plagued all sectors. However, for exposition purpose, we focus on the case of the public sector (which has witnessed significant shifts in the valence of its key functions over time) to illustrate the way organizations and social arrangements may become trapped into some cultural warps that may prove toxic if not actually lethal.

On four key functions of government

The first function of government in modern society is coordination *stricto sensu*: intervening in the allocation of resources by regulation, taxes, subsidies, or modification in the mode or production and distribution of goods or services, etc. to correct market failures and improve the efficiency of the coordination of economic activities (e.g. subsidies to increase the consumption of certain educational services that are collectively valuable but not fully appreciated by individuals).

The second function is stabilization. This pertains to interventions by government to compensate for cyclically fluctuating levels of activities in the private sector. For example, increasing public sector aggregate demand in times of depressed private demand, or reducing public sector demand at times when private aggregate demand risks overshoot the supply potential. This type of intervention is usually associated with Keynesian thinking, and it has acquired widespread legitimacy in the second half of the 20th century.

The third function is redistribution. This entails a transfer of resources from those citizens supposedly better off to those supposedly less well off, through a variety of techniques (from taxation and subsidies to the provision of public goods and services), but also between and among regions, sectors, etc., according to negotiated but often arcane formulae. This function has taken on a new *grandeur* in the post-World War II era, when this sort of transfer of resources – once celebrated only as a convenience for stabilization purposes (e.g. family allowances to mitigate the decline of military expenditures after 1945) – became fuelled by a new progressive philosophy that sanctified such redistributive action as desirable *per se* in the late 20th century.

A fourth governmental function – pedagogical, ideological – has always lurked in the background of government activities, but it has become especially important as we entered our *civilisation du spectacle* (Vargas Lloosa 2015) and as the idea of redistribution became meritorious and canonical *per se*. Of late, this function of governments (either for electoral purposes or for the promotion of a supportive ideology) has come to dominate the perceptions and representations of most political parties and has imbibed the worldviews of a significant portion of the intelligentsia and of the media.

Any democratic government has legitimate responsibility in the affairs of the mind (Tussman 1977). Government is an important producer of information; it also has responsibility to protect citizens against misrepresentation and deception; and to promote collective cognition. However, such state interventions can tumble into a form of propaganda, and become a source of state-centric mass manipulation of public opinion.[18]

We argue in this chapter that the mix of functions of the government has changed over the last 60 years, and that this has been the result of many forces but to a great extent the result of shifts in the culture governance. We also argue that social coordination remains the primary function for government, while the others are sub-functions in aid of social coordination to minimize conflict and inspire innovation.

The coordination-redistribution switch

Since 1973, there has been a long decline of productivity, accompanied by cyclical downturns, which at times were caused either by spurts in oil prices or by financial crises. While a variety of explanations have been proposed about the constellation of problems and the issues that emerged as a result, for our purposes, what is of import is the pervasive sense of helplessness that developed in the face of ill-inspired or ineffective or perverse government interventions that were proposed to deal with such problems.

In the early phase of this period of challenge (1971-1995), coordination concerns still dominated the public sector psyche, along with the sweeping belief that 'New Public Management' was the required remedy. This led to a number of circumscribed structural reforms (federally or provincially) (Paquet 1997; Paquet 2014a, b: chapter 5).

The collective results of those modest restructurings of the production and allocation apparatuses were not always very

---

[18] For example, the active propagation of the views (a) that mass immigration generates massive economic benefits and is needed to correct the demographic impact of the aging of the Canadian population, and (b) that diversity is an absolute good, and pride in multiculturalism is the reason why Canadians have seemingly not reacted negatively (like the rest of the Western world) to mass immigration in the 1990s, can be regarded as disinformation and propaganda that have been perpetrated by the Canadian government and their intellectual accomplices, and have deliberately been foisted on the citizenry with a view to brainwashing it into not resisting these sorts of policies (Paquet 2012).

imaginative or forward looking. Most importantly they lacked a clear understanding of the frameworks, skills and practices of effective collaboration that could be used to foster a more concerted economy.

More recently (1996-2014), the situation began to evolve in a dramatically different direction. Redistribution had become increasingly important during the post-World War II period, but, in the 1990s, it came to be regarded as the solution to three of the most daunting public sector challenges:

- the expanded need for mechanisms for recycling of government surpluses;
- the phenomenal ideological drive toward egalitarianism – evolving from social preference to absolute right and entitlement; and,
- the generalized state of resignation and pessimism on the part of governments – having realized that they had neither the capacities nor the will to transform their unproductive and outdated apparatus of socio-economic coordination – while coupled with an understanding that they could at least retain their legitimacy by compensating the citizenry for the malefits generated by governance failures on the coordination front.

Culture governance

There is a growing consensus (Hamel 2013; Senge *et al.* 2008; Hagel 2009) that modern society has grown so complex, dynamic and differentiated that it cannot be ruled any longer by hierarchies and bureaucracies imposing control over people top down. As the new public management (NPM) experiment also revealed, the sole reliance on the market mechanisms proved of little help in resolving the complex social problems that rely on social interactions and collective innovation for their resolution.

Unlike markets or hierarchies, the mechanisms of social democracy are much better suited to help people with highly diverse perspectives come together to solve complex problems collectively (Farrell and Shalizi 2013), because they allow forms of social learning and innovation that neither price mechanisms nor hierarchical bureaucracy are likely to produce. The cultural underground records such changes. While the cultural underground of beliefs and propensities to act in certain directions is only slowly and cumulatively swayed by the accumulation of experiences, it holds powerful influence on the ways in which individuals, groups and organizations react to new circumstances. Consequently, as the ethos of the time evolves and is recorded by the intelligentsia and the media, it tends to counter or reinforce *l'air du temps*.

For instance, it is neither innocent nor inconsequential that the topic chosen by Janice Stein for her Massey Lectures in 2001 was "the cult of efficiency" (Stein 2001). Her lectures indicted efficiency (i.e., the fight against waste) as a 'virus' and captured well the *zeitgeist* of the time in Canada. They also threw some light on the characteristics of the cultural underground of the period – one that was shifting its focus from value-adding to value-redistributing concerns (shift I), an attitude that later helped to derail Canada's Program Review.[19] By the end of the century, it had become the new gospel of the so-called progressivists.

The anti-efficiency movement continues to this day despite the many dispiriting experiences with redistribution. In fact, and it is only in very recent times that the culture of governance has come to raise suspicions about redistribution masquerading as a panacea. Despite two decades of redistributive profligacy *ex post* as a substitute for the failed quest for efficiency *ex ante*, there appears to be a renewed interest in the coordination game. We see this demonstrated in the growing interest in self-governance, empowerment, participation, and P3s, as well as other culturally charged processes like deliberation and involvement. However, this shift (shift II) – from unbounded redistribution to a focus on value-adding again – is only materializing very slowly (Bang 2003: 243).

---

[19] Program Review is a label connoting an exercise in rationalization of the Canadian federal government program expenditures undertaken in the middle of the 1990s. We refer to it later in this chapter.

On culture governance I:
from coordination to redistribution

It is culture governance that helps steer a collective human system through the use of embedded propensities that have evolved over time, and that comprise socially accepted mechanisms, conventions, and arrangements that make the highest and best uses of all the intersubjective, interactive and cooperative capabilities that are in common currency. To put it in another way,

> *Community is fundamentally an interdependent human system given form by the conversation it holds with itself. The history, buildings, economy, infrastructure and culture are [artifacts] of the conversations and the social fabric of any community* (Block 2008: 30).

Culture governance is a product of those conversations, one that evolves a collective sense of what is possible or not; and what is, or is not, acceptable behaviour, and for instance, what is an acceptable role for government.

The traumatic failures of governments in the 1970s and 1980s generated much in the way of antigovernment attitudes, but they did not succeed in triggering action to transform the flawed, maladapted, institutional structures of the coordination game. This was ascribable to well-entrenched social rigidities and state-authorized structures of all sorts such as corporate property rights, in all sectors (Olson 1965, 1982). This led to a decline in the hopes that government could be relied upon to generate the needed structural reforms, and therefore to a decline in public pressure on governments to unshackle our evolving socio-economy from these aging structures (Kindleberger 1978).

In the face of this perceived incapacity of governments to deal with the coordination problem *ex ante*, and at the very time when the entitlement mentality was becoming ever more legitimate for groups feeling maligned or marginalized, the culture governance shifted (shift I) to embrace a host of redistribution schemes to correct both the real and imagined malefits that were inflicted by an imperfectly coordinated socio-economy.

This increased the propensity of groups on all sides to shift their attention away from the daunting and frustrating efforts to transform the social coordination game, toward making the state the primary tool in the redistribution game – to ensure both protection from anything that could be declared a malefit (and claim requisite compensation when this could not be done), and maximum capture of all possible entitlements, rents and privileges (whether they were morally defensible or not). This has had the effect of redirecting the bulk of citizen and media criticism away from pressing government to reform the coordination terrain, towards pressing government to become ever more involved in the redistribution of tangible and symbolic benefits to compensate for real or imaginary disadvantages.

Indeed, it would appear that, in this new era, all claims for compensation for any inegalitarian outcomes – symbolic or real – would appear to be considered legitimate, automatically promoting everyone to the status of a member of some "disadvantaged group" or other – a vacuous label created by the Charter of Rights that connotes anything one might wish it to mean (Gwyn 1995: Part III; Paquet 2012: 56).

As a consequence, redistribution has slowly evolved from its integrator role in the post WWII period to dominating the national discourse, and by the 1990s, to becoming somewhat sacralised. It is no longer just a single aspect of government's role, but it is now the primary one:

- being regarded as the only legitimate tool available to government in an era of increasing complexity to correct (after the fact) the impacts of social coordination malefits that could not be prevented beforehand; and,
- being able to build on the general acceptance of redistributive and entitlement mechanisms, in a deeply-rooted 'no-fault' culture, that permitted the forgiveness of governments for their lack of *ex ante* coordination interventions, as long as 'appropriate'

compensation was provided (with 'appropriate' being negotiable).

On this slippery slope, most governments have remained blithely unconscious and oblivious to the social rigidities and mental prisons that such a perspective might generate. In particular, they have failed to grasp that redistributive property rights, once granted, cannot easily be withdrawn later; or that redistribution being a process of taking from one person and giving to another is inherently conflict-generating and divisive; or that it does nothing to improve collective innovation or performance – just the opposite. Yet, in the end, this ethos was sufficiently convenient, powerful and popular as to mollify efforts to get the coordination house in order.

1990s: the failed transition to the strategic state

That said, before the long drift into the swamp of unlimited redistribution fully unfolded, there was a moment of truth in the mid-90s in Canada, when the possibility existed to redefine the texture of government through a significant redesign and refurbishment of the way in which the socio-economy was governed.

Program Review came after some ominous warnings by the IMF (Paquet 1993a) that the federal government's budgeting was out of whack. At the time, in response to it and various other coordination failures, a burgeoning literature about governance had surfaced in Canada, and a new vocabulary of governance surrounding the notion of subsidiarity had begun to circulate (Paquet 1994). Yet even then it was recognized that effective work of this sort had to be more than just conceptual. It required new frameworks and the development of new ensembles of working principles, skills and mechanisms. The paucity of such tools in the federal government, however, made any experiment with governance redesign likely to be a doomed one.

Program Review: the failed transition to a strategic state[20]

In Canada, the public finance crisis of the early 1990s provided the federal government with a unique opportunity and motivation to critically analyze the existing governing apparatus because of the real threat of financial insolvency. This assessment was done in the early part of the mandate of the newly elected Liberal government of 1993 under the general label of Program Review.

At that time, however, each federal program was to be subjected to six tests during Program Review:

1. Does this program continue to serve the public interest?
2. Is there a legitimate/necessary role for government in it?
3. Is the current role of the federal government appropriate? Should it be shared with lower order governments?
4. Should the program be transferred in whole or in part to the private or voluntary sectors?
5. Could its efficiency be improved?
6. Can we afford it?

If the entire federal enterprise had been seriously subjected to this battery of tests, quite clearly the whole governing apparatus of the country would have been significantly overhauled and refurbished. Unfortunately, it did not happen because there was, quite simply, no appetite for such a transformation.

This is not the place to develop a full historical analysis of Program Review. Suffice it to say that this was one of the most interesting Cartesian exercises in revamping government (and therefore the governance systems of the country),

---

[20] The notion of strategic state (Paquet 1992, 1996-7) was the subsidiarity-based, 'small g' (governance) template that one of us had succeeded in bringing to the front of the stage in the period leading to the 1993 federal election. It was most certainly well received in certain circles of the Liberal Party of Canada in stimulating debates before the election, and even in the immediate aftermath. It is only later in the decade that financial woes completely displaced this subsidiary agenda, and later on the centralizing phalanx of the Chretien government and the senior federal bureaucracy buried it.

through a philosophy of subsidiarity. Unfortunately, the process was hijacked by the centralizing phalanx of the Chretien Cabinet and the upper federal bureaucracy. As a result, what had been planned as a redesign of government into a strategic state, became, through sleight of hand, simple cover for a federal budget exercise in public expenditure reduction which was achieved primarily on the back of Canada's unsuspecting provinces through cuts in federal-provincial transfers that were, not only not negotiated, but also unannounced until after the fact. The whole exercise was one of deception and imposture (Paquet 1996b; Paquet and Shepherd 1996).[21]

Unfortunately, as it turns out, this was the last serious effort to deal, even theoretically, with the coordination failures within the Canadian governance system as a whole. Even the Social Union Agreement proposed later by the federal government in 1999 – a faint-hearted promise not to meddle unexpectedly with the finances of provincial jurisdictions without serious consultations – proved entirely disingenuous (Paquet 1999a). Neither the Chretien government nor the senior executives during the tenure of Alex Himelfarb as Clerk of the Privy Council had any honest or serious interest in pursuing an agenda of subsidiarity or cooperative federalism, whatever superficial gestures they may have been willing to make in this direction in the aftermath of the traumatic and existential Quebec referendum in 1995.

Without that interest, it was inevitable that the 'new' federalism was bound to count on redistribution to bribe all vocal interest groups into silence or soften provincial partners and cities alike, rather than to address the more complex task of reforming coordination mechanisms to improve the overall effectiveness of cooperation in the federation.

---

[21] This should not be interpreted as a statement that the original subsidiarity-inspired Program Review left no trace. This inspired program was hijacked by Treasury Board away from the Privy Council Office, but one cannot ascertain what it might have been by what it accomplished despite the hijacking (Paquet 1999a)

Perils of egalitarianism and unbounded redistribution
Not only were the 1990s the last hope of achieving a more coordinated strategic state, but the period around year 2000 was also the last one when the perils of egalitarianism and irresponsible redistribution – as articulated so well by de Tocqueville (1840/1961) – were heard in our democracies (Laurent and Paquet 1991; Kekes 2003). Since then, egalitarianism and redistribution have become, like social rights, idolatrized icons, immune to challenge.

Yet de Tocqueville has astutely shown that the passion for equality – *"plus insatiable à mesure que l'égalité est plus grande"* (de Tocqueville 1840/1961: vol. II, p. 144, 189) – would eventually turn toxic. In a world where the greater the equality, the more insatiable becomes the thirst for even greater equality; and the greater the passion for equality, the more the egalitarianism dogma becomes the source of widespread envy (Foster 1972).

After the derailing of Program Review in all but name in the late 1990s, and the closing of minds in government to the development of a strategic state, there was an unbounded celebration of redistribution and egalitarianism as progressive, and a new era in government was established.

It witnessed the replacement of *Type α* anti-government criticism – expressions of discontent *vis-à-vis* government with a view to forcing government to repair the flawed governing processes that were dysfunctional and wasteful (very much along the lines of what Program Review was all about) – with *Type β* criticism of government (that is pressure to effect redistribution in order to assuage the *ex post* malefits generated by the structures of governance now accepted as flawed – structures that now became at least partly immune to reform).

For instance, the disgruntlement about flawed production and governance structures in health and education – that include inefficiencies and ineffectiveness that are well known, have been widely discussed for decades, and have such undue weight on the public purse that they are threatening to bankrupt the state within decades (Levert 2013) – have remained unchallenged, largely because these services have been provided either free or at such highly-subsidized price levels that they have become entitlements over the years.

Despite a flood of *ad hoc* entitlements and claims for redistribution that have been created in recent history, the net long-term effects of these interventions have remained occluded within a complex system. Most people remain blind to the social rigidities and mental prisons that such initiatives have generated, appearing to be satisfied and content to collect on compensation claims of political bribes because the cultural governance underground has upheld their legitimacy (Paquet 2004).

At this point, these arrangements of convenience have become like no-fault auto insurance, and they have been adopted because they dramatically reduce government transaction costs in the short run, even though, in the longer run, they also reduce the mindfulness and responsibility of the citizenry. So it is that when entitlements acquire the status of a right, they constitute a blockage to the modification and evolution of collective behaviour – harmful behaviours need not be discouraged, effective markets need not be fostered and trade-offs need not be considered.

Principles and mechanisms

If 'Big G' (Government) is unlikely to provide effective coordination in a world where power, resources and information are widely distributed, then a call for 'small g' (governance) is warranted ... but it cannot be just a call for change. The 'ownership' of citizens must be re-instilled for if they cannot accept how their actions or reactions contribute to the *status quo*, can they contribute to change? One has to be able to spell out the sort of assemblage of principles, skills, conventions and mechanisms that are likely to provide what one might refer to as the right mix of transparency, sermon, carrot and stick.

While that toolbox of practices was deficient in the 1990s, experience since then has demonstrated what the most useful principles and mechanisms might be.

The sample below is drawn from a recent encyclopedia (Paquet 2014c).

Table 4. Principles and Mechanisms for the Construction of a Governance Regime

Principles	Mechanisms
Maximum participation	Inclusive forums
True prices and costs	Moral contracts
Subsidiarity	Social learning and reframing
Competition and collaboration	Links between beliefs and actions
Multi-stability	Fail-safe mechanisms
Trust	Relational linkages

Since power, resources and information are widely distributed, and no one is fully in charge on any major issue of the day, the coordination challenge is best met by being inclusive, by sticking as much as possible to true prices and costs, and forging moral contracts or conventions to handle the more qualitative dimensions. Subsidiarity calls for delegating decisions to the most local level possible, and designing social learning mechanisms capable of acquiring experience as time goes by.

This sample of principles and mechanisms is not an exhaustive one, but it can serve as a provisional guidepost for designing modes of governance specific to issues and contexts. The notion that an effective assemblage of principles and mechanisms must be created puts design at the core of the governance process (Boland and Collopy 2004; Martin and Christensen 2013), but any effective design must also be equipped with a social learning apparatus that is capable of constantly adapting this assemblage to an evolving environment, and a stewardship capacity to creatively navigate the dual handicaps of mental prisons and system failures.

Transforming public governance may therefore be seen as a design exercise for remixing or recombining the principles and mechanisms that are known to promote collective action. However, the outcomes of this process are never certain because there will always be learning along the way, not to mention the slippages or hijackings of these processes by one or other of the major parties involved. In fact, most collaborative experiments struggle in the tensions between imaginative redesign and the administrative pathologies that stand in their way.

Indeed, even when a smooth drift from 'Big G' to 'small g' could be envisaged 20 years ago with Program Review, this shift is not what happened. At least at the level of formal arrangements, the forces of dynamic conservatism were extraordinarily successful in ensuring the conservatorship of arrangements that have remained wasteful, conflictual, and incapable of ensuring effective social learning and antifragility.

Anyone examining carefully the major issues that have struck the world over the last 15 years (from 9/11 to the financial crisis of 2007-08, to the carnival of instability in the European Union, to the collapse in the price of natural resources, to the psychodramas recently played out about terrorism and inequality) could not help but observe the extraordinary sense of confusion in the minds of experts in all fields, and the even more extraordinary lack of capacity on the part of the nation-states to really do anything about those crises.

The surreal histrionics of nation-states to orchestrate grand spectacles (be it through the Chaplinesque demonstration of international unity of nations against terrorism in Paris after the Charlie Hebdo attacks or the vacuous *grand-messe écologique* around climate change also in Paris in 2015, or the miniature replica of this vaudeville in Canada during the federal election of the fall of 2015) has revealed the extent of our self-promotion, our *civilisation du spectacle*: all showbiz, no substance, a modern version of Nero's fiddling when Rome was burning. Governing has become a form of entertainment, as the US presidential candidacy of Donald Trump so aptly demonstrates – a fraudulent world of *mentir-vrai*, of a vast imposture by the politicians, the media, and the intelligentsia to generate inventive distractions and appropriate deceits to avoid addressing or even mentioning real problems with which they feel completely incapable of dealing.

Fortunately, in the meantime, on the ground, in the life world, a revolution is unfolding that is rarely remarked upon.

From unbounded redistribution to dissipative structures

Given the pathologies of the modern state described above, and the impotence of any government reform movement to press for significant coordination and governance realignments, it is hard not to be cynical. Any call to refocus attention among government actors, stakeholders and the public away from the toxic distractions of redistribution and back to the important value-adding issue of social coordination will not be easy, especially given the vaudeville of inequality issues (Watson 2015).

And yet the frustration generated by the coordination failures and the impotence of governments in effecting the needed repairs will not be denied. As a result of ongoing state failures, non-state actors have been led to grope for alternative ways to deal with the pathologies that infect government. Their search for alternatives to government in addressing chronic issues of social coordination may relieve government of much of its burden of office or it may replace government altogether.

This pent-up frustration with the 'unbearable lightness of the nation-state' can however be channelled into more effective inquiries and explorations once it becomes clear that socio-political-economic systems are open dissipative systems that are constantly changing.

The term 'dissipative system' is drawn from thermo-dynamics, and refers to a non-equilibrium system that is constantly exchanging with its environment. Indeed it maintains itself as an orderly structure by exporting disorder and importing order to continuously renew itself. It is "non-equilibrium that brings order out of chaos" (Prigogine and Stengers 1984: 287).

Non-equilibrium structures, such as living systems and governments, involve many sub-processes which when combined create temporary states of stability that emerge from states that require less energy to maintain. However, it is these same fluctuations among these order producing sub-processes which may cause the system to change and evolve. When these fluctuations occur far enough away from equilibrium, they may self-organize to produce a new more efficient state of temporary stability. Self-organization emerges from dissipative structures due to the fundamental interdependence of structure and function, and the exchange of information and energy with the environment which is one of the most profound laws of physics (Jantsch 1980: 40).

These same conditions ... underlie the possibility of internal self-amplification of fluctuations and their ultimate breakthrough [into a new state of order]. Without such internal self-amplification there is no true self-organization. The possible consequence is the evolution of the system through an indefinite sequence of instabilities each of which leads to the spontaneous formation of a new autopoietic structure (Ibid.: 44).

System change, therefore, involves a process of inducing self-organization that is the result of a three-fold process of interaction involving structure, function, and fluctuation, which together can be thought of as one giant fluctuation. Both chance and necessity move the system to a higher level of organization – chance, through the contributions of individual fluctuations, and necessity arising from the coupling of sub-processes. Since internal sub-processes can also combine to dampen 'innovation' in a system, the point at which new fluctuations overcome these dampening barriers creates great instability, and the need for a new stable structure becomes significant. During transitions, entropy production, or disorder, increases markedly, as the system spares no expense to move to the more stable, lower energy state.

It is not adaptation [learning to dominate] to a given environment that signals a unified overall evolution, but the co-evolution of system and environment at all levels, the co-evolution of micro- and macro-cosmos (Ibid.: 75).

This new dynamic is so profoundly engraved in our practice that we cannot but look at a local newspaper as we did the morning of May 25, 2015 – while putting the not quite final touches to an earlier draft of this chapter – without finding a report that documented change on the fringe of our socio-economy that called for "policy from the bottom up" (Jackson 2015), illuminating the fact that while hundreds of bottom up collaborations are in the process of generating policy change across this country, they remain essentially a *terra incognita*.

On culture governance II: from redistribution to diffraction

Over the last two decades, our culture governance has evolved dramatically as a result of the continual diffraction of power (Naím 2013). Some have stylized this process in three waves:

- first, there was an attack on the citadel of the state in response to the challenges posed by the failure-prone process of top-down hierarchical bureaucratic governing – but in Canada, when alternative service deliveries started encroaching on the traditional notion and turf of the role of the state, there was a strong state-centric pushback that denounced this hollowing out;
- second, the traditional state apparatus sprung back: it realized that it might be able to maintain its dominion by exercising its power in more subtle and indirect ways like redistribution – this meant that pushback by the traditional state became less overt, and it morphed into a form of siren seduction, inviting citizens through bribes and rhetoric to abdicate their co-ownership and to welcome a sort of voluntary submission to the will of the state as a way of self-realization; and,
- third, a further erosion of the 'Big G' notion of state into a somewhat more liquefied notion of contingent cultural

practice – to the point where some announced the emergence of a stateless state – something that was not to be feared but was nevertheless meant to extinguish the anti-government criticism altogether (Bevir and Rhodes 2010) by removing the boundary between the state and citizens, and suggesting co-governance in matters of coordination.

These waves have not only considerably dampened the anti-government hostility considerably by declawing the state, but in the end they have also undermined the 'Big G' vista by attacking its very foundation: the traditional gap between ruler and ruled.

This evolving notion of governance has not only triggered the emergence of a putative notion of a declawed state, but it has also questioned some basic assumptions upon which the 'Big G' (Government) approach was built. In the context of our new complex and uncertain world, it has proclaimed that there exists no shared values and that no one is in charge. It has pointed out the growing number of stakeholders who defend so many different interests that power, resources and information have become so distributed into so many different hands that the very notion of leadership has become senseless sham.

How can such a diversity of interests be coordinated in pursuit of collective innovation? What guidance mechanisms best capture the sort of required wayfinding that one observes in forms of effective stewardship? (Paquet 2013: chapter 2)

These developments may not have been explicitly captured in newspaper headlines, but they have nevertheless percolated in the collective consciousness and then modifying culture governance accordingly, along with the propensities that are built into that culture. The foibles of perfect computation by the state, or of perfect competition in the market, have led most analysts to abandon their lofty ideals of perfect coordination. Simultaneously, however, it has been recognized that some forms of imperfect and temporarily viable coordination would have to be constructed through processes of 'learning while doing' in order to deal with the fractured socio-economies *par morceaux,* if society and the ship of state were to keep on going.

There is probably no better illustration of working, multiplex, improvised governance on the margin becoming a substitute for the 'Big G' (Government) of the traditional state than that of Belgium. It holds the world record for a democracy going without an elected governing executive – 589 days in 2010 and 2011 – because opposing Flemish and Walloon parties were unable to agree on how to form a governing coalition following an election that resulted in several minority parties. During that 20-month period, the six million Flemish and five million Francophones (despite no one being in charge) exhibited largely indifference to the political impasse, even taking pleasure when the country broke the European record for coalition talks in January 2011.

In the short run, neither group was punished by the electorate for their inability to produce a working government. Eventually, a government was formed in December 2011. And then, obviously unchastened by that experience, Belgians went again to the polls in May of 2014, once again electing a divided Parliament that formed a new government only in October 2014 after a five-month interregnum. Belgians clearly did not see a functioning, cohesive, elected government as being all that critical.

The Belgian experience clearly puts a lie to the hyperbolic claims that without someone in charge of government, all will be chaos and lost. So if this fundamental assumption can be relaxed, then are there others that can also be eased?[22]

[22] Another distinctive urban myth is that government alone is capable of setting policy, of having a public mandate embodied in its elected members and a range of expertise in its technocrats. Yet the Canadian Partnership Against Cancer Corporation (CPAC) is a not-for-profit organization that is a partnership among federal, provincial and territorial government health authorities. It also includes several voluntary sector organizations, like the Canadian Cancer Society, as part of its decision-making board (Foster and Wilson 2014). When it comes to establishing cancer fighting strategies, it has policy authority and the financial resources to develop new approaches and policies that are subsequently implemented by the public agencies. CPAC is unique in this way in Canada. As a result of the federal Cabinet decision, CPAC may be the first non-profit organization that has been delegated *de*

On distributed governance: strategic state redux

The most important transformation of the last 20 years has been a mutation of the governance culture into a subtle and powerful Quantum cosmology that is driven by uncertainty, probability and relationships. We are only now beginning to recognize that we do not live in a Newtonian world order. It is difficult or impossible to determine predictable cause and effect except in probabilistic terms, and that, in our diffracted and diverse world, it is only by experimentation, collaboration with others, and social learning *par morceaux* that our inquiring and wayfinding systems can hope to tackle some of the large, chronic, complex problems we currently face, such as climate change, perpetual economic growth, access to basic resources, security, health care, migration and over population.

Governments are fundamentally mechanisms of social coordination. That said, other actors, using the tools of telecommunications, the Internet, universal education, and social media have begun to wrestle a significant amount of coordination legitimacy away from traditional, centralized governments. Clearly governments no longer have a monopoly on social coordination and innovation, while citizens and non-governmental organizations of all types are now learning to generate coordination without government. As a consequence, we can now observe a growing number of competing alternatives to government that are being created.

Three examples of efficiency initiatives

We offer three examples of efficiency initiatives that have been experimented with and have slowly gained ground over the

facto policy authority to implement a national strategy. "CPAC represents" (according to Claude Rocan) "an attempt to establish a different type of relationship. This may well be unprecedented in modern times in the health sector" (Rocan 2011). All three major political parties supported the Canadian Strategy for Cancer Control in the 2006 election campaign, suggesting a consensus that the CPAC approach allowed a degree of operational flexibility and an opportunity for relationship building that was more difficult in the existing government apparatus, where any government's claim to be 'in charge' would be universally challenged.

last two decades, focusing on coordination: including private-public partnerships (or P3s), community-based initiatives, and whole of government approaches.

P3s have been used for many purposes: to build bridges (e.g. The Confederation Bridge linking PEI to the mainland), highways (such as Toronto's Highway 407), and hospitals (such as the Royal Ottawa Hospital) as well as service delivery to citizens (such as BC's health card). These partnerships between governments and business have had varying degrees of success (Hubbard and Paquet 2007) depending on the attention to partnership dynamics and the participants' willingness to step beyond the traditional client-vendor relationships in government.

Community-based initiatives (Wilson 2007, 2008), such as the Vancouver Agreement that was in place between 2000 and 2010, and that brought together local businesses and agencies along with federal, provincial and municipal authorities, to tackle the health, economic and social problems that appeared intractable to any party working alone. Community-based initiatives were often led and driven by local stakeholders working with various governments and their departments which chose to align their respective mandates to achieve locally defined goals. In the end, the Vancouver Agreement was terminated because governments could not lay claim fully to any of its successes nor could they fully distance themselves from any of its collaborative shortcomings.

Similar to community-based initiatives are whole of government approaches, such as the UK's Local Strategic Partnerships (LSP) initiative. In the face of the inability of siloed governments to make progress on complex problems, initiatives such as the LSP created *de facto* unified local government entities independent of existing bodies to address the needs and priorities of specific communities. These independent bodies would refine central policies and distribute locally targeted funding on the basis of those local priorities.

According to Levesque, one of the reasons for the lack of integration in regards to these sorts of coordination experiences was that they created a sense of loss of control within the political cadres. This arose from a rift between the political (steering) and the administrative (rowing) functions in government created by the new public management model that generated their increased mutual autonomy, and a disintegration of cohesive departmental bureaucracies in favour of more independent and specialized units (Lévesque 2012). Thus the decentralization encouraged by NPM only added further complexity to public institutions (Christensen and Laegreid 2004). This additional fragmentation helped to further erode the notion of who's 'in charge,' fostered a competition between the steering and rowing elements of government, and thus contributed to a further lessening of public confidence in government.

These isolated attempts at reform by inventing alternative coordination mechanisms, notwithstanding public confidence in government globally, has continued to decline. Global trust in government has declined from its high in the 1970s, and according to Edelman's *2015 Trust Barometer,* it now stands at 48 percent. At 63 percent, NGOs remain the world's most trusted institutions. While businesses are generally perceived as being more trustworthy than government at 57 percent, the least trusted employee groups were CEOs and government officials at 43 and 38 percent, respectively.

Blockchain and cryptocurrencies

Some of the most interesting of the emerging alternatives to government involve blockchain applications which, for instance, support cryptocurrencies (like Bitcoin), and which can be used, like canaries in a coal mine, to assess the public's attitude to government and its appetite for alternatives (Plansky, O'Donnell, Richards 2016).

Until very recently, our national economies were absolutely underpinned by the concept of 'money' – coins or paper that were controlled by the authority of the government and the central banks. When we exchanged something of value, that exchange was mediated by a dollar bill or credit card that was backstopped by a bank and the reputation and power of a national government. These central authorities were trusted (not that we had much choice) to work on our behalf to develop monetary and fiscal policies, as well as regulatory, security and enforcement policies that would maintain public confidence in the stability and predictability of the value of 'money' as a store of value and an intermediary of exchange. Consequently, the management of the economy and the money supply has long been considered as a core function of government. In order to maintain public trust in the economy, governments used significant layers of oversight and regulation to ostensibly prevent abuse or corruption among those few in the centre and to offset market failures of one sort or another.

Enter cryptocurrencies in 2008. Cryptocurrencies like Bitcoin, and over 500 others like it, operate using a public record of digital transactions called the 'blockchain'.

The 'blockchain' is essentially a distributed database – a sort of public online ledger that records digital exchanges between people without the need to resort to trusting some central authority like a bank or government clearinghouse. The entries in the blockchain ledger are listed in chronological order, and may be added to by network members, for instance, those running Bitcoin software. Transactions between two parties are broadcast to this member network who then can validate them, add them to their own copy of the ledger, and then rebroadcast these additions to others.

Bitcoin is not 'money' (Ramasastry 2014) in the traditional sense as it is not issued by a sovereign state, and it does not rely on the user to trust in some central authority.

Since each network member stores their own copy of the blockchain, any and all Bitcoin transactions can be independently verified along the entire chain of ownership.

In a network environment that lacks central oversight, it is this combination of a frequent exchange of data entries and a shared public history that is used to validate each transaction and to prevent double spending, that is, spending the same amount more than once.

The security model of blockchain currencies is decentralized. There is no center to the network; no central authority; no concentration of power; and no actor in whom complete trust must be vested. Instead the core security functions are put in the hands of the end users of the system (Antonopoulous 2014).

Since exchanges between parties can occur without the direct or indirect involvement of a central authority, there is no need for government to manage a supply of money or provide regulation around its use. With cryptocurrencies, the 'money' supply can be predicted decades in advance and therefore economic policies that in the past were used to manipulate it (often to the benefit of incumbent governments) are completely unnecessary. The blockchain provides this without compromising a user's privacy or identity, or relinquishing transactional security or system trust.

While Bitcoin advocates, such as Andreas Antonopoulos, are clearly optimistic that cryptocurrencies can help reduce the growing public concerns regarding the safety of online transactions, privacy and identity theft, these digital currencies clearly lessen the risks associated with rich database targets of centralized private information that have been amassed by the work of central authorities in every country.

Furthermore, citizens no longer have to pretend that these authorities will always work in their best interests even when there is long standing evidence that suggests otherwise. Antonopoulos argues that, "we cannot protect consumers by removing their ability to control their own privacy and then ask them to entrust it in the same intermediaries who failed them so many times before" (*Ibid.*).

In addition, according to Tapscott and Tapscott (2015), the blockchain's digital ledger

can be programmed to record not just financial transactions but virtually everything of value and importance to humankind: birth and death certificates, marriage licenses, deeds and titles of ownership, educational degrees, financial accounts, medical procedures, insurance claims, votes, transactions between smart objects, and anything else that can be expressed in code. This ledger represents the 'truth' because mass collaboration constantly reconciles it.

Fundamentally the blockchain is all about replacing the power of central authorities with distributed knowledge, computing power and data storage that is available to all of us through networks. "Every network", says Rosenberg, "requires what programmers call a 'single source of truth'– the authority that says, 'this is real,' 'this user is who she claims to be,' 'this transaction occurred'" (Rosenberg 2015). Until now that 'single source of truth' has been provided by centralized authorities usually in governments and in ways that differ only slightly from feudal times. On the other hand,

the blockchain turns the entire network into its [own] source of truth. It's a mechanism for us to collectively confer legitimacy on one another. That's why it appeals to the same people who fell in love with the Internet and the Web 20 years ago: no individual or company owns it, and anyone can participate in it (Ibid.).

Other initiatives

In many other small ways, citizens have already begun to participate in activities and functions that have long been associated with or dominated by governments. Here are just a few well known illustrations:

- **Education:** e.g. Kahn Academy, Scolaris.ca, the Student Room, Gooru Learning and MOOCS;
- **Health:** e.g. MumsNet, PatientsLikeMe, We Are.Us, MedHelp or SickWeather;
- **Public transportation:** e.g. Zipcar, Uber, FixMyStreet, and a Better Place;
- **Garbage collection:** e.g. Let's Do It Estonia and SeeClickFix;
- **City planning**: e.g. The City 2.0;
- **Oversight:** e.g. citizen journalists via Twitter or YouTube;
- **Disaster relief:** e.g. Ushahidi-Haiti, and Virtual Alabama, and,
- **Space exploration:** e.g. Galaxy Zoo and the X-Prize.

Certainly there is growing evidence that when citizens can use Internet-enabled tools, they do cooperate more. Bring your own solution, the new BYOS, is increasingly the hallmark of social coordination. As a result citizens are developing collaborative solutions for specific issues, but also collaborative solutions for government's traditional turf of social coordination.

Here are some interesting examples:

- **OpenParliament.ca** when the Canadian Parliament wouldn't provide parliamentary data to citizens in an accessible, easy to read format, a single citizen did it himself;
- **TheyWorkforYou.com,** a UK initiative trying to bridge the democratic disconnect through greater transparency and public engagement;
- **Loomio.org,** an open source web application for making group decisions that was originally created during the Occupy Wall Street period;
- **iCitizen Corp.** helps people to stay up-to-date on issues and legislation; helps them rate and connect with elected officials, as well as participate in issue polls, the results of which are then sent to elected officials;
- **Citizen-attache.github.io,** a citizen hackathon to generate insights and analysis for Canada's international aid community;
- **RandomHacksOfKindness,** an international network of events to build solutions that address challenges faced by non-profits, humanitarian and community organizations by making use of public data from all levels of government;
- **Laboratório Ráquer,** or "Hacker Lab," inside the Brazilian Chamber of Deputies that is open for access and use by any citizen so they can utilize public data in a collaborative fashion for actions that enhance citizenship; and
- **DemocracyOS,** an open-source platform created in Argentina that is both Web- and smartphone-based and

can be used for voting and political debate that political parties and governments can download, install, and repurpose in a manner similar to WordPress blogging software.

Consequently, it is not unreasonable to expect that if citizens continue to participate in social coordination in these and other ways, they will eventually demand a larger share of societal governance as real partners-with-government, instead of being just passive recipients of government paternalism.

With the proliferation of online tools to connect, communicate and cooperate, it is likely that we may see a development of a further round of anti-government attitudes, although one based more on the failures of social coordination rather than those currently based on self-interested claims for redistribution.

Those who are most engaged in the development and use of these new alternative modes of communication and coordination have come to regard traditional government as somewhat of an encumbrance – too slow, too corrupt, too lacking in innovation, and benefitting too few. But their response as a consequence, is much less anti-government (in the hopes of reforming government) than it is dissociative anti-government (in the way of failing to see its value adding contribution).

On secession from 'Big G' Government

The movement against the *"Stop Online Piracy Act"* or SOPA of 2012 is an illustration of this shift in mindset. SOPA was solidly supported by American business leaders and key representatives of the US government. But rallying against it was a combination of rag tag, grass roots individuals and a who's who of Internet companies including: Craigslist, Flickr, Google, Mozilla, Reddit, Tumblr, Twitter, Wikipedia, and WordPress. On January 18, 2012, 115,000 websites went offline in protest of SOPA, most notably Wikipedia, in the largest protest action in human history, involving millions of people worldwide, including over 10 million US voters. Said one protester, "The Internet has injected itself into the very fabric of society, [and] it feels like you're fighting the future if you're trying to regulate the Internet like this" (*Seattle Times* 2012: January 18).

According to Yochai Benkler at Harvard University,

the blackout was a very strong public demonstration to suggest that what historically was seen as a technical system of rules that only influences the content industry [through intellectual property regulation], has become something more," adding, *"You've got millions of citizens who care enough to act. That's not trivial" (Ibid.).*

Overnight US Senators went from 80 for SOPA and 31 against to 65 for and 101 against, and SOPA was essentially dead. Millions of people with the means to connect and have their voices heard were enough to override the wishes of their elected representatives.

This new anti-government voice can also be heard among Internet and social media leaders who have begun to fundamentally challenge the existing 'power elites' of government.

Some of these leaders, such as Balaji Srinivasan, the co-founder of Counsyl, Inc. a Silicon Valley DNA testing corporation, have suggested (Leonard 2013) that those citizens dissatisfied with the *status quo* of government are in effect seceding from the 'paper belt' of US power centres (Boston, New York, Washington and Los Angeles) through such online innovations like MOOCs, Kickstarter, Uber, Bitcoin, YouTube, and Blogger. As online innovations continue unabated, virtual secession, he argued, is a natural evolution. In the past, people seeking better lives 'exited' their broken countries, and emigrated to countries like the USA and Canada. Today their descendants can emigrate again, except that now they don't need to go anywhere physically – just into the cloud.

According to Srinivasan,

Exit means giving people the tools to reduce the influence of bad policies over their lives without getting involved in politics ... It basically means building an opt-in society, run by technology, outside government. It's no longer clear," he said, "that [government] can ban something it wants to ban anymore" and without that coercive power and with value generation shifting online, the voices of the established 'paper' powers are becoming less credible in society. "This is how Silicon Valley sees itself now – not just as the delivery vehicle of innovation, but as the avant-garde of a new society unburdened by broken government" (Ibid.).

When Srinivasan says 'exit', he means "building an opt-in society run by technology." In effect what he's describing is the creation of a 'proof of concept' for an online society that operates separate from but parallel to the existing one. In it no one person, no central agency is directing it, and social coordination is a self-emergent property that evolves on the basis of many individual contributions. This is government by other means. For more details, see Tapscott and Tapscott (2016).

It is not only from the availability of new non-governmental social technologies of collaboration, or the emergence of online societies that one may expect disruptive moves in the social order. The cumulative change in the context, in the social representations in good currency, and in the culture governance has transformed Western socio-economies in such a way that Canadian society may be said to be in an unstable state – akin to the phenomenon of supercooling in physics – a phenomenon that points to the fact that a minor disturbances may trigger an instant transformation from liquid to solid at this juncture. In any system in a state of surfusion (the French term for supercooling) even minor shocks to the socio-economic system may trigger major reframing, restructuring and retooling effects – and do so very quickly (Paquet 1993b: 280).

The physicist Hubert Reeves (1986) has used the examples of the horses in Ladoga Lake as an illustration of the phenomenon. In 1942, in Russia, forest fires caused by bombardments forced 1,000 horses to jump into Ladoga Lake to save their lives. Even though the temperature had dropped sharply over the previous few days, and it was very cold, below the freezing point, the water was still liquid. But while the horses were swimming to the other side of the lake, the lake froze suddenly. The day after, the horses had become ice monuments in the middle of the frozen lake. The explanation of this phenomenon is that, when the drop in temperature is too rapid, water does not have time to congeal into ice, and remains liquid at a temperature below zero. But this water was in quite an unstable state: a small disturbance triggered a process of instant ice crystallization.

One may regard the present state of the Canadian socio-economy as close to this state of instability. In such a situation, not only an election may cause a surprise, but new sensitivities may generate a reaction quite different in 2016 to what occurred in 2014 when Federal Minister Tony Clements announced that he would like to demand four competences from federal public servants to increase productivity, and that they would guide him in forthcoming negotiations with the unions: showing integrity and respect, thinking things through, working effectively with others, taking initiative and being action-oriented. This may sound common-sensical to ordinary citizens, but this was not the reaction of public sector unions. The reaction of 17 public service unions was to take the government to court for "disguised discipline." This Kafkaesque scene generated not a scintilla of reaction either in the media or in the intelligentsia in Canada in the spring of 2014 (May 2014), but one may imagine that it might trigger turmoil in a world if the degree of surfusion were a bit higher ... in 2016. Buoyed by recent wins of 'election by spectacle', but nevertheless bereft of the collaborative tools to enhance social coordination, and mired in complex chronic issues that will just not go away, we may hope to see the new governments reach out in ways rarely seen as partners and collaborators in efforts towards co-governance.

Quo vadis?

In a Quantum-like world (Becker 1991), one does not know exactly how the next move toward a more collaborative strategic state might unfold – a crystallisation of a new temporary equilibrium as a result of an ensemble of forces evoked above that are occurring on society's fringe; the result of an unanticipated shock in the global scene that might shake culture governance in the Western democracies out of their somnolence and redistributive rut; the value adding possibilities opened by the new coordination technologies within the light of the current crises; or the spontaneous explosion of anger at a minor Kafkaesque event.

The fact that one cannot predict the way such a transition may unfold does not mean that one cannot anticipate its inevitability, given the growing dysfunctions of our socio-economies, and the fast approaching financial limits to our redistribution schemes and their social acceptability.

There is a sense that the present may be a time in the life of government when the fundamentals are about to change – a strategic inflection point – as Andrew Grove, one of the founders of Intel, might have put it. And at such times, "when not everything is known and when all the data aren't in yet ... you're caught in the turbulence ... and the sad fact is that instinct and judgement are all you've got to guide you through" (Grove 1996: 35).

Recent electoral outcomes, be they in Greece or in Alberta or Canada nationally, have shown us signs that the legitimate frustration among citizens is giving rise to a surprising new appetite for change. However, it may take some time for that anger to find a way to express itself wisely. Inevitably though, after much erratic probing, usually, but not always, bad ideas and their defenders get set aside. But

> *even if any strategic action changes the trajectory on which the [organization] moves by only a few degrees, if those actions are consistent with the image of what the [organization] should look like when it gets to the other side of the inflection point, every one of them will reinforce every other (Ibid.: 147).*

Our intent in this chapter (very much like in the work at the Centre on Governance over the last 20 years) has not been to offer a recipe or to show a mechanical way out of whatever crisis is most current, but to establish the basic conditions of a process that could help us find a way to grow beyond the present situation.

These conditions pertain to:

1. the complex context (showing the ground in motion);
2. the unduly narrow representations we have of the context (more or less crippled by the mental prisons inherited from the past); and,
3. the culture governance or socio-cultural underground (that defines the propensities of our socio-economies to adopt certain types of arrangements or reject them, and to adapt in certain directions rather than others) that constrain or welcome future possibilities.

On the first front, the governance literature has already established beyond reasonable doubt that the context is indeed best approximated as a world where the ground is in motion (Paquet 2005) where:

a. there is an irreversible move from 'Big G' (Government) toward 'small g' (governance);
b. the ever greater degrees of distributed governance are generating more turbulence and instability;
c. there is no one in charge, and there are no shared values; and,
d. where politics and the evolution of society have a quantum quality, where unpredictability and uncertainty are the rule of thumb, and where order is generated from chaos in a largely self-referral manner.

On the second front, current debates are increasingly exposing the crippling epistemologies at the source of the most toxic mental prisons and assumptions that threaten to generate a perpetuation of governance failures (Paquet 2009a/b) by encouraging:

e. the displacement of leadership by stewardship;
f. shared governance over the conservatorship of top-down authorities;
g. social learning that takes us beyond the technical rationality of what we already know; and,
h. progress away from resilience to antifragility.

On the third front, we are only beginning to explore the shift in the culture governance underground in which our socio-economies are anchored, and which shapes to a very great extent the sort of propensities and sensitivities likely to be encouraged by our collective humanity, and the arrangements likely to be most easily adopted or rejected. On this front we are still very much in *terra incognita*, in a world filled with taboo topics like, among others:

i. the unbearable lightness of citizenship (Paquet 2008);
j. the uncritical deference to some forms of authority, in particular superbureaucrats (Paquet 2014a);
k. the well-known paradoxical nature of Canada's national character (Ross 1954); and,
l. the peculiar fabric of the Canadian *habitus* or propensities to react (Paquet 2014b: chapter 5).

These elements constitute not only a challenging program of academic research but also a challenge for practitioners to develop the requisite skills, behaviours and practices to properly surf the waves of change.

In summary

This chapter has taken the view that we find ourselves at a strategic inflection point where what has served us well in the past no longer does so. That in itself has an element of anti-government challenge in it.

What we need is a public conversation on the importance of reframing government via critical thinking:

1. toward the convergence of coordination and collaboration challenges in the inquiring manner we have hinted in chapter 6; and,
2. away from divergent and divisive redistribution issues – which are unlikely to bring forth cooperation, effectiveness, innovation and antifragility.

The new promising, non-state mechanisms that are emerging might help to bring back coordination and collaboration to the centre of the governmental stage by providing alternatives to the state. The open questions are (1) whether the governments will actively fight them and try to sideline and delegitimize them on the coordination front; or whether they will reach for accommodation with them; and (2) what will be the ultimate outcome of this conflict among different avenues for social coordination.

The challenge now is to build on an old idea introduced in public discussion by Albert Hirschman in 1971 – the idea of "possibilism" (Hirschman 1971).

It consists in a deliberate investment in the discovery of paths, however narrow, leading to an outcome that appears to be foreclosed on the basis of probabilistic reasoning alone, in an approach that is built on the possibility of increasing the number of ways in which the occurrence of change in the status quo can be visualized (Paquet 1993b: 280).

After decades of governance failures, it is our view that we have learned enough from past mistakes to be tempted to turn those daring experiments at the fringe of the socio-economy into assets and use them as a spur to reimagine and reinvigorate government and those that inhabit it.

References

Antonopoulos, Andreas M. 2014. "Bitcoin and Cryptocurrencies," presented to the Senate Committee on Banking, Trade and Commerce, *Study on the use of digital currency*, 11th session, October 8, 2014. www.youtube.com/watch?v=xUNGFZDO8mM [Accessed March 24, 2016].

Bang, Henrik P. 2003. "A new ruler meeting a new citizen: culture governance and everyday making" in H.P. Bang (ed.). *Governance as social and political communication*. Manchester, UK: Manchester University Press, p. 241-266.

Becker, Thomas L. 1991. *Quantum Politics – Applying Quantum Theory to Political Phenomana*. New York, NY: Praeger.

Bevir, Mark and R.A.W. Rhodes. 2010. *The State as Cultural Practice*. Oxford, UK: Oxford University Press.

Boland, Richard J., and Fred Collopy (eds.). 2004. *Managing as Designing*. Stanford, CA: Stanford University Press.

Block, Peter. 2008. *Community: The Structure of Belonging*. San Francisco, CA: Berrett-Koehler.

Christensen, Tom and Per Lægreid. 2004. *The Fragmented State – The Challenges of Combining Efficiency, Institutional Norms and Democracy*, Working Paper 3. Bergen, NO: Stein Rokkan Centre for Social Studies, Unifob AS, March, http://cms.uni.no/media/manual_upload/65_N03-04.Christensen-Lagreid.pdf [Accessed March 24, 2016].

de Tocqueville, Alexis. 1840/1961. *De la démocratie en Amérique*, vols. I and II. Paris, FR: Gallimard.

Edelman Trust Barometer. 2015. *Annual Global Study*, Vancouver, BC: Edelman, January 19, www.edelman.com/news/trust-institutions-drops-level-great-recession/ [Accessed March 24, 2016].

Farrell, Henry and Cosma Shalizi. 2013. "An Outline of Cognitive Democracy," in *LaPietra Dialogues, Social Media and Political Participation*, May 10-11, www.lapietradialogues.org/area/pubblicazioni/doc000071.pdf [Accessed March 24, 2016].

Foster, G.M. 1972. "The Anatomy of Envy: A study of symbolic behavior," *Current Anthropology*, XIII (2): 165-202.

Foster, Wayne and Christopher Wilson. 2014. "Illustrations in Public Health of a More Collaborative Public Service," *www.optimumonline.ca*, 44(4): 21-44.

Grove, Andrew. 1996. *Only the Paranoid Survive*. New York, NY: Currency-Doubleday Books.

Gwyn, Richard. 1995. *Nationalism without Walls – The Unbearable Lightness of Being Canadian*. Toronto, ON: McClelland & Stewart.

Hagel, John. 2009. "A Labor Day Manifesto for a New World," *Edge Perspectives*, September 7. http://edgeperspectives.typepad.com/

edge_perspectives/2009/09/a-labor-day-manifesto-for-a-new-world.html [Accessed March 24 2016].

Hamel, Gary, quoted in Lucas Mearian. 2013. "The next corporate revolution will be power to the peons," *Computerworld*, June 4, www.computerworld.com/article/2497414/it-management/the-next-corporate-revolution-will-be-power-to-the-peons.html [Accessed March 24, 2016].

Hirschman, Albert O. 1971. *A Bias for Hope*. New Haven, CN: Yale University Press.

Hubbard, Ruth and Gilles Paquet. 2007. "Public-Private Partnership and the 'porcupine' problem" in G.B. Doern (ed.). *How Ottawa Spends 2007-08, The Harper Conservatives – Climate of Change*. Montreal, QC and Kingston, ON: McGill-Queen's University Press, p. 254-272.

Jackson, Edward. 2015. "Policy from the bottom up is needed," *Ottawa Citizen*, May 25, C5.

Jantsch, Erich. 1980. *The Self-Organizing Universe*. Oxford, UK: Pergamon Press.

Kekes, John. 2003. *The Illusions of Egalitarianism*. Ithaca, NY: Cornell University Press.

Kindleberger, Charles P. 1978. *The Aging Economy*. Kiel, DE: Institute für Weltwirtschaft.

Laurent, Paul and Gilles Paquet. 1991. "Intercultural Relations: a Myrdal-Tocqueville-Girard Interpretative Scheme," *International Political Science Review*, 12(3): 173-185.

Leonard, Andrew. 2013. "Silicon Valley dreams of secession," *Salon*, October 28, www.salon.com/2013/10/28/silicon_valley_dreams_of_secession/ [Accessed March 24, 2016].

Levert, Stéphane. 2013. *Sustainability of the Canadian Health Care System and Impact of the 2014 Revision to the Canada Health Transfer*. Ottawa, ON: Canadian Institute of Actuaries, www.cia-ica.ca/docs/default-source/2013/213075e.pdf [Accessed March 24, 2016].

Lévesque, Benoît. 2012. *Social Innovation and Governance in Public Management Systems: Limits of NPM and Search for Alternatives?* Montreal, QC: Centre de recherche sur les innovations sociales (CRISES), Université du Québec à Montréal, Collection Études théoriques - no ET1116, March: 25, https://crises.uqam.ca/upload/files/publications/etudes-theoriques/ET1116_GS.pdf [Accessed March 24, 2016].

Martin, Roger and Karen Christensen (eds.). 2013. *Rotman on Design*. Toronto, ON: Rotman-University of Toronto Press.

May, Kathryn. 2014. "Unions grieve new PS performance rules," *Ottawa Citizen*, April 6, A1.

Musgrave, Richard A. 1959. *The Theory of Public Finance*. New York, NY: McGraw Hill.

Naím, Moisés. 2013. *The End of Power – From boardrooms to battlefields and churches to states, why being in charge isn't what it used to be.* New York, NY: Basic Books.

Olson Jr., Mancur. 1965. *The Logic of Collective Action – Public Goods and the Theory of Groups*. Cambridge, MA: Harvard University Press.

Olson, Jr. Mancur. 1982. *The Rise and Decline of Nations – Economic Growth, Stagnation and Social Rigidities*. New Haven, CN: Yale University Press.

Paquet, Gilles. 1992. "The Strategic State," in J. Chrétien (ed.). *Finding Common Ground*. Hull, QC: Voyageur Publishing, p. 85-101.

Paquet, Gilles. 1993a. "Maybe the IMF can save us from our debt," *Ottawa Citizen*, January 17.

Paquet, Gilles. 1993b. "Sciences transversales et savoirs d'expérience: the art of trespassing," *Revue générale de droit*, 24(2): 269-281.

Paquet, Gilles. 1994. "Reinventing Governance," *Opinion Canada*, 2(2): 1-5.

Paquet, Gilles 1996a. "La grisaille des institutions," in S. Coulombe and Gilles Paquet (eds.). *La ré-invention des institutions et le rôle de l'État.* Montreal, QC: Association des économistes québécois, p. 395-423.

Paquet, Gilles. 1996b. "Le fruit dont l'ignorance est la saveur," in A. Armit and J. Bourgault (eds.). *Hard Choices, No Choices: Assessing Program Review.* Toronto, ON: IPAC/Canadian Plains Research Centre, p. 47-58.

Paquet, Gilles. 1996-1997. "The Strategic State," *Ciencia Ergo Sum,* 3(3): 257-261, (Part I); 4(1): 28-34, (Part 2); 4(2): 148-154, (Part 3).

Paquet, Gilles. 1997. "Alternative Program Delivery: Transforming the Practices of Governance," in Robin Ford and David Zussman (eds.). *Alternative Service Delivery: Sharing Governance in Canada.* Toronto, ON: RIPAC/KPMG, p. 31-58.

Paquet, Gilles. 1999a. "Innovations in Governance in Canada," *www.optimumonline.ca,* 29(2-3): 71-81.

Paquet, Gilles. 1999b. "Tectonic Changes in Canadian Governance," in Les lie Pal (ed.). *How Ottawa Spends 1999-2000 – Shape Shifting: Canadian Governance Towards the 21st Century.* Toronto, ON: Oxford University Press, p. 75-111.

Paquet, Gilles. 2004. "If every desire becomes a right, the real rights are devalued," *Ottawa Citizen,* June 18.

Paquet, Gilles. 2005. *The New Geo-Governance – A Baroque Approach.* Ottawa, ON: University of Ottawa Press.

Paquet, Gilles. 2008. *Deep Cultural Diversity – A Governance Challenge.* Ottawa, ON: University of Ottawa Press.

Paquet, Gilles. 2009a. *Crippling Epistemologies – A Plea for Experimentation.* Ottawa, ON: University of Ottawa Press.

Paquet, Gilles. 2009b. *Scheming Virtuously: The road to collaborative governance.* Ottawa, ON: Invenire Books.

Paquet, Gilles. 2012. *Moderato cantabile: Toward principled governance for Canada's immigration policy.* Ottawa, ON: Invenire Books.

Paquet, Gilles. 2013. *Tackling Wicked Policy Problems: Equality, Diversity, and Sustainability.* Ottawa, ON: Invenire Books.

Paquet, Gilles. 2014a. "Super-bureaucrats as *enfants du siècle*," *www.optimumonline.ca*, 44(2): 4-14.

Paquet, Gilles. 2014b. *Unusual Suspects: Essays on Social Learning Disabilities.* Ottawa, ON: Invenire Books.

Paquet, Gilles. 2014c. "Gouvernance," in Frank Tannery *et al. Encyclopédie de la stratégie.* Paris, FR: Vuibert, p. 645-656.

Paquet, Gilles and Robert Shepherd. 1996. "The Program Review Process: A Deconstruction," in G. Swimmer (ed.). *How Ottawa Spends 1996-97 – Life Under the Knife*, Ottawa, ON: Carleton University Press, p. 39-72.

Paquet, Gilles and Christopher Wilson. 2011. "Collaborative Co-Governance as Inquiring Systems," *www.optimumonline.ca*, 41(2): 1-12.

Paquet, Gilles and Christopher Wilson. 2015. "Collaboration in the absence of *affectio societatis*," *www.optimumonline.ca*, 45(1): 40-48.

Plansky, John, Tim O'Donnell, and Kimberly Richards. 2016. "A Strategist's Guide to Blockchain," *Strategy + Business*, January 11, p. 20.

Prigogine, Ilya and Isabelle Stengers. 1984. *Order Out of Chaos: Man's new dialogue with nature.* Toronto, ON: Bantam Books.

Ramasastry, Anita. 2014. "Is Bitcoin Money? Lawmakers, Regulators and Judges Don't Agree," *Verdict*, September 9, https://verdict.justia.com/2014/09/09/bitcoin-money [Accessed March 25, 2016].

Reeves, Hubert. 1986. *L'art de s'enivrer.* Paris, FR: Le Seuil.

Rocan, Claude. 2011. "The Voluntary Sector in Public Health," *www.optimumonline.ca*, 41(4): 18-40.

Rosenberg, Scott. 2015. "There's a Blockchain for That," *Backchannel*, January 13, https://medium.com/backchannel/how-bitcoins-blockchain-could-power-an-alternate-internet-bb501855af67 [Accessed March 25, 2016].

Ross, Malcolm (ed.). 1954. *Our Sense of Identity*. Toronto, ON: Ryerson Press.

Seattle Times. 2012. "Internet's dark day: Anti-piracy bills take a beating," *Seattle Times*. January 18. www.seattletimes.com/nation-world/internets-dark-day-anti-piracy-bills-take-a-beating/ [Accessed March 25, 2016].

Senge, Peter *et al.* 2008. *The Necessary Revolution: How Individuals and Organizations are Working Together to Create a Sustainable World*. Toronto, ON: Doubleday.

Srinivasan, Balaji. 2013. "Balaji Srinivasan at Startup School 2013," www.youtube.com/watch?v=cOubCHLXT6A [Accessed March 25, 2016].

Stein, Janice G. 2001. *The Cult of Efficiency*. Toronto, ON: Anansi.

Taleb, Nassim N. 2012. *Antifragile – Things that gain from disorder*. New York, NY: Random House.

Tapscott, Don and Alex. 2015. *What's the Next Generation Internet? Surprise: It's all about the Blockchain!* March 12, www.huffingtonpost.com/don-tapscott/whats-the-nextgeneration-_b_6859156.html [Accessed March 25, 2016].

Tapscott, Don and Alex. 2016. *Blockchain Revolution – How the technology behind bitcoin is changing money, business, and the world*. Toronto, ON: Portfolio/Penguin Canada.

Tussman, Joseph. 1977. *Government and the Mind*. New York, NY: Oxford University Press.

Vargas Lloosa, Mario. 2015. *La civilisation du spectacle*. Paris, FR: Gallimard.

Watson, William. 2015. *The Inequality Trap – Fighting Capitalism Instead of Poverty*. Toronto, ON: University of Toronto Press.

Wilson, Christopher. 2007. *Attention to Place: An International Comparative Review of National Community-Based Policies for Social and Economic Development.* Prepared for Strategic Policy Research Branch. Ottawa, ON: HRSDC.

Wilson, Christopher. 2008. "Attention to Place to Correct Policy Imbalance," *www.optimumonline.ca*, 38(1): 17-25.

CONCLUSION

| Governing Intelligently

"... l'immense chemin qui passe entre plusieurs mondes"
Denis Grozdanovitch

Social and issue complexity entails that there are a number of persons or groups committed to change, that they hold different values, and are in pursuit of different goals. Moreover, no one is fully in charge, and therefore there is no such thing as an objective function that clearly defines the so-called 'collective goals' or public interest. Since the path-breaking work of Kenneth Arrow, we know that one cannot aggregate the diverse preferences of a multitude of individuals and groups into a coherent and consistent order. One has to be satisfied with seeking access to feasible and viable avenues that would appear not to violate too blatantly the different sets of constraints of too many of those disparate groups (Wilson 2011).

Another consequence of this complexity is the persistence of fundamental uncertainty: the recognition that the state of the world is not given, or static, or even statistically ascertainable. It is continually evolving due to the ongoing interactions among its existing components. Moreover, this environment is further disturbed by our very human actions that attempt to nudge organizations or social systems in certain directions. Consequently the environment itself is in motion.

Intelligent governing is, in a way, nothing less that finding a road to dynamic accommodation between these two evolving worlds – the evolving human organization and the evolving external environment.

As suggested in Paquet and Wilson (2011), this requires the design of an inquiring system that needs to be interactive, reflexive, adaptive, dialectically evolving, and engaged in wayfinding, while simultaneously seeking accommodation among the different groups that hold portions of power, resources and information, in a manner that secures their continued participation and contribution. Such inquiring systems are engines of discovery and social learning but, at the same time, they are engines of coordination and collaboration through the harmonization of the diverse conceptual frameworks and knowledge repositories of each partner who cannot succeed without working with others.

In such a complex, uncertain and heterogeneous world, progress on complex issues can only be accomplished by *tâtonnement,* or trial-and-error, through a search process that builds on ever improved inputs and outputs via ever more intelligent sets of processes. This may include: more stakeholders having a part of the power, resources and information, more effective cognitive learning rules, a broader design of hybrid networks capable of weaving coordination and collaboration arrangements, etc. And all are in the throes of a dynamic that combines self-organizing forces with deliberate nudging to influence those ever emerging processes.

In this world, governing is not about asserting control but it is concerned with the construction of communication patterns that encourage collective learning, and enable coordination and cooperation through various families of linkages, making use of principles, mechanisms, conventions, moral contracts, etc.

As Helmut Willke (2007: 25) puts it, "governance produces patterns of communication and the need to organize communication creates the demand for governance." Good governance creates collective coherence and coordination through effective communication and learning. It is not solely an exercise of making choice and imposing will. Organizations and social systems are assemblages of people, architectures of relations, routines and cultures: all are not equally malleable in the short run – relations and routines (and sometimes the mix of people) may be more readily modified than culture. Yet the 'right' mix of people, relations and routines will generate a change in culture.

In the tradition of Kenneth Boulding

One of the main challenges for intelligent governance is to ensure the requisite degree of coordination through networked ecologies of governance (Paquet 1995).

This fluid and dispersive organizational/institutional reality is made up of three generic ensembles of organizations, dominated by different informational mechanisms – *quid pro quo* exchange (market economy), coercion (polity), and reciprocity (community and society). Kenneth Boulding (1970) used a simple triangle as a mapping device – with each of these families of integrating mechanisms in their purest form at one of the apexes, and all the inner territory representing organizations and institutions embodying different mixes of these different informational mechanisms.

There is a tendency for modern society to be seen as instituted process to elicit the development of an ever larger number of mixed-signal arrangements, blending these different mechanisms in order to provide the necessary signposts and orientation maps in our complex and confusing world. This translates into a much denser filling of the Boulding triangle: mixed arrangements capable of providing the basis for mediation, cooperation, harmonization, concertation, and even co-decision making involving agents or organizations from the three sectors (Laurent and Paquet 1998).

One can stylize this development via a series of emerging concentric circles within which there are different degrees of institutional and organizational mixing. This is depicted in Figure 5.

Figure 5. An Adapted Boulding Triangle

Economy

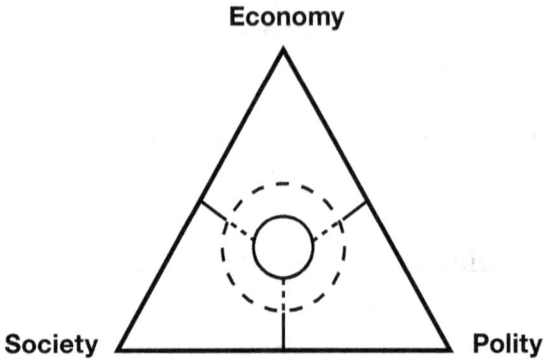

Society   **Polity**

Source: Boulding, 1970.

Two centrally important characteristics of these parallel processes of co-evolution (of the system and its environment) and joint evolution (economy, society, polity) are resilience (the capacity for the economy-polity-society nexus to spring not too badly damaged from the pressures or shocks emerging from the environment, through some rearrangements that do not modify the basic nature of the overall system), and learning (the capacity to improve current performance – however defined – as a result of experience, through a redefinition of the existing arrangements to ensure coordination but also of the overall objectives; and a modification of behaviour and structures as a result of new circumstances).

These two characteristics exist in creative tension, since resilience calls for preservation, whereas learning implies change. They must be kept in some sort of balance. Managing well this tension demands agility – i.e., a capacity to switch to a greater or lesser dependence on one family of integrative mechanisms or another as circumstances change. To cope with an environment that is turbulent and generates surprises, organizations and societies must be able to use their environment and institutions strategically in much the same way as the surfer uses the wave to adapt more quickly. This calls for "un-centralization" (Cleveland 2002) and subsidiarity for two reasons.

Firstly, because the game of learning is going to generate more innovation if component parts of a system are empowered to take decisions on the spot due to their superior awareness of the circumstances. In fact, the best learning experience of this kind can be carried out through highly decentralized and flexible teams, woven by moral contracts and reciprocal obligations, and negotiated in the context of evolving partnerships (Lester and Piore 2004).

Secondly, when faced with turbulent environments, organizations can only govern themselves effectively by experimenting, by becoming capable of learning both what their goals are, and the means to reach them as they proceed. To do so, they must include as many of the relevant stakeholders as possible in that conversation, and bring forward each bit of knowledge and wisdom from each person who has a bearing on the issue (Piore 1995).

However, reconciling resilience and learning can ultimately have but one result: learning overtakes resilience and 'transforms' it into antifragility, i.e., a capacity to spring back not only undamaged from shocks but also be more capable to overcome more powerful, ever faster, more effective, and stronger future shocks (Taleb 2012).

Building on this approach

Organizations are complex adaptive systems and not simple linear amalgamations of agent-principal relations. They can have outcomes which no agent of the system may have intended – emergent outcomes that one cannot make sense of without an understanding of what the system is about, of what processes underpin it, how it works in reality, and how it evolves in ways that are not necessarily simple, or linear, or predictable (Paquet 2014a: 177ff).

This is as true for understanding why an organization may have evolved in certain ways, or failed in others, as it is for understanding why the elephant has evolved a trunk. Therefore, developing an appreciation of an organization as a system entails not being satisfied with a snapshot of one of its dimensions (like its organizational chart or financial statements), but focusing on an appreciation of the organization as a whole and of the nexus of forces that underpin its dynamics – something that cannot be accomplished without a blending of its many perspectives and approaches to its many facetted characteristics.

Two of these blending efforts (among the many that exist in systems thinking) may be singled out as being particularly important for the sort of explorations typical of inquiring systems: the one is the blending of stakeholder perspectives into a synthetic one that transcends the myopic tyranny of reductive analytical modes of inquiry and partial information, and the other is the reconciliation of the agonistic tensions among the different agents and groups in order to generate a broader and more encompassing and effective organizational capacity than any one partner may have.

   a. The synthesis perspective stands in contrast to what Valerie Brown has described as the dominant form of Western culture that shines brightly on individualism, competition, hierarchy, and analytical thinking. Tools for synthesis-based thinking, collaborative inquiry, and integrative governance lie in the shadows (Brown 2008). This analytical bent has led to efforts to 'solve' problems by slicing issue domains into ever smaller segments where simple formal cause-effect and instrumental rationality relations can be more easily imagined. This has fuelled a representation of the world as fractured and disjointed, characterized by isolated local zones of pseudo-instrumental rationality and certainty. In this manner, disciplines have imposed their dominant lenses, based on axiomatic systems, and claiming to be able to deduce what forms institutions and organizations should have from partial but supposedly universal principles.

The belief that knowledge of the parts predicts the knowledge of the whole is a notion that has been falsified in every scientific discipline. And yet, it retains its currency with the social sciences wherein disciplines remain anchored in very narrow conceptions of humans, and in very reductive methods of inquiry (Katouzian 1980; Paquet 2009: 32ff).

Synthesis, by contrast, maintains the advantages of specialized inquiry, but finds better ways to foster holism by:

- developing synoptic perspectives that combine and blend different points of view on any given theme;
- reclaiming the capacity of contributors to construct a whole, and develop a synergy by their constructive interactions;
- generating both a fresh and sometimes unpredicted whole from unit parts, and incomplete knowledge and integrative thinking capable of constructing collective decisions (open-ended, future-directed, etc.); and,
- nudging successful change as a result of the recognition that the parts exist in dispersive relationship to each other, even as they form an effective whole.

By ensuring that integrative thinking is given its proper place (which should be large), new ways of scoping the context, new principles, and new tools will emerge. Synthesis is an approach that tries hard to ensure the parts find a way back to the whole, to put Humpty Dumpty back together again if you will.

b. The more synoptic reconciliatory view encompassing many perspectives and many points of view is bound to produce an appreciation that goes much beyond the narrow ambit of the rationalist ideology and its dreams of a universal method, a perfect language, or a unitary system. Much of the last century has lived under the theoretical charm of rationalism, but *de facto* what has emerged in parallel is a process of inquiry that has proceeded in a zigzag fashion – building on the interaction of rationalist forays with empiricist inquiries that fed on one another, not in search for *characteristica universalis,* but of a promising language of inquiry likely to generate workable stewardship and wayfinding to enable the capacity to work together (Vickers 1965).

Toulmin (2001) makes a powerful call to redress the balance between the imperatives of narrow instrumental rationality and of reasonableness, and argues for the need to confront the challenge of an uncertain and unpredictable world by returning to a more humane and compassionate form of reason, one that accepts diversity and complexity as integral and essential parts of human nature, and establishes this as the wellspring of all intellectual inquiry.

This is the sort of roadmap for instance proposed by Valerie Brown and her group in Australia (Brown *et al.* 2010). However, not all the work advertised under this rubric is so focused. Much that is advertised as new, open and collaborative, under the guise of network governance, can often be regarded as rhetoric and window dressing around some thinly camouflaged defence of old style leadership promising to 'tackle wicked problems,' be more collaborative, and to be open to learning and sharing power.[23]

Four additional design challenges

Boland and Collopy (2004: 10) have attempted to move beyond the traditional management focus on efficiency (doing the thing right) and effectiveness (doing the right thing) when they emphasized the distinction between the decision attitudes (that choose from the alternatives that are already at hand) and the design attitudes (that strive to construct a more satisfying possibility than that previously proposed or readily available).

The design process is more fluid, more open, more novelty-oriented, searching outside the box, as it explores new alternatives. 'Governing as designing' represents a more comprehensive view of social coordination, and *Rotman Magazine* has done much to propound that point of view (Martin and Christensen 2013).

---

[23] This variegated literature – even at its best in the works of Valerie Brown and consorts – seems to be most reluctant to completely abandon the language of leadership (with all its baggage), and consequently has generated much confusion in allowing the impression that wicked policy problems could be tackled through the traditional approaches if those were slightly more open and adjusted (Goldsmith and Eggers 2004; Nickerson and Sanders 2013; Eggers and Macmillan 2013, 2015).

Intelligent governance as a design process gambles on a broader worldview and looks at a longer time horizon. It aims at nurturing not only the organizational resilience but the antifragility of the organization to continually adapt through innovation – i.e., an improved capacity to overcome (Taleb 2012).

This entails not only self-referential contextualization, but also taking into account both the organization and its circumstances: a broader and richer context, a longer time horizon, and a more comprehensive notion of the relevant worlds the organization is facing or could potentially face.

But intelligent governance digs deeper still: to its roots in interpersonal resources (Foa 1971). Design calls for more than simple technical rationality, but for *Wertrationalität à la Max Weber* (i.e., value rationality) in order to probe 'the good' and not just 'the functional': indeed for exploring where only human imagination can go (Ramos 1981: 6-7, 24-27).

The sort of journey of inquiry, through which intelligent wayfinding takes us, goes much beyond the efficiency-effectiveness world of exploitation of existing knowledge into an exploration of entirely new territories like smart governance, wise governance, cognitive governance, and heuristic governance.

Governing smartly brings forth references to 'goodness of fit' with the broader context in order to enable the stewardship to operate opportunistically both in the short and medium run; governing wisely carries with it the imperatives of 'goodness of fit' brought forth by the notion of burden of office (Tussman 1989; Paquet 1997) – therefore it is an echo of broader cultural and ethical dimensions; governing cognitively opens up exploration of the unknown – thereby factoring in the *terra incognita* that one may imagine but not yet touch; and governing heuristically carries with it the willingness to go even further and to gamble on the possibility of uncovering, through experimentation, not only what had heretofore been regarded as unknowables, but also new paths and possibilities that one may not yet have even imagined.

Intelligent governance is within reach

The reader may have come to appreciate during this book-length voyage to intelligent governance that obstacles are important. Indeed, they are important, but they are not impossible to overcome. Many mental prisons are toxic, and the lack of critical thinking is debilitating. And yet those governance failures have been sufficiently costly and citizens are becoming aware of the fact that the existing arrangements are unsatisfactory.

This explains the variety of alternative arrangements that have blossomed over the last while.

Some additional levers have also recently become available, including: the need for a more comprehensive goodness of fit, some path-breaking work in Australia, and some promising exploratory work done in Canada.

In the name of ever more comprehensive goodness of fit

All these labels (efficiently, effectively – dealt with earlier – and smartly, wisely, cognitively, heuristically) are abbreviations for ever more ambitious ensembles of principles, mechanisms and stratagems capable of infusing improved and richer forms of coordination back into the exigencies of a collective human system in real time, while taking into account an ever broader context and richer environment (Willke 2007). We have already mentioned many of these principles, mechanisms and stratagems in chapter 7, but we have developed them more extensively in recent works (Paquet 2011: Part I; Paquet 2014b).

These contraptions point in several general directions. But at minimum they translate into mechanisms to ensure that organizations and social systems are well-adjusted to all their circumstances – internal and external.

The mechanisms that inspire cooperation (moral contracts, reframing of perspectives to accommodate divergent views of the world, modifying the conceptual framework, etc.) as well as the behaviours that inhibit it (denial, cognitive dissonance, contagion, cumulative causation, mimesis, herd movements, cascades, synchronicity, etc.) produce different results depending on specific circumstances, and consequently, they can either accelerate or decelerate adjustments.

Some principles, (maximum participation, true prices and costs), have easily identifiable mechanisms associated with them that are likely to be operative and helpful in most situations in the short run. For instance, maximum participation may encourage the creation of forums or the facilitation of dialogues. In the same manner, efforts to make costs and prices close to true prices and costs may be encouraged by the removal of artificial protective measures. That said, many of the usual subterfuges (transparency, sermon, carrot and stick) are likely to be tractable in the short run, and to have some degree of impact.

However, other principles (subsidiarity, competition, multi-stability) may require some modification of the structure and operations of government, including legislative changes or changes in basic rules or conventions, and this may take some time.

The whole process of mechanism design may, therefore, become even more delicate and challenging when one no longer focuses only on the organization as an independent entity, but also on:

1. the interfaces between the organization and its environment (like the labour-management interface, the different interfaces among segments of the value chain, the world of externalities, the management-governance interface, etc.); and,

2. the ways in which one might be able to deal with particular organizational failures by identifying specific mechanisms at particular interfaces within the organization (Paquet and Ragan 2012).

This new unbounded outside (beyond the frontiers created by the milieu, the socio-cultural ethos, and the leaden wall of ignorance) is in a way a denial of the very notion of organizational limitations. Its only limits are those of the creative powers of its designers, and those imposed by the collective consciousness of society, reflected in all the potentialities of the different components of the governance apparatus that an imaginative designer can pull together.

This type of governance challenge is akin to the voyage of discovery that began when partners and stewards came to recognize that the assumptions, which they were not aware they were making, constituted important mental prisons. This constituted an invitation to escape from the trappings of traditional corporate governance with its crew of usual suspects (shareholders, managers, committees, and boards of directors) and the plumbing that connected them (Gomez 2015). It allowed them to focus on a basket of co-governance rules that enabled them to confront a broader world of stakeholders and a much richer world of flexible purpose organizations which were calling out to be invented (Segrestin and Hatchuel 2012; Paquet 2013: chapter 6).

That sort of re-orientation is an inevitable part of intelligent governance, but it can only begin when, architecturally speaking, one no longer feels trapped into replicating the dull modernism of Le Corbusier architecture any longer, and everyone feels compelled to enter a post-Gehry world where even the very notion of 'what is a house?' is an open question.[24]

In this vein, organization design becomes the new definition of governing.

Brown and the Australian gambit

In this context, Valerie Brown and her colleagues have been one of the few groups involved in governance redesign that have dared to put imagination at the centre of their research program. It is a dimension that underpins much of their work because creative design means using imagination to go beyond the simple recombination of established principles and mechanisms, to view the terrain of operations differently

---

[24] Le Corbusier was a Swiss-French architect (1887-1965) well-known for the purity and harmony of the forms he designed. Frank Gehry is a Canadian born/American architect (1929-) who has been boldly experimenting and has sought to escape from the Le Corbusier so-called Modernist style.

and with new eyes. It does not simply look over the wall of ignorance, but it uses imagination to detect, beyond the flow of new data, some new patterns of potentialities and possibilities.

Such ambitious design efforts have helped to develop capabilities and capacities that use collective learning as a method for transformational change by Brown's group in Australia (Brown et al. 2010; Brown and Lambert 2013).

The basic comparative advantage of this team was two-fold: first, the fact that the Australian government has taken seriously the notion of wicked problems, and has been willing to fund research on how to tackle policy problems defined as wicked; and second, the fact that Brown et al. have focused their interest on a family of wicked problems related to environmental issues.

In Brown et al. (2010), the team explored ways to tackle such wicked problems in 15 separate studies. In Brown and Lambert (2012), the team created a guide for collective action. However, in both cases, their emphasis on the mechanics of collective action and how to mix different sorts of knowledge has meant that their *problematique* remained all too often trapped within the language and narrow framework of synoptic thinking. This meant that their focus on coordination dominated over the equally important focus on shared discovery and innovation, in terms of practical new collective arrangements, as well as problem solutions.

We believe that this has resulted in planning and leadership traps being incompletely exorcised, in addition to the efficiency and optimization challenges that flow from them. Indeed, the complexities of their inquiring system were unduly simplified as a result.

Far from insisting on the emergent nature of the problem definition and on the necessary *tâtonnement* process imposed by this emergence, the focus on a synoptic view tended to allow an artificial coalescence of the problem definition as if it could and would mechanically lend itself to the requirements of collective action once synoptically stated. The process of emergence was, therefore, somewhat smothered. The multidimensional wickedness of the problem was assumed to dissolve when the disparities of partial perspectives, one dimension of wickedness, were resolved by synoptic harmonization. Unfortunately things tend to be not that simple – relational, temporal and evolutionary dimensions still exist to confound attempts at changing the *status quo*, especially during implementation phases. Thus, the presumption that the harmonization of points of view by itself resolves the difficulties inherent in coordination and collaboration is ill-founded. Wicked problems pose two sets of difficulties (situational and representational), and a synoptic perspective handles only the representational challenge.

Yet Brown's pioneering work has thrown some most useful light on the work ahead on collaboration.

Some explorations at the frontiers

The work at the Centre on Governance of the University of Ottawa has focused on the blockages to the development of intelligent governance and on the various pathologies that have ensued.

For instance, Paquet and Ragan (2012: 92-93) have shown that a recent study by Dov Seidman[25] of some 5,000 managers and executives in the United States indicated that we already know what organizational form works best, but that we seem to be prevented from acting on the basis of this evidentiary knowledge by cultural/moral forces.

Seidman discovered that companies fit into three categories: Type I (blind obedience) organizations relying on top-down command-and-control; Type II (informed acquiescence) organizations that have clear-cut rules and procedures based on rewards and punishments; and Type III (self-governance) organizations where people at all levels are trusted to act on their own initiative to collaboratively innovate, and common norms and principles guide employee and company behaviour.

---

[25] "The Thought Leader Interview of Dov Seidman" by Art Kleiner, *Strategy+Business*, Issue 67, Summer 2012 (published on May 29, 2012). The results of the study have been vindicated in 17 other countries. Our summary here draws freely from a portion of chapter 5 in Paquet and Ragan (2012).

This study found that Type III organizations outperformed the others substantially on many fronts as can be gauged from Table 5 below.

TABLE 5.

Performance of Organizational Forms

	Type I	Type II	Type III
Above average			
Financial performance	52%	77%	92%
Reporting of misconduct	26%	62%	94%
Superior			
Rapid adoption of new ideas	18%	67%	94%

Yet, of the companies surveyed, it was discovered that Type I organizations made up 43 percent; Type II made up 54 percent; and Type III made up only three percent of the companies surveyed.

The accumulation of oblique evidence of a link between sociality/morality and performance (through a very different shaping of governance) is such that, despite some looseness of these relationships, their connection has come to be regarded as important for organizations to reshape their culture and ethos (even though such actions have proven to take time and to be very difficult on occasion) or at least to recognize that the ethos has an impact on performance (O'Donovan 2007; Willke 2009).

This intermingling of cultural and moral forces has been casually dismissed by those extreme secularists intent on completely exorcizing any moral or cultural dimension from discussions of public affairs in the world of 'Big G' Government. However, this is an unrealistic attitude. The central forces that shape the burden of office of partners in any organization are in part inspired by beliefs and morality, even if no homogeneous, shared values exist. Both of these contribute to the common public culture, and it is neither easy nor necessary to insist on a neat partitioning of the social and the moral: both matter.

The Canadian federal public service: a vignette in the spring 2016

The sort of cultural freeze evoked at the end of the last section often blocks the smooth evolution of governing arrangements. Indeed, this explains the extraordinary inertia one can notice in the ways in which the Canadian federal public service adapts to new circumstances.

There is a particular tradition in public administration defending the view that the primary function of the bureaucracy is to protect, maintain and preserve the administrative institutions in a manner consistent with constitutional processes, traditions, values and beliefs – whatever these may mean. For those holding this view, the notion of 'administrative conservatorship' shapes the manner of the role career executives are defined by: "balancing the inherent tension in the political system between the need to 'serve' and the need to 'preserve'" (Terry 2003: 29).

This conservatory bias may seem to be rather innocuous, but it has proved rather toxic: over time, the need to 'preserve' has often overshadowed the need to 'serve' for the bureaucracy. This attitude has had an important impact on the Canadian scene where the tradition of an independent, professional, public service has been revered, so a fair number of opinion-molders have seized on it to provide legitimization for regarding the senior public service as a quasi-clergy, while some version of this gospel has come to be popularized.

This worldview has fed a most unhealthy tendency to sacralize the role of the bureaucracy as the guardian of the fundamental principles of democracy, and to allow the bureaucratic clergy to define what has to be preserved. This sort of hijacking has been anointed by a plurality of public administration academics. However, since the bureaucracy is not, in reality, a selfless clergy – whatever may be said by those who regard bureaucrats as missionaries (Kernaghan 2007) – this perspective has guided the bureaucracy's strategy in defining what needed to be preserved. It has led the bureaucracy to insist on preserving most things that helped in maintaining its own power base and putative dominion.

This has seemingly immunized the Canadian federal public service against any significant efforts at reform – either during recurrent internal attempts at change over the last decades, or when outsiders have revealed its ineffectiveness and failing collaboration role (Hubbard and Paquet 2014). This does not mean that the failures of the bureaucracy have gone unnoticed, only that such diagnoses have never led to significant corrective action.

Indeed, in a recently published interview in the *Ottawa Citizen* (May 2016a), the new Clerk of the Privy Council, Michael Wernick, has suggested that the federal public service is in much need of repair.

Wernick described the public service as "a bit of a fixer-upper in the sense that the foundations are good." Not surprisingly then, he describes a public service that is unproductive ("load of rules, bureaucracy and process that isn't productive"); that is lacking is agility (structures and processes that make it so difficult to difficult to "move dollars, people and information around, within and across departments"); that is somewhat learning impaired (hobbled by structures that make it too slow, rigid and risk-averse); that is worn out ("we are too slow and not very nimble" and a public service workplace that is old, outdated and tired).

In his mind, the problem, however, is not with public servants *per se*, but with the structures, processes and culture of government that are no longer properly aligned to the realities of the day. Wernick identifies the principal challenge for public servants as the escalating pace of change, including technological change and the complexity of the issues being wrestled with.

What is the source of the problem?

In his view, governments no longer have all the knowledge, resources or power to realize what they intend to realize. Governing is no longer solely in government's hands; governance has become widely distributed in society among many institutions, organizations, and actors, and pertains to a significant degree to forces entirely external to government, over which government has little or no control.

"All the important issues facing Canada," Wernick says, "are multifaceted and [that] require collaboration, and we have to get better working across silos internally. One of the real challenges … is [the need for] a lot more space to collaborate and work with people outside the public service" (Wernick 2016).

On these basic points, one can only be in full agreement. But what this actually means in practice for the sort of necessary public service reform is not entirely clear.

This is especially the case since it is not unreasonable to surmise, given the history around PS reform, that conservatorship will again prevail, and that nothing meaningful will be done to reform the public service. The conventional wisdom on governing is likely to find ways to exculpate the governing arrangements and the bureaucrats. Indeed, the Clerk already seems to have found the culprit and announced his diagnosis and cure (*Ibid.*) – he intends to put dealing with the mental stress and mental illness in the federal public service as his top priority – thus hinting at the fact that this is the source of the bureaucracy's dysfunction (May 2016b).

In our view, Wernick's diagnosis and solution for the problem are somewhat off-base.

Our book has been designed to help persons like the Clerk in dealing with this gap between realities and representations. It has been constructed as a guide to interested parties to assist them in escaping mental prisons, reframing the way traditional governance is approached, refurbishing their governance toolbox, and scheming virtuously in our complex and uncertain world.

The presentation of topics was sequenced so that it could be shown that the 'intelligent governance' approach we describe is based on solid foundations: a sound criticism of the conventional but outdated or flawed governing practices; a presentation of emerging alternatives to conduct the business of governing; and a promising way to explore even better ways in the future.

The disadvantage of such a coherent approach to 'intelligent governance' is that it may not have emphasized sufficiently or revealed forcefully enough the foundational skeleton of the book through identifying upfront both the need to revisit the conventional assumptions and to accept the controversial theses on which our critique of the conventional approach and our sketch of ways to improve it is based.

In closing this book, it has become clear to us that it might be useful to underline explicitly the heretical nature of our work, the sort of Augias stable cleansing of conventional thinking that it requires, and the fact that the reader must become conscious that the extensive reframing, restructuring and retooling of the governing apparatus that is required, cannot be envisaged seriously without some sort of accompanying 'revolution in the mind', unless reform proceeds on the basis of new assumptions and theses about the art of governing – no matter how controversial they might be.

We have played down these features in our book to make the presentation less argumentative and conflictual. But it appears essential in closing this book to ensure that the set of assumptions and practices on which our scheme of thought is based are clear, so as to make the reader fully conscious of the full extent to which our alternative set of assumptions stand in conflict with the conventional literature.

Our alternative assumptions have led us to identify critical theses about the ways in which conventional governance practices contribute to the current dysfunctions of government that weaken its capacity to address issues of importance to citizens. One cannot seriously imagine tackling the enormous task of generating intelligent governance practices and more efficient, effective, smart and wise government, unless conventional assumptions are discarded. Otherwise, one might be led to fantasize about the sources of the problems of the

Canadian public service, and to suggest spurious remedies that will do nothing to refurbish the actual processes of governance. Our theses have been clearly identified throughout the text, but it may be useful to restate them in a lapidary way.

A. About the basis for the dysfunctions of the conventional governance practices
- reliance on technical rationality, the myth of shared values and other mental prisons;
- futile strategic planning, the fraud of leadership, and unaccountable accountability;
- misplaced focus on redistribution rather than on coordination.

B. About what is required for intelligent governance practices
- learning while doing;
- renewed focus on coordination and collaboration;
- stewardship by design for wayfinding;
- practical systems of inquiry and integrative thinking; collaboration in the absence of *affectio societatis*;
- A fuller appreciation of the blockchain revolution.

C. About the possibilities beyond the present state of affairs
- imaginative transdisciplinary, multi-stakeholder inquiry;
- experimentation and social learning;
- self-organizing co-governance catalyzed by government.

No organization – private, public and social – can experience dysfunction and continue to fantasize about change without actually changing. In the current light, governments, therefore, should expect to have to change radically in recognition that they cannot control anything of consequence in the lives of their citizens. This must mean shifting from the top-down 'Big G' Government approaches to a 'small g' governance practices that are geared towards more of a guiding and steering role to reduce social conflict and maximize social innovation. This would also have the effect of significantly revitalizing the value-adding legitimacy of both politics and technocracy. Such a shift would entail developing the tools, the skills and the trust that are essential to experiencing a distributed, 'co-governance' approach that would be inclusive and focused primarily on learning.

In adopting an 'intelligent governance' approach, Canadian governments would likely be:

- adding new value as collective brokers, facilitators, educators, angel investors, and conflict mediators, inspiring new relationships with businesses, not-for-profits and citizens that foster social learning and innovation; and,
- developing the skills, processes, mechanisms and practices that promote collective stewardship by design, and using technology to connect to citizens and groups of citizens to co-learn, help generate new resources, conduct joint experiments, co-develop prototypes, be mutually accountable, and co-govern.

It is fair to say that little of this type of action would appear to be predictable from the sibylline public statements of the Clerk – even though he is regarded as one of the most enlightened of federal bureaucrats.

In describing the public service, he says it's "a bit of a fixer-upper ... It is a fixer-upper in the sense that the foundations are good" (May 2016a). He regards the foundations of the Canadian Public Service – the people, the mission, the benefits of government – as good. And consequently, it would seem, he does not feel that radical reforms are needed. We don't know how most readers would react to this metaphor, however, if we were buying a house and the realtor started emphasizing "it's a fixer-upper" and talking about how good the foundations were, we'd suddenly be thinking of a tear down.

Unfortunately, at is point in time, to get the best results from the people and the mission of government, one has to engage in serious redesign and rebuilding and not, as the Clerk's predecessors have done, simply focus on interior redecoration.

Conclusion

At a time when the 'Big G' fortress has come under assault in all sectors, and alternatives are becoming sufficiently numerous that the 'exit Government' motto has become thinkable (as we saw in chapter 7), it must be acknowledged that many of the 'Big G' fantasies still dominate the scene. Some may venture to say, therefore, that there is a quixotic quality to our efforts to defend a gospel of intelligent governance, or to issue a call to arms to construct a system of governance that is smart, wise, cognitive and heuristic.

We do not come to these conclusions at the end of this book. We rather sense that we have made a strong and persuasive case for intelligent governance. Even if we must admit that there has been an immense amount of cognitive dissonance, willful blindness, and disingenuity in reaction to the argument of intelligent governance, evidence is accumulating that unintelligent governance is not a defensible stand, and that there are reasons to believe that its rearguard action is weakening.

It is hardly surprising that the cadre of intermediate level bureaucrats in the public sector, who are most clearly challenged by a change in the governance regime, would also be those most stridently opposed to a transformation that would threaten their own petty security. In the private sector, resistance at this level can only be temporary; in the not-for-profit sector, it may last a bit longer but not much, since ineffectiveness soon yields curtailment of funds. In the public sector, the capacity to extend the life of a most ineffective regimen is much longer, although one cannot count on the benevolent patience of semi-disinterested politicians for ever.

But these pathological defence mechanisms of intermediate level officials in the public sector are threatening the public safety and public health of Canadians and they have to be exposed – as we have – because their willful blindness and dilatory action is putting Canadians at risk. It may well be called, in the face of future crises, criminal negligence, i.e., a form of unsettling or rash lack of concern.

In parallel, less obtuse officials with a better survival instinct must be persuaded to examine and evaluate anew what were the sources of success and failure in collaborative governance in the recent past, and to establish on the basis of social learning from such evaluations what might be regarded as the appropriate prerequisites for intelligent collaborative governance.

It would be unwise to presume that because earlier attacks have not completely weakened the 'Big G' citadel, renewed efforts will not either. In the case of business enterprises, sensitivities have been modified over time. It is now regarded as inappropriate to act in ways that are environmentally, socially and ethically irresponsible, and in order to retain their social licence, new legal forms have developed as a result of this emerging 'code of honour.' So to the extent that something as ethereal as a 'code of honour' for those in government might be a significant game changer; reframing the debates around it may represent a promising new gambit (Appiah 2010).

Changing the notion of what is considered honourable is neither easy nor formulaic. And it need not be based on imposing directly and coercively the eradication of reprehensible behaviour. It need not be a total revolution in the mind triggered by a Copernican theoretical upset either. It may simply involve an emotional reaction to some specific feature of the present situation that would transform perceptions or interpretations.

Previous and existing regimes have proven vulnerable to such innocuous changes in our worldview in surfusion. For example, in a francophone high school in Quebec where schoolyard bullying and violence were problematic, some professors suggested that imposing the use of 'vous' instead of 'tu' in all interpersonal exchanges on the whole territory of the school ground might help. It worked marvelously, even though no one could really explain fully what made it work. Reintroducing a basic sense of civility in this most perfunctory way seemed to help temper school violence dramatically.

The real governance challenge, therefore, is in imagining ways to reintroduce a sense of ownership and responsibility, together with a sense of limits, within the citizenry, and nudging behaviour back within cultural and moral corridors that would encourage their cooperation by way of redefining what is the honourable thing to do.

It is that simple and that complex!

References

Appiah, K. Anthony. 2010. *The Honor Code – How Moral Revolutions Happen*. New York, NY: Norton.

Boland, Richard J. and Fred Collopy (eds.). 2004. *Managing by Design*. Stanford, CA: Stanford University Press.

Boulding, Kenneth E. 1970. *A Primer on Social Dynamics*. New York, NY: The Free Press.

Brown, Valerie A. 2008. *Leonardo's Vision – A guide to collective thinking and action*. Rotterdam, NL: Sense Publishers.

Brown, Valerie A. *et al.* (eds.). 2010. *Tackling Wicked Problems – Through the Transdisciplinary Imagination*. New York, NY: Routledge.

Brown, Valerie A. and Judith A. Lambert. 2012. *Collective Learning for Transformational Change – A Guide to Collaborative Action*. London, UK: Routledge.

Cleveland, Harlan. 2002. *Nobody in Charge*. San Francisco, CA: Jossey-Bass.

Eggers, William D. and Paul Macmillan. 2013. *The Solution Revolution*. Boston, MA: Harvard Business School Press.

Eggers, Willam D. and Paul Macmillan. 2015. "Cognitive Government," *Nesta*, May 8.

Foa, Uriel. 1971. "Interpersonal and Economic Resources," *Science*, January 29, 171(3969): 345-351.

Gallie, W.B. 1964. *Philosophy and the Historical Understanding*. London, UK: Chatto & Windus.

Goldsmith, Stephen and William D. Eggers. 2004. *Governing by Networks*. Washington, DC: The Brookings Institution Press.

Gomez, Pierre-Yves. 2015. *Référentiel pour une gouvernance raisonnable des entreprises*. Lyon, FR: IFGE.

Hirschman, Albert O. 1971. *A Bias for Hope*. New Haven, CT: Yale University Press.

Hubbard, Ruth and Gilles Paquet. 2014. *Probing the Bureaucratic Mind – About Canadian Federal Executives*. Ottawa, ON: Invenire.

Katouzian, Homa. 1980. *Ideology and Method in Economics*. New York, NY: New York University Press.

Kernaghan, Kenneth. 2007. *A Special Calling: Values, Ethics, and Professional Public Service*. Ottawa, ON: Canada Public Service Agency.

Kleiner, Art. 2012. "The Thought Leader Interview of Dov Seidman," *Strategy & Business*, 67, Summer.

Laurent, Paul and Gilles Paquet. 1998. *Epistémologie et économie de la relation: coordination et gouvernance distribuée*. Lyon/Paris, FR: Vrin.

Lester, Richard K. and Michael J. Piore. 2004. *Innovation – The Missing Dimension*. Cambridge, MA: Harvard University Press.

Martin, Roger and Karen Christensen (eds.). 2013. *Rotman on Design*. Toronto, ON: University of Toronto Press.

May, Kathryn. 2016a. "PS needs to pick up pace of reforms: Privy Council Clerk," *Ottawa Citizen*, March 25.

May, Kathryn. 2016b. "Mental Health set as PS priority," *Ottawa Citizen*, April 4.

Nickerson, Jackson and Ronald Sanders (eds.). 2013. *Tackling Wicked Government Problems: A Practical Guide for Developing Enterprise Leaders*. Washington, DC: The Brookings Institution Press.

O'Donovan, Gabrielle. 2007. *The Corporate Culture Handbook: how to plan, implement, and measure a successful culture change.* Dublin, IR: Liffey Press.

Paquet, Gilles. 1995. "Institutional Evolution in an Information Age" in T.J. Courchene (ed.). *Technology, Information and Public Policy: The Bell Canada Papers on Economic and Public Policy 3.* Kingston, ON: John Deutsch Institute for the Study of Economic Policy, p. 197-229.

Paquet, Gilles. 1997. "The Burden of Office, Ethics and Connoisseurship," *Canadian Public Administration*, 40(1): 55-71.

Paquet, Gilles. 2009. *Crippling Epistemologies and Governance Failures: A Plea for Experimentalism.* Ottawa, ON: University of Ottawa Press.

Paquet, Gilles. 2011. *Gouvernance collaborative : un antimanuel.* Montreal, QC: Liber.

Paquet, Gilles. 2013. *Gouvernance corporative – une entrée en matières.* Ottawa, ON: Invenire Books.

Paquet, Gilles. 2014a. *Unusual Suspects – Essays on Social Learning Disabilities.* Ottawa, ON: Invenire.

Paquet, Gilles. 2014b. "La problématique Gouvernance," in F. Tannery, J.P. Denis, T. Hafsi, and A.C. Martinet (eds.), *Encyclopédie de la stratégie.* Paris, FR: Vuibert, p. 645-656.

Paquet, Gilles. 2014c. "Super-bureaucrats as *enfants du siècle*," *www.optimumonline.ca*, 44(2): 4-14.

Paquet, Gilles and Tim Ragan. 2012. *Through the Detox Prism: Exploring Organizational Failures and Design Responses.* Ottawa, ON: Invenire Books.

Paquet, Gilles and Christopher Wilson. 2011. "Collaborative Co-governance as Inquiring Systems," *www.optimumonline.ca*, 41(2): 1-12.

Piore, Michael J. 1995. *Beyond Individualism*. Cambridge, MA: Harvard University Press.

Ramos, Alberto G. 1981. *The New Science of Organization*. Toronto, ON: University of Toronto Press.

Segrestin, Blanche and Armand Hatchuel. 2012. *Refonder l'entreprise*. Paris, FR: Seuil.

Taleb, N. Nicholas. 2012. *Antifragile – Things that gain from disorder*. New York, NY: Random House.

Terry, Larry D. 2003. *Leadership of Public Bureaucracies – The Administrator as Conservator*. Armonk, NY: M.E. Sharpe.

Toulmin, Stephen. 2001. *Return to Reason*. Cambridge, MA: Harvard University Press.

Tussman, Joseph. 1989. *The Burden of Office*. Vancouver, ON: Talonbooks.

Vickers, Geoffrey. 1965. *The Art of Judgment – A Study of Policy-Making*. London, UK: Chapman & Hall.

Wernick, Michael. 2016. *Twenty-Third Annual Report to the Prime Minister on the Public Service of Canada*. Ottawa, ON: Privy Council Office, March 31 [Accessed at: http://www.clerk.gc.ca/eng/feature.asp?pageId=431].

Willke, Helmuth. 2007. *Smart Governance – Governing the Global Knowledge Society*. Frankfurt, DE: Campus Verlag

Willke, Helmuth. 2009. *Governance in a Disenchanted World – The End of Moral Society*. Cheltenham, UK: Edward Elgar.

Wilson, Christopher. 2011. "On Collaboration," *www.optimumonline.ca*, 41(1): 15-30.

About the Centre on Governance of the University of Ottawa

The Centre on Governance (COG) was created by Gilles Paquet at the end of 1997 as a joint venture of the Faculty of Administration (now the Telfer School of Management) and the Faculty of Social Sciences at the University of Ottawa. From its inception, it was seen as an umbrella organization – a hub for the work on governance taking place in all the faculties of the University of Ottawa. The main objectives of the Centre were to develop: conceptual frameworks for analyzing coordination problems, tools to better analyze governance issues, and a critical approach for repairing governance failures. It was meant to bring together persons who are committed to seeking better responses to contemporary problems of governance in the private, public and civic sectors both within and outside of the University of Ottawa. It aimed from the beginning to be an observatory of emerging trends and experiments in the world of governance.

From the beginning, the COG has been responsible for the publication of *www.optimumonline.ca* – a refereed quarterly on governance and public management. Fellows of the Centre have produced hundreds of papers over the years and generated large numbers of books published under different banners. What follows is a list of the main books and reports produced by the Centre, under the banner of the University of Ottawa Press, then under the banner of Invenire – The Idea Factory, and also under the banners of other publishers. All these books are available from www.amazon.ca.

The University of Ottawa Press (1999-2010)

D. McInnes. 1999. *Taking it to the Hill – The Complete Guide to Appearing before Parliamentary Committees*

G. Paquet. 1999. *Governance through Social Learning*

L. Cardinal & C. Andrew (sld). 2001. *La démocratie à l'épreuve de la gouvernance*

L. Cardinal & D. Headon (eds.). 2002. *Shaping Nations – Constitutionalism and Society in Australia and Canada*

P. Boyer *et al.* (eds.). 2004. *From Subjects to Citizens – A hundred years of citizenship in Australia and Canada*

C. Andrew *et al.* (eds.). 2005. *Accounting for Culture – Thinking though Cultural Citizenship*

G. Paquet. 2005. *The New Geo-Governance: A Baroque Approach*

J. Roy. 2005. *E-government in Canada*

C. Rouillard *et al.* 2006. *Re-engineering the State – Toward an Impoverishment of Quebec Governance*

E. Brunet-Jailly (ed.). 2007. *Borderlands – Comparing Border Security in North America and Europe*

R, Hubbard & G. Paquet. 2007. *Gomery's Blinders and Canadian Federalism*

N. Brown & L. Cardinal (eds.). 2007. *Managing Diversity – Practices of Citizenship*

J. Roy. 2007. *Business and Government in Canada*

T. Brzustowski. 2008. *The Way Ahead – Meeting Canada's Productivity Challenge*

G. Paquet. 2008. *Tableau d'avancement – Petite ethnographie interprétative d'un certain Canada français*

P. Schafer. 2008. *Revolution or Renaissance – Making the transition from an economic age to a cultural age*

G. Paquet. 2008. *Deep Cultural Diversity – A Governance Challenge*

L. Juillet & K. Rasmussen. 2008. *A la défense d'un idéal contesté – le principe de mérite et la CFP 1908-2008*

L. Juillet & K. Rasmussen. 2008. *Defending a Contested Ideal – Merit and the Public Service Commission 1908-2008*

C. Andrew *et al.* (eds.). *Gilles Paquet – Homo Hereticus*

O.P. Dvivedi *et al.* (eds.). 2009. *The Evolving Physiology of Government – Canadian Public Administration in Transition*

G. Paquet. 2009. *Crippling Epistemologies and Governance Failures – A Plea for Experimentalism*

M. Small. 2009. *The Forgotten Peace – Mediation at Niagara Falls 1914*

R. Hubbard & G. Paquet. 2010. *The Black Hole of Public Administration*

P. Dutil *et al.* 2010. *The Service State: Rhetoric, Reality, and Promises*

G. DiGiacomo & M. Flumian (eds.). 2010. *The Case for Centralized Federalism*

R. Hubbard & G. Paquet (eds.). 2010. *The Case for Decentralized Federalism*

Invenire (2009-2016)

R. Higham. 2009. *Who do we think we are: Canada's reasonable (and less reasonable) accommodation debates*

R. Hubbard. 2009. *Profession: Public Servant*

G. Paquet. 2009. *Scheming Virtuously: The Road to Collaborative Governance*

J. Bowen (ed.). 2009. *The Entrepreneurial Effect: Ottawa*

F. Lapointe. 2011. *Cities as Crucibles: Reflections on Canada's Urban Future*

J. Bowen. 2011. *The Entrepreneurial Effect: Waterloo*

G. Paquet. 2011. *Tableau d'avancement II – Essais exploratoires sur la gouvernance d'un certain Canada français*

R. Chattopadhyay & G. Paquet (eds.). 2011. *The Unimagined Canadian Capital – Challenges for the Federal Capital Region*

P. Camu. 2011. *La Flotte Blanche – Histoire de la Compagnie de la navigation du Richelieu et d'Ontario 1845-1913*

M. Behiels & F. Rocher (eds.). 2011. *The State in Transition – Challenges for Canadian Federalism*

R. Clément & C. Andrew (eds.). 2012. *Cities and Languages: Governance and Policy – International Symposium*

R. Clément & C. Andrew (sld). 2012. *Villes et langues : gouvernance et politiques – Symposium international*

C.M. Rocan. 2012. *Challenges in Public Health Governance: The Canadian Experience*

T. Brzustowski. 2012. *Why we need more innovation in Canada and what we must do to get it*

C. Andrew *et al.* 2012. *Gouvernance comunautaire : innovations dans le Canada français hors Québec*

M. Gervais. 2012. *Challenges of Minority Governments in Canada*

R. Hubbard *et al.* (eds.). 2012. *Stewardship: Collaborative decentred metagovernance and inquiring systems*

G. Paquet. 2012. *Moderato cantabile: Toward principled governance for Canada's immigration policy*

G. Paquet & T. Ragan. 2012. *Through the Detox Prism: Exploring organizational failures and design responses*

G. Paquet. 2013. *Tackling Wicked Policy Problems: Equality, Diversity, and Sustainability*

G. Paquet. 2013. *Gouvernance corporative : une entrée en matières*

G. Paquet. 2014. *Tableau d'avancement III – Pour une diaspora canadienne-française antifragile*

R. Clément & P. Foucher. 2014. *50 years of official bilingualism: challenges, analyses and testimonies*

R. Clément & P. Foucher. 2014. *50 ans de bilinguisme official : défis, analyses et témoignages*

R. Hubbard & G. Paquet. 2014. *Probing the Bureaucratic Mind: About Canadian Federal Executives*

G. Paquet. 2014. *Unusual Suspects: Essays on Social Learning Disabilities*

R. Hubbard & G. Paquet. 2015. *Irregular Governance: A Plea for Bold Organizational Experimentation*

L. Cardinal & P. Devette (eds.). 2015. *Autour de Chantal Mouffe – Le politique en conflit*

R. Higham. 2015. *What would you say? … as guest speaker at the next Canadian citizenship ceremony*

D. Gordon. 2015. *Town and Crown – An Illustrated History of Canada's Capital*

G. Paquet & R.A. Perrault. 2016. *The Tainted-Blood Tragedy in Canada: A Cascade of Governance Failures*

G. Paquet & C. Wilson. 2016. *Intelligent Governance: A Prototype for Social Coordination*

Editions Liber

G. Paquet. 1999. *Oublier la Révolution tranquille – Pour une nouvelle socialité*

G. Paquet. 2004. *Pathologies de gouvernance – Essais de technologie sociale*

G. Paquet. 2005. *Gouvernance : une invitation à la subversion*

G. Paquet. 2008. *Gouvernance : mode d'emploi*

G. Paquet. 2011. *Gouvernance collaborative : un anti-manuel*

Éditions Vrin

P. Laurent & G. Paquet. 1998. *Épistémologie et économie de la relation – coordination et gouvernance distribuée*

Éditions H.M.H.

G. Paquet & J.P. Wallot. 2007. *Un Québec moderne 1760-1840 : Essai d'histoire économique et sociale*

Government of Canada

G. Paquet. 2006 (en collaboration). *The National Capital Commission: Charting a New Course*

Report of the NCC Mandate Review Panel

Special research reports

COG. 1999. *The Borough Model: Municipal Restructuring for Ottawa*

COG. 2000. *The Governance of the Ethical Process for Research – A study for the Tri-council*

COG. 2000. *Governance in the 21st Century* (The Royal Society of Canada)

G. Paquet. 2001. *Si Montfort m'était conté … Essais de pathologie administrative et de rétroprospective*

A. Chaiton & G. Paquet (eds.). 2002. *Ottawa 2020 – A synthesis of the Smart Growth Summit*

G. Paquet & Kevin Wilkins. 2002. *Ocean governance … An inquiry into stakeholding*

J. Roy and C. Wilson. 1998. *Strategic Localism and Competitive Advantage*

COG. 1999. *Corporate Governance & Spin-in Ventures*

COG. 1999. *The Borough Model: Municipal Restructuring for Ottawa*

COG. 2000. *The Governance of the Ethical Process for Research – A study for the Tri-council*

COG. 2000. *Governance in the 21st Century*, Lead role in the annual symposium of the RSC

G. Paquet. 2001. *Si Montfort m'était conté ... Essais de pathologie administrative et de rétroprospective*

Talentworks Project (under the supervision of Christopher Wilson)

COG. 2001. *Evaluating TalentWorks: Creating a Foundation for Successful Collaboration*

COG. 2002. *Ottawa's Workforce Environment, Report I of Ottawa Works: A Mosaic of Ottawa's Economic and Workforce Landscape*

COG. 2002. *Profiling Ottawa's Workforce, Report II of Ottawa Works: A Mosaic of Ottawa's Economic and Workforce Landscape*

COG. 2002. *Ottawa's Workforce Development Strategy, Report III of Ottawa Works: A Mosaic of Ottawa's Economic and Workforce Landscape*

A. Chaiton and G. Paquet (eds.). 2002. *Ottawa 2020 – A synthesis of the Smart Growth Summit*

G. Paquet and Kevin Wilkins. 2002. *Ocean governance ... An inquiry into stakeholding*

B. Collins, *et al.* 2003. *Assessment of Public Internet Access in Ottawa: Report of Key Findings*

COG. 2003. *SmartCapital Evaluation Guidelines Report*

COG. 2003. *SmartCapital Baseline Assessment*

R. Hubbard, G. Paquet and C. Wilson. 2004. *CIPO: Reaching the World of SMEs*

COG. 2004. *SmartCapital: A Smart Community Assessment*

G. Paquet and J. Roy. 2005. *CIPO as an Innovation Catalyst*

www.ingramcontent.com/pod-product-compliance
Lightning Source LLC
Chambersburg PA
CBHW062049270326
41931CB00013B/2999